Business Organization

R. J. WILLIAMSON
MA, MInst.M(Dip), MIMC, FCCA, ACIS

Published on behalf of
The Institute of Marketing and the CAM Foundation

HEINEMANN: LONDON

30220556

William Heinemann Ltd
10 Upper Grosvenor Street, London W1X 9PA

LONDON MELBOURNE TORONTO

JOHANNESBURG AUCKLAND

First published 1981

Reprinted 1982, 1984

434 92262 5

Typeset in Great Britain by
Supreme Litho Typesetting, Ilford, Essex

Printed in Great Britain by
Redwood Burn Limited
Trowbridge, Wiltshire.

Acknowledgements

To the ladies in my life whose company has been so sorely missed during the writing of this book: Evelyn, Phyllis, Jennie, Sylvia, Clare, April and Holly.

To Mr Ted Jenner whose patience, good humour, and practical suggestions during editing helped to bridge the gap between London and Bangladesh where most of the book was written. The contributions of the readers of the Institute of Marketing are also gratefully acknowledged.

To my friends and colleagues in PA Management Consultants who have contributed so much advice, technical expertise, and experience to the book.

Sources

Grateful thanks are due to the following for permission to reprint extracts, diagrams and cartoons: *The Financial Times*, *The Economist*, McGraw-Hill Book Company Ltd, The General Electric Company Ltd, Turner and Newall Ltd, and the Brockhouse Group.

Preface

In recent years the divisions between the traditional business disciplines have tended to become blurred; the accountant, the engineer, the buyer, and the marketing manager have left their watertight compartments in the interest of co-ordinating and integrating all the functions of a business into one effective operation.

The individual manager needs to understand much more about the workings of other parts of his organization than ever before. The training policy at the Institute of Marketing is to regard Marketing as a cross-functional operation; in addition to knowledge of the sophisticated techniques of market research, forecasting, and promotion, the manager needs an appreciation of company-wide business administration since his activities may well involve action by a number of other specialists or departments.

This book is therefore designed to provide both the specialist manager and the student with a means of broadening their knowledge and understanding of the organization of business, and in particular of the influences that determine the degree of success or failure of their own activities.

Many students preparing for qualifications issued by the Business Education Council (BEC) and the Council for National Academic Awards (CNAA), particularly in the Diploma in Management Studies (DMS) will benefit from the contents of the book. It has been written specifically, however, for students preparing for the 'Business Organization' paper of the Institute of Marketing's Certificate examinations, and includes all the questions set between May 1975 and January 1979 in an appendix of revision exercises. IM Diploma students will also find it helpful in dealing with the organization aspects of their final papers. It will also be directly useful for students preparing for the 'Marketing' and 'Business Environment' papers of CAM. Many professional institutes now include this topic in their examinations, and this book is particularly suitable for students of:

The Institute of Chartered Secretaries and Administrators
The Association of Certified Accountants
The Institute of Cost and Management Accountants
The Institute of Administrative Accounting
The Institution of Industrial Managers
The National Examinations Board in Supervisory Studies.

The general reader will find it a logical and easy-to-read explanation of what goes on under the surface of the company reports published in the Press.

R.J. Williamson

Contents

		Page
Acknowledgements		v
Preface		vi
Introduction		viii
1	Principles of Organization	1
2	Functions of Management	17
3	The Structure of Business	31
4	Channels of Communication	50
5	Planning and Control	65
6	Business and the Law	80
7	Financial Management	102
8	Sources of Funds	123
9	Sources and Materials Management	139
10	Production Management	158
11	Management of Human Resources	178
12	Industrial Relations	200
13	The Role of Marketing	221
14	Management Change	244
Revision Exercises		252
Further Reading		261
Index		268

Introduction

The traditional organization of business has tended to be on functional lines. The production manager has regarded himself as a 'factory man', the accountant as a 'money man', and the personnel manager as a 'people man'. Each developed his own techniques and disciplines, sometimes breeding a sense of exclusiveness or even inter-functional rivalry that worked against the overall interests of the company.

In many firms the little boxes on the conventional organization chart accurately represent the watertight containers in which people work, and there is often friction at the interface between departments that is accepted as just another aspect of the working day. Perhaps Sales will resent the financial restrictions placed on its activities by Accounts; R & D may feel their creativity is blunted by the disciplines of Corporate Planning; or Production may resist the frequent schedule changes required by Marketing to keep up with the fluctuations of demand.

Each in his own way is right, but each is working to different objectives. Efforts to maximize sales, to economize on working capital, and to minimize factory costs, are all praiseworthy in their own context, but may well be mutually counter-productive if followed to their *nth* degree without adequate co-ordination with the other departments concerned.

Taking a corporate view is difficult for the individual manager because his day-to-day responsibilities and duties make it hard for him to 'see the wood for the trees'. Managing a business has been compared with driving a troika, the three-horse Russian carriage; success depends on getting everybody to pull in the same direction at the same time. In order to do this the driver needs a knowledge of where he is going and what the road is like, effective controls over his horses, and a means of checking that he is in fact going in the right direction. By analogy the manager needs an operating plan in sufficient detail to guide each unit or department towards what it is trying to achieve; systems and procedures as a basis for purposeful activity; an organization structure within which to operate; and a mechanism of controls to monitor what is being done.

A business organization is a series of arrangements made to enable the manager to do these things in an on-going way. It is designed to employ available resources to achieve objectives set in advance as economically and cost-effectively as possible. Obviously corporate objectives change from time to time and there may be conflict between short and longer term goals. It is therefore necessary to review organization structures from time to time, particularly if major changes in objectives take place. An organization is not a monolith with an existence independent of what it is designed to achieve. In one sense it may be like a building that is torn down and reconstructed when its use changes, but it may also be like a living organism with a definite life-cycle. The study of business organizations is still at a formative stage, but it is clear that the health of the main structure relates to the quality of the relationships between the individuals who work in it. In this sense people are the organization and it only exists to serve their needs and aims.

Business performance is monitored by comparing these aims or objectives with the results actually achieved in the period under review. The most common method of measuring a company's efficiency is to compare the results obtained with the amount of resources used. The ratio of profit earned to capital employed is one way of doing this. The manager's job may be defined as achieving these results by getting things done through other people. People are a resource like any other that must be used economically. Although they have special characteristics that demand specific recognition by the manager, they represent an expense that must be met out of the working capital that he has available for his operation. The function of the business organization is to provide an environment in which he can carry out this role effectively in pursuit of the objectives that have been set for him.

The manager differs from the specialist in the important respect that he is responsible for results. This is a function that involves him in a wide range of activities, spreading beyond the boundaries of his own specialism. He must integrate and co-ordinate the activities of his people to reach definite goals. The techniques he uses may be drawn from many disciplines. He is likely to be a bit of a planner, cost accountant, and personnel officer; in most companies it is customary to involve the line manager in the selection of personnel for his department even if there is also a specialist Personnel Department already.

The modern approach to business emphasizes this management approach, and the individual needs to obtain knowledge and appreciation of the other departments in his organization to enable him to operate effectively. The trend in business organization is away from watertight functions towards ones which overlap in some respects and are closely integrated in the activities of the departments with which they have working contact. The traditional activities of Purchasing may now be included in the broader responsibilities of Materials Management that take the buyer into Production, Research and Development, and Marketing through such techniques as Value Analysis for example. Similarly the old style Transport Manager finds his job integrated in the new discipline of Physical Distribution Management (PDM).

Marketing is the pre-eminent example of this trend. Peter Drucker makes this point in his book, *The Practice of Management*:

> 'Actually marketing is so basic that it is not just enough to have a strong sales department and to entrust marketing to it. Marketing is not only much broader than selling, it is not a specialized activity at all. It encompasses the entire business. It is the whole business seen from the point of view of its final result, that is from the customer's point of view. Concern and responsibility must therefore permeate all areas of the enterprise.'

The marketing manager entrusted with the implementation of the marketing plan must have sufficient knowledge of the working of those areas and sufficient appreciation of their problems and viewpoint to be able to steer the plan, monitor its progress, and hopefully make a positive contribution on the way.

He will be involved with Corporate Planning because it is his view of the opportunities in the market that should determine the scale of the company's operation. His sales forecast will be the basis for Production Planning, and his

interpretation of market demand will have an influence on the activities of Quality
Control. Similarly Research and Development should be carried out in the context
of what the market needs in the short and long term. The nature and scale of
Distribution will depend on the selected sales strategy and the channels chosen to
carry it out. Because of the central role of the sales forecast in cash and working
capital planning, the importance of advertising and promotion expenditure in many
profit and loss accounts, and the need to ensure that marketing plans are efficiently
appraised in financial terms, Marketing has a close relationship with Finance and
Accounts; in fact a new breed, the Marketing Accountant, has appeared to manage
the interface between the two.

The aim of this book is to provide the manager in general and the Marketing
student manager in particular with the knowledge of company administration and
management that he needs to think in a cross-functional way, appreciating the
company-wide implications of his actions. This involves some theoretical and
some practical knowledge, with an appreciation of some of the main techniques
of management in current use. The logic of the book therefore follows the scheme
below:

1 *Principles and Theory*
  Principles of Organization
  Functions of Management

2 *Organization in Practice*
  Structure of Business
  Channels of Communication

3 *Planning and Control*
  Business Planning and Control
  Business and the Law
  Financial Management
  Sources of Funds

4 *Management*
  Sourcing and Materials Management
  Production Management
  Management of Human Resources
  Industrial Relations

5 *Co-ordination*
  The Role of Marketing
  Managing Change

Inevitably a single chapter focussed on a particular aspect of business tends to
give it an importance out of proportion to its day-to-day significance. This is
particularly true of 'Business and the Law'; the average company is not constantly
involved in litigation, usually avoiding legal action if it can. The same applies to
the chapters dealing with management techniques; these are of course designed for
use when needed, as a single weapon would be selected from an armoury.

To restore a sense of perspective an imaginary group of companies, Consumer & Electrical Ltd, has been invented to represent the average competently and sensibly managed enterprise that predominates in business today. Its decision-making is in no sense optimal, and its practices are not intended as a model to others. It is intended to provide an example of life in the real world outside the hot house of business theory.

C & E is in fact an amalgam of five companies with whom the author has worked as a consultant. It has an annual turnover of about £50 million, and has interests in consumer and industrial electrical products; it has manufacturing and wholesaling interests, as well as a retail sales force; and it has a significant share of its business overseas. It makes its first appearance in Chapter 1, but is also featured in the conclusion to subsequent chapters where a further practical example may be helpful.

1. *Principles of Organization*

The organization of men and women at work is fundamental to the success of any business, and touches the lives of almost everybody in some way or other. 'Parkinson's law' and the 'Peter principle' are now part of the English language. Yet our knowledge of how business organizations work is far from complete, in spite of the attention that the topic has received in recent years. The starting point is nevertheless encouragingly, if deceptively, straightforward.

To organize a business is at its simplest to provide it with everything it needs in terms of material, human, financial and management resources for the achievement of its objectives. The resulting structure can be drawn on an organization chart, where jobs and roles may be specified in detail; formal relationships between roles may be defined; and procedures may be rigidly standardized. Yet only part of the story has been told. An organization is not a static framework or skeleton but is really more like a social system with characteristics deriving from the reactions and attitudes of the human beings who form its component parts. Their personal goals may well be distinct from the corporate objectives of the organization, but each will react on the other in ways that cannot be ignored. Informal relations inevitably supplement the formal ones recorded on the chart, and informal groups emerge with their own roles, codes of behaviour, and leadership patterns. These may play a major part in the functioning of the organization, helping or hindering the achievement of organizational objectives.

An organization has been compared to a living body because it is dynamic and it may grow or contract. In addition, however, it can restructure itself in the short term and one role of management is to plan and implement organizational development to make the best use of formal and informal elements. It is now recognized that organization is not an end in itself but a means of optimizing management performance and achieving planned results. Conversely, an unsound structure may seriously hinder business performance and put success at jeopardy.

1.1 Criteria for a Sound Organization

The criteria for a sound organization may be summarized as follows:

1. It enables productive work to be performed efficiently without wasted effort. It does not distract the individual with onerous procedures and it provides a harmonious work environment.
2. It utilizes to the full the human power and experience at its disposal. This implies effective motivation and staff development policies, as well as enlightened recruitment and personnel management practices.

1

3   It makes central control really effective, employing appropriate degrees of
     decentralization and delegation of responsibility. Effective management
     information systems are a pre-requisite.
4   It has the flexibility to adapt to changes in its environment and to facilitate the
     planned level of corporate growth and business expansion.
5   It is not distorted to accommodate the personal characteristics of individuals,
     being more permanent than the people who comprise it. Jobs are specified and
     responsibilities grouped to permit the recruitment of staff to perform them.
     Otherwise, personnel changes may force a major reconstruction.

The prime justification of any organization is its ability to create synergy. If 2 plus
2 does not equal 5, that is, if a better overall outcome than could have been expected by all the component factors considered in isolation is not achieved, then the
impact of the organization is at best neutral and may even itself be a counter-
productive element.

The individual employee may not see things in these terms, but the health of
organization affects his performance intimately.

In a malfunctioning organization he is likely to feel little commitment to organizational objectives and to place high value on minimizing risks.

He sees things going wrong and does nothing about them, preferring to hide
problems and mistakes. His personal needs and feelings are not considered important and his judgment is not respected outside the narrow limits of his job. He feels
locked into his current position and seems stale and bored. Poor performance is
glossed over or handled arbitrarily. Problem-solving is complicated by factors like
status and an excessive concern for management.

The manager himself is not immune. People at the top try to control as many
decisions as possible and staff complain about irrational decisions. He feels un-
supported in trying to get things done and is very jealous over his area of responsibility. He tightly controls small expenditures and allows little freedom for making
mistakes.

Peter Drucker focuses attention on three symptoms of malorganization which
indicate lack of observance of the right structural principles wherever they are
present. They are:

1   Growth of levels of management and numbers of co-ordinators and assistants
     with no clear job responsibility of their own. Inadequate objectives, over-
     centralization and lack of proper activities analysis are causes of this condition.
2   A tendency 'to go through channels' rather than direct to the man who has or
     needs the information concerned. This insulates the individual and stifles
     initiative.
3   A lop-sided age structure of predominantly old or predominantly young
     management. There must be enough older men to ensure opportunities for
     younger men and enough younger men to ensure continuity.

1.2   Establishing the Organization Structure

The pursuit of an agreed goal or objective may be the central theme, but the
establishment of a business organization cannot be confined to the setting of

corporate objectives and the choice of an appropriate structure to achieve them. A confusing welter of relationships, roles, responsibilities and communication channels need to be sorted out so that the people involved can work effectively together and so constitute a coherent working force.

E. F. L. Brech defines the main steps in the establishment of an organization structure as:

1   The determination of the responsibilities to be allocated to the particular positions concerned.
2   The allocation of responsibilities to the individual person who is to hold the managerial position concerned.
3   The establishment of certain formal relationships between managers and the emergence of informal relations among them.

1.3   Types of Organization

It is possible to identify three types of organization, although, in practice, most businesses do not fall into one or other category in a clear-cut way.

A *Line* organization is one in which the lines of authority and responsibility between senior and subordinate within the organizational structure are direct in the sense that a higher authority may give valid orders to those within its area of responsibility.

A Works Manager has a line relationship with the Departmental Foremen reporting to him.

A *Functional* organization is one in which relationships exist between specialists or functional managers in their respective spheres of activity and those responsible for carrying out the main operation. They have a responsibility for the effective performance of the service concerned but have no authority over the people who use the service in the course of the company's business.

A Personnel Manager, for example, is responsible for the implementation of personnel policy, but has no line authority except within his own functional department.

Most organizations contain both line and functional elements and are described as *Line and Staff.* The simple line organization has developed in such a way that one or more ancillary services have become functionalized.

1.4   Formal Relationships

Within the organization structure various formal relationships exist between those holding posts at different levels or on the same level.

Executive, line, or direct relationships are those between senior and subordinate, whilst a functional relationship is one between a functional specialist and managers with direct executive responsibilities. These relationships follow closely the types of organization bearing the same names.

Relations between executives and managers operating at the same level are known as 'lateral' relationships. No one manager is senior to another, but all are responsible to a common superior and they all need to co-operate and co-ordinate their efforts. This type of relationship is at the boundary between formal and informal organization and may not appear on a formal chart. It nevertheless exists and can have significant impact on the effectiveness of management. Managers who cannot co-operate among themselves in a real sense are not managers at all.

A fourth category is the Staff relationship which exists, for example, between a managing director and his personal assistant. The latter has no authority in his own right but carries out duties as an extension of the principal's role in the organiation. The co-ordinator in a major or multi-national company is another example. Here, the authority derives from head office, and the function is, at least in theory, facilitating rather than executive in nature.

1.5 Organization Charts

The structure of the organization may be represented in chart form. The traditional family tree is a convenient way of presenting an established structure of posts and responsibilities with an indication of the status of individual managers and direct lines of communication. It can be an important aid in analysing organizational strains, but its value should not be over-stated:

a chart cannot show the content of the responsibility allocated to each position
it may over-stress status difference and the hierarchical nature of organization;
it ignores informal relations and structure, and does not show 'shared' responsibilities;
it tends to perpetuate out-of-date organization. The following is an example of the traditional 'tree' form of chart. It provides a valuable means of reference to who does what in the company, but it only *represents* the organization; it is not *the* organization. Its importance should be seen as that of an organizational tool of limited application (Figure 1.1).

The following concentric organization chart (Figure 1.2) goes one step further. The circles indicate the echelon level of the jobs connected by them. Thus the Sales Manager and the Chief Accountant are on a par, for example. The straight lines indicate the flow of authority, clearly showing the pivotal position of the Managing Director.

A matrix form of organization chart indicates the roles of individuals and groups in various activities in a way that the other forms of chart cannot. It gives a good visual picture of job relations and highlights overloading of staff or over-manning on particular activities. It shows particularly clearly how functional responsibilities relate to those of executive managers, for example when project organization cuts across the lines of the formal organization. Such a chart, sometimes called a linear responsibility chart is shown on page 6 (Table 1.1).

But Wilfred Brown has the last word on this topic. He recognizes four interpretations of organization and defines them as follows:

1   The *Manifest* organization is the organization described formally on charts and supporting responsibility schedules and job descriptions.

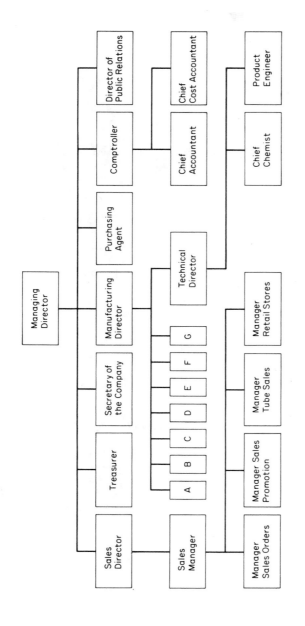

Figure 1.1

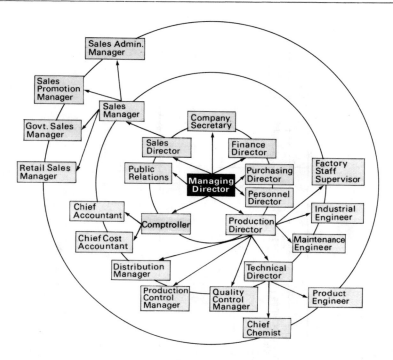

Figure 1.2

Table 1.1: Linear Responsibility Chart

		Role		
Objective	*Board*	*Chairman*	*Managing Director*	*Finance Director*	*Marketing Director*
Determine Policy	—	A	D	D	D
Implement Policy	A	A	—	D	D
Approve Executive appointments	—	A	D	E	E
Control overall operations	A	A	—	F	F

Key: *Function*
A General Supervision
B Direct Supervision
C Specific Decisions
D Consultation
E To be kept informed
F May be called in

2 The *Assumed* organization is how an individual believes it to be, recognizing that reality differs from the formal description.
3 The *Extant* organization is the organization revealed by systematic exploration and analysis.
4 The *Requisite* organization is the organization as it would have to be to accord with the real properties of the field in which it exists.

A chart can show only the first, but the differences between description and reality are great, and if we could pull them together it would affect our lives beneficially in many ways.

1.6 Theory of Organization

It is often easier in business management to diagnose the symptoms of malfunction than to provide the cure. Organizations are highly complex and we do not know enough about them to have developed comprehensive theories about how they work and why they behave in particular ways. Theorists have tended to approach the topic from one of three standpoints:

the 'classical school' regards organization as a formal structure subject to definable principles;
the 'human relations school' considers organizational problems in terms of the behaviour of the people employed;
the 'systems school' regards the organization as a series of sub-systems, inter-relating to each other and to the outside environment.

The three approaches are not mutually exclusive, but complement each other in a way that can be positively helpful to the manager. It is quite legitimate to pick and choose between them when tackling a particular problem in a way that is quite impossible in the case of many technologies and theories. It is thus worth looking at each in a little more detail.

1.61 *The Classical School*

The 'classical school', including writers like F. W. Taylor, J. D. Mooney, L. F. Urwick, Henri Fayol, E. F. L. Brech and Mary Parker Follett among others, regarded organization as a formal structure and attempted to define a set of principles that had universal validity in designing business organizations and making them work.

Henri Fayol outlined fourteen principles of business organization in his book, *General and Industrial Management*, and much of what was subsequently written was discussed under these headings. The major concepts of the 'school' are summarized below:

1 *Division of Labour*
   Efficiency can best be attained by sub-dividing work into the smallest possible elements with each element performed by separate personnel, thus allowing expertise to be developed and productivity to be increased.

2   *Unity of Command*

Each man should have only one boss with no other conflicting lines of command. However the right to issue commands must be accompanied by an equivalent responsibility for its exercise. Similarly, discipline is a two-sided process, since employees would only obey orders if management play their part by providing good leadership.

3   *Unity of Direction*

People engaged in the same kind of activities must have the same objectives in a single plan. It is important that the interests of individuals be subordinated to the general interest, and management must see that the goals of the firm are always paramount. Nevertheless, allowing all personnel to show their initiative in some way is a source of strength for the organization, even if it involves a sacrifice of 'personal vanity' on the part of many managers.

4   *Scalar Chain*

A hierarchy is necessary for unity of direction, but lateral communication is also fundamental, conditional on superiors knowing that it takes place. Three kinds of formal relations, 'line', 'functional' and 'staff', exist within it.

5   *Span of Control*

The number of subordinates reporting to one superior should be kept low with five or six a widely quoted maximum, although Brech saw that it could vary with the manager concerned and the tasks he has to perform.

6   *Centralization*

Fayol regarded centralization as 'one of the laws of nature', with decision-making concentrated in one command if effective co-ordination is to be maintained.

7   *Staff Management*

    (a) A 'combination of kindliness and justice' is needed in treating employees if equity is to be achieved.
    (b) Stability of job tenure can make a major contribution towards a successful business.
    (c) Management must act positively to foster the morale of its employees, co-ordinating effort, encouraging keenness and rewarding merit without arousing jealousies.
    (d) Remuneration is an important motivator.

Some of these concepts appear seriously dated and subject to qualification. Division of labour is an example; we now know that over-specialization can de-motivate workers, and companies like the Swedish car manufacturer Volvo are successfully increasing the variety in production line jobs in the quest for higher productivity. Similarly with the span of control. It is now considered that there is no ideal span but that it should depend on such factors as the similarity of subordinate jobs, the discretion exercised by subordinates, the degree of stability, and the type of co-ordination. A broad span has certain major advantages, including shorter lines of communication up and down the management hierarchy. The main weakness of classical theories is that they are static and tend to be rigid when it is now appreciated that organizations must continuously change and develop if they are to survive. They tend also to understate the importance of behavioural aspects and the inter-relationships between component parts of the organization. They are 'closed' systems in the sense that they pay scant regard to the outside environment.

1.62 *The Human Relations School*

The 'human relations school' looks at organizational problems in terms of the people who are employed there. Recognizing that the effectiveness of an organization is sensitive to the ways in which staff work together, it analyses why people at work behave as they do and what factors influence their behaviour. Starting with the famous Hawthorne studies at the Western Electric company in Chicago in the 1920s, social scientists like Elton Mayo and Joan Woodward have studied how organizational structures work in practice and have identified many behavioural factors that can influence the type of formal organization that is adopted.

Chris Argyris, Rensis Likert, Douglas McGregor and Robert Blake have also made major contributions in this field.

The major significance of the Hawthorne experiments was in discovering the informal organization that it is now realized exists in all organizations. A number of employees in the Bank Wiring Room were observed to enforce a standard for output that was not exceeded by any individual, appearing indifferent to the company's promised incentive scheme. The group was highly integrated with its own social structure and code of behaviour that clashed with that of management in ignoring the organization's formal allocation of roles. Not too much work would be done as that would be 'ratebusting', while not too little would be done as that would be 'chiselling'.

A series of investigations at the Glacier Metal Company, an engineering factory in London, during the 1950s added *inter alia* two important conclusions. Firstly, specific individual behaviour at work is as likely to arise from the nature of the role that the individual occupies, its relation with other roles, and its position in the social system at work, as from the personality of the individual. Secondly, in order to create an environment that will encourage social rather than antisocial behaviour at work, there is a need to develop means of communication between people so that they share a common view of the environment in which they take up different roles.

The individual was recognized to feel a need to have his role and status clearly defined in a way that is acceptable both to himself and to his colleagues.

Where there is some confusion over role boundaries or where multiple roles occupied by the same person are not sufficiently distinguished, insecurity and frustration result. The study of the Divisional Managers meeting showed that it functioned sometimes as an executive committee taking decisions for the London factory, sometimes as a group for non-decision-making discussions with the Managing Director and sometimes as a concealed Board of Directors for the whole company. Its powers differed, depending on the particular capacity in which it was functioning. These powers were not clear, and this was disturbing to the members.

Even when a role has been defined, it may have elements that the individual finds unacceptable or difficult to fulfil. In these circumstances, he may attempt, perhaps subconsciously, to avoid responsibility and authority. Some mechanisms identified by the study were:

> exercise of a merely consultative relationship when a role of executive leadership was envisaged by the executive hierarchy;
> misuse of joint consultation in avoiding responsibility for immediate subordinates;
> 'pseudo democracy', where a senior might avoid a leadership role by excessive delegation.

There is a distinct leadership role in groups that members expected to be properly filled, and organizations do not as a rule function well unless it is.

These examples are only representative of the work done in this field. They serve, however, to illustrate that the behaviour of members of an organization affects both its structure and its functioning as well as the principles upon which it can be managed. Above all, human beings affect the aims of organization in which they participate, not merely the methods used to accomplish them. The technique of Organization Development (OD) attempts to induce changes in individual and group beliefs, attitudes, values, and behaviour that will improve organizational effectiveness by blending informal and formal organizations in such a way that all the social forces present aid the achievement of the organization's corporate objectives.

The commonest uses of OD are:

> as a way of managing change. It works closely with the people affected by the change, examining and questioning their own assumptions about other employees, the management and the organization. In the process, their agreement and commitment to the change are obtained;
> as a discipline for focussing human energy on specific goals. The wants and needs of individuals are seen as essential ingredients in goal-setting for the group;
> if each member participates in this process and subscribes to these goals, a considerable share of his energy begins to move towards the common purpose.

A common theme in OD is training in interpersonal and group membership skills. Methods tend to be personal and introspective, examining why individuals behave as they do in group situations and attempting to influence the pattern of their relations with other members of the group. Joint participation by all interested parties is seen as a critical factor in implementing a voluntary change in methods, roles, or procedure.

Fordyce and Weil include a 'toolbox' of OD methods in their book, *Managing with People*. One example is the Manager's Diagnostic Team Meeting, designed to make a periodic assessment of the effectiveness of the organization and to appraise the need for and possibility of change. The team consists of a top manager or principal assistant, an outside consultant and a number of managers with organization-wide responsibilities. It has no executive or formal fact-finding power; it meets once or twice a year and should consist of people respected in their organizations who are strongly interested in change. The procedure is shown in the following chart:

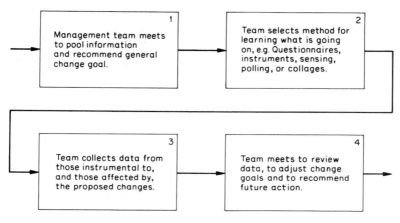

Figure 1.3

The second box includes some specialist OD means of eliciting information that is not contaminated by organizational defects like status or an over-concern for management. Thus:

Sensing consists of unstructured discussions with groups of employees designed to give the manager a feel for their attitudes and get a better understanding of their complaints.

Polling is a means of taking the opinion of a group on a topic either involving its own attitudes or on the performance of the group as a team.

Collages are a means of allowing group members to express themselves on a fairly deep personal level. Collages are produced, using paper, crayons, glue and felt to answer such questions as 'What is happening to this organization?'

1.63 *The Systems Approach*

The systems approach views an organization as a web of interacting variables. Its components are not independent but have interfaces with each other and with the outside world that can materially influence their success in performing their appointed roles. Organization health depends on these inter-relationships and study of them can provide insight into how individual organizations work.

1.631 *Cybernetics*

The systems approach to management evolved from operational research and its best known theory is cybernetics, the science of communication and control. In simple terms, the principle of cybernetics is to provide methods of control by studying the relationship between animal and machine. Automation is an example with machines capable of imitating an animal's ability to carry out a process and to be self-regulating through the feedback of information. An organization is compared with a thermostatically controlled physical system, or perhaps to an automatic pilot keeping a vessel on course by reacting to any changes that might cause deviation. The concept is of interest to managers not only because they may have charge of machines with feedback control systems, but also because the organizations in which they manage may for some purpose be regarded as comparable with cybernetic systems.

1.632 *Social Systems*

In many ways, however, the analogy is not totally satisfactory. The business system has more in common with a social organization in which people have roles to play. A second group of systems theorists have regarded the organization as a social system and have emphasised the interactions between the different aspects of the organization, its people, technology, formal structure and environment. In a series of mining studies, Eric Trist of the Tavistock Institute of Human Relations, found that it was possible, within set technological and economic constraints, to operate different systems of work organization with different social and psychological effects. The manager thus has a considerable degree of organizational choice when taking account of social and psychological aspects. He developed the concept of the working group as being neither a technical nor a social system, but as an interdependent socio-technical system. The business organization is thus seen as an open socio-technical system, because it obtains inputs from its environment and exports outputs to it, as well as operating the conversion process in between.

1.633 *Information Systems*

An organization can alternatively be looked at as a mechanism for processing information, and the traditional staff function in organization is really concerned with the provisions of information appropriate to the different levels of management. A manager can be thought of as a decision centre who may be overloaded by a flow of information and requests for information as an electrical switch may be overloaded. The routes of information flows can be studied and may indicate the health of the organization, replacing the classical principles of organization on one side and the behavioural considerations of the human relations school on the other as the main focus for attention.

1.7 Applying Organization Theories

The theories discussed so far are not mutually exclusive, and all tell us something about the nature and workings of organizations. They deal with different aspects of the same problem. Starting from a set of formal propositions, an analytical study of the organization on both behavioural and systems principles could sensibly be made, although different aspects would inevitably receive differing degrees of emphasis.

Thus, in approaching the problem of setting up a group organization for three small confectionery companies who had decided to integrate their activities, the project leader might use three specialists:

George, taking a classical approach, would design the formal organization structure, defining jobs and responsibilities, calculating manning levels, analysing authority structures and reporting lines, ensuring a correct balance between staff and line roles, and setting formal objectives.

Mike, the social scientist, would probe staff and management attitudes to the new organization, attempting to assess how informal relationships will develop. He would consider conditions of work and how authority will be exercised in practice, particularly with reference to possible conflict between expectations and reality. He would seek to cultivate better understanding between the management and staff, and examine where personal roles and aspirations might clash with job definitions and the formal structure.

Peter, the systems analyst, would analyse the flow of information between head office and the constituent establishments in the group, perhaps using a computer model to help determine the optimum flows. He would examine the decisions that need to be taken, awarding a priority, and assessing the need for data in each case. The routes by which information travels would be studied and a formal Management Information System (MIS) designed. A manager would be regarded as a decision centre and information flows therefore become the sinews of the organization.

All three could provide the Project Leader with valuable insight into the group's needs and problems when he came to the tasks of making recommendations on the type of organization most likely to meet its corporate objectives.

1.71 *Development of an Effective Organization*

Whether a classical, behavioural or systems approach is taken, there are several major requirements on which the effectiveness of a given structure depends:

1 *Corporate Objectives*

Although it is no longer maintained that an effective organization can be built from scratch by simple reference to its objectives, the structure must be appropriate if goals are to be achieved. Size, ownership, geographical location, technology, production systems and, of course, the business environment will influence the selection of corporate objectives and will correspondingly affect the type of organization that will be most effective in each case.

2 *Planning*

The organization must take account of the different levels of planning, and aid rather than hinder their development. The structure needs to recognize the separate roles of production planning, marketing planning and strategic planning in the development of the corporate plan. The purpose of the organization has to be kept currently in view, and its capability to perform the key tasks identified during the planning process is an important standard of effectiveness.

3 *Decision-Making*
Decision-making is an important barometer of organizational health. If decision-making is hampered by ineffective communications, by complex approval channels or by any of the factors identified earlier as disincentives to the manager in taking responsibility, the operation of the company will move more slowly and less efficiently in any or all of these vital areas. Thus over-centralization, for example, may stifle initiative in making operating decisions, whilst the quality of strategic planning may be debased if control is too widely dispersed.

4 *Delegation*
The whole concept of organization is based on delegation but middle-managers find it notoriously difficult to delegate effectively. They need to be able to free themselves for their most significant tasks and to spread the work-load as evenly as possible. Failure to delegate may be a symptom of organizational malfunction or it may itself be a cause of strain elsewhere.

5 *Communications*
An organization depends on a network of communications to co-ordinate its activities and to provide forward momentum. Formal communications may be downwards from superior to subordinate in the form of instructions, information about the job, or feedback of performance ratings; it may be upwards, through reports from the subordinate, suggestions or complaints, procedures, or the formal channels of industrial relations or it may be lateral between equals or through participation in committees. An informal system, the 'grapevine', is likely to subsist alongside the formal channels. If these channels become blocked, or if the balance between formal and informal flows is upset, the ability of the organization to operate effectively is seriously reduced.

6 *Growth*
Perhaps the acid test of an organization's effectiveness is its ability to provide the degree of flexibility to accommodate the firm's innovation and growth strategies. Three major stages typically occur in the growth and development of companies:

In Stage I a single owner organizes and takes all decisions. There is usually a single product or product line with a uniform set of distribution channels. Little or no delegation takes place, but communications are easy and informal.

As the business grows, the owner becomes overworked, being involved in too many decisions and having too many people reporting to him. As a result, the decision-making process is slowed down.

In Stage II reorganization of the Stage I company leads to a basic functional structure with tasks usually grouped together by functions for which authority is delegated to individual managers. Vertical communication is established by the structure, and management performance assumes importance. The Managing Director co-ordinates all functions.

The structure allows for considerable expansion within the same markets and product ranges. However, top management tends to suffer from too much detail and too broad a span of control as growth takes place through an increasing number of functional departments. Functional units start to act independently and managers get out of touch with operations.

In Stage III the move to multi-product, multi-channel operations gives rise to the replacement of Stage II's structure by product divisions each contributing a major profit centre. Each division is organized functionally, undertaking group corporate planning. Staff groups from the centre give advice to divisions and operating units.

Of course, this is not the end of the process, and Stage III difficulties may prove more complex and intractable than in the preceding stages. Administration costs tend to mushroom; there may be considerable duplication of activity, and some loss of direction and drive may appear. The degree of control to be exercised at corporate level and the selection of activities to be carried out at this level rather than in the divisions become major questions.

1.8 Conclusions

A body of principle needs to be set firmly in the context of normal business practice. Most companies make very few changes to their organization structures except when major developments occur. Fine tuning is seldom possible and tinkering can often do more harm than good. It may be maintained that 'change for change's sake' helps to keep people on their toes, but it may also upset successful methods of operation and prevent the individual developing experience within his own job. Nevertheless an organization must be able to meet the challenge of change in its markets and its general environment. It must be sensitive to organizational strains as they appear and be prepared to make appropriate modifications, often of a radical nature. This is not easy to do in practice, and many companies make a point of carrying out an organizational review whenever major new objectives are introduced. It clearly makes sense to ask from time to time whether the company's people and resources are adequately organized to obtain optimum results in a changing world.

Our guinea-pig company, Consumer and Electrical Co. Ltd, attained its current form in the mid-1950s through a series of amalgamations and acquisitions. Each member company retained its old shape, subject to a high degree of control from head office. By the mid-1970s major organizational strains had begun to appear. Decision-making at the centre had become slow, and the growing diversity of the group had made it increasingly bureaucratic as more and more reports and control forms were required to enable it to operate. Inevitably central management had become remote; leadership was lacking in the operating units. There was an unhealthy reluctance to take responsibility, and a rash of committees and co-ordinating bodies had appeared, diluting the role of the manager further.

Following a report from Management Consultants, the Board decided to restructure the group and to increase greatly the authority delegated to the units. The twenty-seven constituent companies were regrouped into three divisions:

C & E (Distribution) carried on the retailing and wholesaling activities of the group;

C & E (Manufacturing) took over the production of small appliances and components;

C & E (International) brought together all overseas interests.

A Chief Executive with a high degree of personal authority was appointed for each division, and the powers of central office were restricted to matters of group-wide interest, notably corporate planning and finance. A new computer based management information system was introduced, and new systems were designed to ensure that an effective degree of co-ordination between the activities of the divisions occurred.

Consumer and Electrical thus obtained a structure more suited to its current needs than the preceding one, broadly in line with the theories and principles discussed in this chapter. However these are only of value if they provide a structure within which a manager can operate and which helps him both to understand the organizational forces determining the success of his efforts and to harness them to his own endeavours. In the next chapter a closer look will be taken at the manager's job, function, role and responsibilities in this context.

2. Functions of Management

The final acid test of an organization structure was seen at the end of the last chapter to be its ability to provide an environment within which the manager can work effectively. Throughout the discussion management and managers were treated as vague synonyms and it was generally assumed that they were sufficiently universal elements to be recognizable in all or at least most business organizations. In fact the term 'manager' covers a very wide range of roles and functions.

At the end of the scale Harold Geneen, the recently retired Chief Executive of the giant multi-national company ITT, headed an organization structured around 250 divisions and 1,000 subsidiaries that operates in half the countries of the world and has sometimes seemed to be more powerful than national governments. He pieced together one of the most intricate and centralized systems of management that has ever been introduced on such a large scale ensuring that he had control of all the important levers affecting its activities.

On the other hand the average British manager, according to a recent BIM *Profile of the British Manager*, is far from being an elite apart. By the time he is 17 he is in full-time employment and will change jobs and functions two or three times in his career. He has some qualifications in Business/Management, but is not a graduate, and feels serious concern over the erosion of salary differentials, his loss of authority in the face of manual unions' militancy and an increasing volume of legislation that seems designed to debase his position further. He may consider himself first an engineer, accountant, or scientist and only secondly as a manager.

Apart from his British birth, our humble 'average' manager appears to have little in common with Harold Geneen. In fact managers come from such a wide variety of educational backgrounds, techniques, disciplines, and career progressions that it may be unwise to refer to 'managers' as an homogeneous group at all.

2.1 The Common Element

The common element running through the work of all these executives is that they are responsible for 'getting things done through other people'. This deceptively simple definition provides the basis for the modern study of management. It covers the full gamut from the board of directors with its responsibility under the Companies Acts for the determination of the overall policy of the company to the lower levels of managers controlling a single operation or process.

2.2 Functions of Managers

A French mining engineer, Henri Fayol, published an analysis of the basic functions common to managers in every type of enterprise in 1916 following a work-study type survey of the activities of the managing director of an iron and steel corporation. He identified the following seven functions:

1 *Planning:* Selecting objectives and policies for the future.
2 *Organizing:* Establishing an organizational structure to implement policies.
3 *Staffing:* Developing policies for recruitment, promotion, training, remuneration and welfare.
4 *Directing:* Supervizing and helping subordinates to make the maximum contribution to the objectives of the organization.
5 *Co-ordinating:* Identifying deviations from plans, devising means of correcting errors and of taking corrective action to ensure that similar errors do not recur.
6 *Reporting:* Ensuring that senior management has sufficient information to enable it to direct the enterprise.
7 *Budgeting:* Preparing detailed estimates of expenditure and income to facilitate control and to enable forecasts to be made of future trends.

Fayol regarded responsibility as an essential element in management that could not be delegated. The manager could require a subordinate to perform certain functions, and was obliged to allocate authority to him commensurate with the job to be done, but he himself remained accountable because he had accepted responsibility in the first place. In this sense managers have legal responsibilities to their shareholders, operating responsibilities to senior and subordinate managers, and also wider responsibilities to other employees and the public.

Fayol's list includes some activities that are more in the nature of administrative tasks than management functions. In essence the manager:

plans
organizes
co-ordinates
controls

and these distinguish him from the accountant, the engineer, the actuary, the scientist or other professional men whose functions consist of defined disciplines and techniques. In so far as they fulfil these roles, they too are managers, even if their professional affiliation seems to dominate their managerial identity.

2.3 Management in Practice

When a professional man is asked what he actually does, the answer should be definite and concise. The work of the accountant or architect for example concerns specific tasks, is governed by a code of conduct or by statute, and is guided by standards of best current practice. When a manager is asked what *he* does, the list is usually very long and seldom fits neatly into these four functions. If management is to become a science or a profession, the manager should be able to operate validly determined procedures of universal application, and should take rational and fully thought-out decisions based on comprehensive and objective facts. It is in fact sometimes maintained that an effective manager should have no regular duties so that he can concentrate on planning and delegation.

In practice the manager's job is not like this. He works under pressure, reacting to short-term events, with inadequate time even to absorb the management inform-ation that has been produced specifically for him. He is the meat in the sandwich between on the one hand his senior directors and shareholders and on the other his subordinates who increasingly expect to participate in the planning and decision process. The author has carried out a series of studies of managers in the course of their work. They included managers in a clearing bank, a multi-national office equipment company, and a confectionery manufacturer. By continuous observa-tion, by the use of job diaries completed by the respondents themselves, and with the use of the electronic **PARAMETER** device that enables the subject to punch a card whenever a random bleep sounds, he was able to record exactly what each manager was doing during his working day.

Results differed from job to job and from individual to individual but the following conclusions emerged clearly:

> The manager has many duties that are strictly not management at all and which may account for over 50% of his time.

Thus the field sales manager may visit important customers, and the purchasing manager may negotiate important contracts. Similarly the managing director may sit on industry committees and the bank manager grant loan facilities himself.

Communications are an essential part of the job, and a manager will often spend between one-half and three-quarters of his time in meetings, in face-to-face discus-sion, or on the telephone. Yet typically he will spend less than one-fifth of his time with his superiors. His main contacts are with subordinates and outsiders.

His day is continuously punctuated by interruptions from subordinates, cus-tomers and other outsiders. Thirty minutes without interruption is a rarity during business hours and many managers make a point of arriving early or staying late to make time for a specific task.

The manager seldom plans his time in an effective way. His individual activities tend to be brief and to lack continuity. His programme may be dominated by a steady flow of callers during the day, and typically he will maintain that it is not possible to make better use of his time because of his vulnerability to the unfore-seen event.

2.4 A Broader View

These findings do not contradict Fayol's analysis, but they do suggest that manage-ment is a more complex question than his four elements imply. The manager is a trouble-shooter, an entrepreneur, a decision maker, and a disseminator of operating information all rolled into one. In addition he needs developed interpersonal skills if the people with whom he has contact are to contribute their best to the general effort. Thus the manager's job has been described in terms of ten roles. As shown in the following chart (Figure 2.1), formal authority gives rise to three interpersonal roles concerning the manager's relationship with other people. As the nerve centre

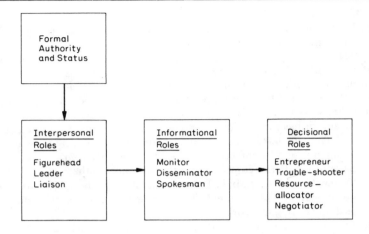

Figure 2.1   The Manager's Roles
(Source: H. Mintzberg, *Harvard Business Review*, July–August 1975)

of his unit the manager also has the role of distributing information, but information is not an end in itself, and the manager plays a major role in the decision-making process.

2.5   Formal Authority

The formal authority vested in the manager gives him the power to require subordinates to work with him and establishes the nature of the demands he may place upon them, but his success will seldom depend simply on his use of this structural authority. Two other factors may be as important in directing the efforts of his subordinates:

personal authority derives from the manager's own characteristics, his standing as an individual, and his skills in dealing with people;
sapiential authority derives from his technical or professional knowledge, skill or expertise.

Managers will use these different authorities in varying combinations depending on the situation and their own inclinations. In an experimental research laboratory sapiential authority will tend to predominate, whilst in field sales management personal and structural authority will be more important.

2.6   Leadership

Leadership and authority are closely related, and management thinking has been much influenced by research into leadership and its impact on group behaviour. Groups tend to appoint their own leaders, and it is probably best if the person appointed officially is one that the group would choose itself. The traditional view of the born leader based on an exhibited profile of characteristics has been supplemented by an understanding that there may be different styles of leadership appropriate to different situations. Thus a wartime crisis was necessary for Winston Churchill to emerge as a great leader. A manager needs to be able to assess the situation and provide the type of leadership that is appropriate. Three different styles of leadership are generally recognized:

Dictatorial leadership: the leader determines policy, decides what needs to be done and how it is to be accomplished, and allocates work to individuals or group.

Democratic leadership: the group is encouraged to participate in decisions and discuss policy. A choice of work-companions is permitted, and a friendlier atmosphere prevails.

Laissez-faire leadership: the group is left largely to its own devices and has to tackle problems as best it can, with little control being exercised from above.

There is no one best style of leadership in management. If a task is either very easy or very difficult, leadership that is primarily seen to be directed towards achieving the task will tend to be accepted, while with tasks of intermediate difficulty a style more concerned with interpersonal relations may be more appropriate. In either event, subordinates and other managers will be quick to recognize any discrepancies between the manager's leadership role in the organization and his ability to perform it.

Personal qualities are of great importance in the manager as a leader since he must be capable of providing the motivation and encouragement necessary to reconcile the individual employee's personal needs and aspirations with the objectives of the organization.

2.7 Liaison

The role of liaison consists of the manager's activities in making contacts outside his vertical chain of command. The average manager spends as much time with people outside his unit as he does with his subordinates, largely in order to build up his own external information system. Clients, suppliers, government and trade organizations, professional bodies, and managers in similar organizations provide him with his perspectives on the outside world. Bankers, management consultants, and general city contacts provide another dimension to his internal sources of information. His effectiveness in disseminating it in a digestible form to his subordinates will be one important influence on their own efficiency.

2.8 Decision-Making

Making decisions is the starting point for all management action and the manager who is indecisive either through personal weakness or in a semi-conscious attempt to avoid this aspect of his role can seriously inhibit the operation of his unit.

H. Igor Ansoff identifies three classes of decision in the firm:

Strategic decisions are those that concern the relation between the firm and its
environment, being concerned with external rather than internal problems
and specifically with the product mix which the firm will produce and the
markets to which it will sell. They cover the firm's objectives, goals and policies,
and tend to be non-repetitive and taken centrally.

Administrative decisions are concerned with organizing the firm's human and
material resources in a way that creates maximum performance potential. They
cover the 'structuring' of authority, work patterns, information flows, and
distribution channels, for example.

Operating decisions deal with budgeting, scheduling operations, supervision of
performance, and exercising control. Examples are setting prices, drawing up
production schedules, and determining inventory levels. Many tactical sales
and marketing decisions fall into this category.

Most managers will make decisions of each of these kinds, but only strategic
decisions are specifically managerial. They concern the threats and opportunities
that face a firm and have to be consciously sought out and identified by positive
action as the insensitive manager may well miss them altogether until it is too late.
This is why Peter Drucker discounts a problem-solving approach to decision
making. He points out that the really difficult job is to select the right question
to ask rather than to provide the right answer, which may be no more than a choice
between relatively obvious options.

The mechanics of decision-making are straightforward enough. The first step is
to identify the real problem and to define it, since the symptoms that are immediately apparent are often not the root cause. Thus, for example, a decline in
production standards may have its origins in unacceptable management styles and
attitudes rather than in the symptoms observed directly on the factory floor. The
facts of the situation need then to be established, and alternative solutions
developed. The next steps are to decide on the best solution and convert the
decision into effective action. Each step has a number of components that will
differ from case to case. The value of this step-by-step approach is that the
manager is forced to consider each aspect of the situation separately, which
improves the quality and incisiveness of his decision-taking.

There are several techniques available to help the manager in reaching decisions.
By utilizing standardized OR (Operational Research) techniques, a manager may
feed data to a computer and rapidly receive guidance as to the outcome of particular courses of action. But he remains responsible for his actions, and the success of
these techniques depends on his skill in defining his objectives and designing the
model of the conditions under which he expects to operate. Thus the marketing
manager of an ethical pharmaceutical company when constructing his market
model would need to estimate the sensitivity of his customer's demand to all the
practical options in the decision variables open to him, i.e. those of price, product,
promotion, and distribution. The computer would deal with the lengthy calculations involved, but the final decisions on the action to be adopted would remain
the manager's alone.

2.9 Delegation

Delegation is closely related to decision-taking. It entails giving authority to a subordinate for a specific task. The superior confers on him a clearly demarcated area of action and control. He retains an overriding responsibility for seeing that the job is done while the assistant accepts accountability for its performance.

Only in the smallest business can a manager retain a personal responsibility for all managerial decisions. As the business grows, he needs to delegate to avoid being overwhelmed with detail. One form of delegation is to bring in specialist knowledge, but a more important aspect is to widen the base of decision-making and at the same time to develop the experience and skills of subordinates.

Many middle managers find effective delegation extremely difficult and the following 'code of practice' outlines some of the conditions for delegating successfully:

1 The tasks delegated must be within the capability of the subordinate
2 Similarly delegation should not extend the manager's span of control beyond his own capabilities.
3 In many cases training may be necessary if delegation is to succeed
4 The senior cannot shed responsibility for the tasks delegated and needs to supervise to ensure that work is being carried out according to his instructions
5 To be effective the delegation needs to be announced so that the subordinate's authority to perform the delegated tasks is generally recognized
6 The subordinate needs the freedom of independent action in the delegated tasks, as delegation implies authority to take decisions without reference back.

2.10 Committees

A committee is a form of delegation that enables concentrated specialist knowledge to be applied to one area of the business. In principle, time can be saved, the involvement of directors can be more widely spread, and the subject can be considered in more detail. Committees may, however, be time-wasting, may be dominated by one strong personality, or may simply be an excuse for delaying decisions unjustifiably. Moreover, a weak manager may hide behind a committee decision.

2.11 The Manager and Results

At the beginning of this chapter management was defined as 'getting things done through other people'. The roles, functions and activities involved in this deceptively simple statement have been described in static mode. Decision-making provided one motor element and delegation began to harness subordinates and other staff to the management process. But the real dynamic of management is only implied in the definition; it is the manager's responsibility for the results of his unit. Achievement of results is the predominant justification for management, and separates the manager quite clearly from other professional executives. The accountant can justify himself in terms of procedures and analyses carried out; the salesman has the job of making sales; and the architect is employed to design buildings. They differ from the manager in that they can point to evidence of a job well done and their organization may yet fail. The manager is much more vulnerable. His planning may be faultless, his accounting techniques immaculate and his personnel management right up-to-date, but if his company fails, if he does not achieve the expected results, these things are to no avail.

The professional football manager illustrates the point excellently. A Don Revie may apply the management experience of many successful years with major clubs like Leeds United, but if his team does not win matches, the fans will soon bay for his blood. Success in most management jobs is not nearly as clear cut as in football, and lack of clarity in defining what constitutes acceptable managerial performance is a major failing in many companies.

2.12 Management by Objectives (MBO)

MBO is a results-oriented approach to management. John Humble in his book, *Improving Business Results*, quotes the following answer from a typical manager when asked what he would need to perform his job better:

> 'Tell me what you expect from me.
> Give me an opportunity to perform.
> Let me know how I'm getting on.
> Give me guidance where I need it.
> Reward me according to my contribution.'

MBO's first step is to attempt to clarify the goals of management activity to see that responsibility for achieving these goals is reasonably distributed among the managers of different grades. The objectives of each unit are defined by the Chief Executive and his senior team. They are in fact asking themselves what they expect the unit to achieve in each of the main areas in which it operates and are identifying those results that are critical to its overall success. Key result areas are defined for each manager's job, and the expected performance in each is expressed in finite terms that should wherever possible be quantified with a time set for achievement. It is customary to involve the manager in this process so that he is personally committed to the standards set.

The essence of key result areas is that they represent the most important activities and tasks of the manager during the period under consideration. He may also have other more general objectives, but these represent the standards of success on which he will be judged. Clearly only a limited number can receive top priority, and five is generally considered a maximum. These goals then form the basis of the manager's personal performance plan, and he works during the agreed period to achieve them. At regular intervals review meetings are held with the aims of monitoring his progress, and of providing any guidance or assistance needed. Objectives may also be modified on these occasions if unforeseen circumstances have made them inappropriate or unachievable. A system of controls that is sufficiently accurate to compare actual performance with that planned in a way acceptable to both the manager and his superior is an important pre-requisite of an MBO scheme.

Table 2.1 is taken from the personal performance plan of the marketing manager of a group of companies manufacturing steel hand precision and cutting tools.

Table 2.1

Key result area	Planned performance	Control
(i) Sales	Achieve the budgeted sales value of £23m representing a 5% increase in volume	Monthly Sales Return
(ii) Product Mix	Increase sales of precision tools from 25% to 30% of total revenue, with a resulting increase in gross margin from 36% to 39%	1) Monthly Sales Return. 2) Quarterly Analysis of product profitability
(iii) Distribution	Achieve distribution of the screwdriver range in 72% of retail ironmongers	Retail Audit Data
(iv) New Products	Carry out market tests for the new micrometer in the Midlands and produce action plan agreed with Board	1) Monthly Progress Report 2) Existence of Plan
(v) Sales Training	Examine the training needs of each salesman and produce proposals for performance improvement	1) Monthly Progress Reports 2) Existence of Proposals

Efforts have been made to make the planned performance as clear and unequivocal as possible and to include only results that depend mainly on the manager's own efforts. Sales achieved are really the job of the whole company, and a number of eventualities, like non-availability of stock, could invalidate this objective. Nevertheless this approach provides a reasonable answer to the manager's requests quoted earlier and applies a valuable discipline for planning into the bargain. The objectives set for each key result area at different levels in the organization provide steps towards achievement of the overall corporate objective. At least in theory, if all individual performance plans are achieved, the company will achieve its own goals.

This approach has been extremely influential, and many other schemes have followed the same lines under different titles. Target Management in Post Office Telecommunications is one example. Targeting is carried out at two levels. The Managing Director reviews proposals and agrees targets with each of his ten Regional Directors after they in turn have gone through a similar process with the General Managers of their telephone area; each region on average has seven areas and 3,000 staff each. Targets cover a wide range of factors under the main headings of revenue, expenditure, demand/supply, quality of service, and manpower. Control is exercised through productivity measures in most cases.

Performance against these targets (except revenue) is monitored monthly at all levels, and the process involves the production and review of a mass of actual performance ratios and outturn predictions. It is left largely to the Regional Director to motivate his staff to meet their regional targets. He is responsible for his region's overall results, and has a wide range of powers to enable him to be so.

2.13   Management Style

The emphasis placed on such aspects of management as leadership, decision-making, delegation, and interpersonal skills indicates that the personal qualities of a manager are extremely important. It is now accepted that there is no one most effective style. The manager has room for some individuality in his approach, and in fact has a degree of choice in the style he adopts. His dress, bearing, attitudes, speech, personal characteristics and general approach to life will affect the impact he makes. Although he will be partly programmed by his upbringing, education, and experience, he can to some degree analyse his impact on others and modify his style to the needs of given situations.

Management theory has tended to represent styles in terms of their position on a scale between two extremes. The main examples are:

concern for production *v* concern for people
leadership (personal strength) *v* bureaucracy (organizational strength)
autocracy (authoritarian) *v* democracy (participative)
innovation (entrepreneurial) *v* stability (avoidance of risk)

These are not mutually exclusive. Most managers will have elements of each, and have the task, consciously or unconsciously of making an effective balance between them. The different demands of the civil service, private business, and the armed forces illustrate the variety that exists. Arnold Weinstock, Lord Robens, Sir Peter Parker, and Tiny Rowland demonstrate the range of personal styles that can serve top managers well.

2.131   *Blake's Management Grid*

Robert Blake used a two-dimensional grid in which the horizontal axis represents the degree of concern for production and the vertical axis the degree of concern for people. On each axis there are nine gradations resulting in a possible eighty-one combinations, although in practice only the five at the corners and the centre of the grid are used. Thus any style can be located by plotting its value on the vertical axis against its value on the horizontal axis. This is shown in Figure 2.2.

The minimum concern for production and for people is denoted by 1.1, whilst 9.9 records the maximum concern for both. The 9.9 manager obtains his results from highly motivated workers operating in a planned and technically effective organization. A 5.5 manager on the other hand is typical of large organizations run bureaucratically. The morale of workers is satisfactory and is balanced by a moderate need to achieve production.

It is possible to classify managers into their positions on the grid with the use of questionnaires designed to record their attitudes towards people and production respectively. Blake suggested a six-phase programme of development to move managers in the directions of the preferred 9.9 ranking. He includes Organization Development techniques of the type described in Chapter 1.

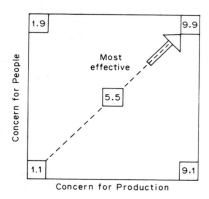

Figure 2.2

2.132 *Theory X and Theory Y*

Douglas McGregor identifies two attitudes towards management, typifying them as Theory X and Theory Y. Theory X assumes that the average human being has an inherent dislike of work and will avoid it if he can. People therefore have to be coerced to make the effort necessary to achieve corporate objectives. It follows that the average human being wishes to avoid responsibility and prefers to be directed, wanting security above everything else. Thus Theory X management is autocratic and discourages participation in the decision-making process by employees.

Theory Y on the other hand assumes that work is as natural as play or rest to the average human being. Rather than inherently disliking work, the individual may find it a source of personal satisfaction and may realize his own self-actualization needs as he directs effort towards organizational objectives. He learns under proper conditions not only to accept but to need responsibility, and lack of ambition and emphasis on security are the results of conditioning and not an inherent trait of human nature. From this approach Theory Y management styles are participaitve, attempting to increase human collaboration and co-operation in the organization as the best means of achieving its corporate goals.

2.14 Management Training and Development

There is undeniably a substantial body of opinion in business that believes that the last thing a manager needs is training. One in four companies in London and the South East offers its managers no training, according to a recent survey by the Manpower Services Commission, and among smaller companies employing fewer than 100 people, management training is provided in less than half. The Commission concluded that for the great majority of the 389 companies surveyed, learning by trial and error was considered the most important part of a manager's education.

It is true that management cannot be taught in the way that other professional disciplines can. As Drucker puts it, 'one cannot as a young man learn what managing managers means, nor managing workers and work. Nothing is as futile as the young man who has learned "personnel management" in a business school and then believes himself qualified to manage people'. Nevertheless knowledge about management is an essential part of management-training and the theoretical study of management techniques and related disciplines like accountancy is essential for the well-rounded manager. Courses are available at most universities, at management training centres like Sundridge Park, Ashridge, and Henley Staff College, at the Polytechnics and correspondence colleges, to cater for the business education needs of the managing director and the school-leaver alike. Many companies run tailor-made courses designed to meet their own special needs, using these colleges or consultants to supplement their own training staff. Major companies like ICI, Barclays Bank, and the Commercial Union have their own training centres, often set in luxurious country-house surroundings. A typical course programme lasts between one week and a fortnight and might include in addition to specific aspects of the company's business, such topics as:

managing human resources and getting the best out of staff;
management information systems and use of the computer;
developing communication skills;
staff appraisal and feedback skills and methods.

Courses tend to be highly participative, with the use of such techniques as closed-circuit television, tape recordings, criticism from other course members and Organization Development (OD) to make the trainee conscious of his performance as a first step towards improving it.

2.15 Developing Management Performance

The essence of management is business performance, and experience in real or simulated operating situations plays a major part in modern management development.

2.151 *Managers of the Future*

The young manager needs actual management responsibility in an autonomous position early in his career. Functional experience is of course also important, but alone it will narrow a manager if he is not put into a position where he can at least see the whole of an operation, even if he does not have actual responsibility for its results. This may be effected by:

appointing him personal assistant to a senior director;
rotating him between departments for a fixed period;
giving him a job with responsibilities designed to meet these needs.

2.152 *Simulated Experience*

There are a number of ways in which management experience can be re-created in classroom conditions and used as a training aid for groups of managers:

computer models can simulate business conditions to demonstrate to trainees the likely effects of their decisions;

business games, like the *Financial Times'* national management games can enable trainees to operate as management teams;

case studies of actual problems and situations can provide trainees with a fund of historical experience.

2.153 *Managers in their Jobs*

The major advance in recent years has been in the design of schemes to improve the performance of the manager actually in his job.

2.1531 *MBO training.* The most widely applied schemes have been based on the MBO approach, and include the 'Improving Business Results' programmes of Urwick Orr and the Management Development schemes of PA Management Consultants. A typical framework of steps in this approach would be:

(a) Advisers are trained, managers are briefed, and at least as important, the support of the Chief Executive is gained.
(b) Present unit objectives are examined to identify scope for improvement.
(c) Key results for each manager are analysed by the manager himself and by an adviser before being agreed by his senior and also by the senior's senior.
(d) At this stage top management reviews conclusions so far and determines the priorities for improvement.
(e) A unit improvement plan is produced and is broken down into specific opportunities for each manager to improve his job.
(f) The results achieved by each manager are reviewed at regular intervals and discussed with him.

As this programme proceeds the manager's development needs are considered and training is planned. In the process top management obtains a much clearer view of his capability and can determine career prospects. This evidence is also extremely valuable in making salary reviews and succession planning.

2.1532 *Action centred training.* Action Centred Programmes have achieved wide acceptance as an alternative to MBO Schemes for management development. Here a manager is set a project that is a real and important part of the company's business, but is designed to give the manager experience, broaden his outlook, and increase his managerial effectiveness. There is nothing simulated about this approach: the manager is faced with all the pressures of a real situation and his career prospects can be affected very radically by his success or failure.

GEC is one company that has made extensive use of this method. A chemist might be given responsibility for the results of a development project, including staff, financial, and marketing aspects. Alternatively a divisional manager might be appointed managing director of a subsidiary. In both cases the experience would stretch the individual and the manager's skills and abilities could be strengthened by a series of progressively more demanding projects over the years. Phased experience of this kind can be difficult to control and the risks and wastage involved can be high. However it does overcome the objection to much management training that it is too theoretical and too remote from the results that the manager needs to achieve in his workplace. Moreover the motivation of a manager who knows that his future depends on the success of his current project tends to be encouragingly positive.

3. The Structure of Business

Traditional theories of economic organization group economic systems into two categories:

3.1 Capitalism

Capitalism has been defined as a system in which the greater part of economic life and in particular new capital investment is carried out by private agencies under conditions of active and substantially free competition with the making of profit as the major incentive. The level and direction of business activity is controlled by the forces of the market which apply the disciplines of market demand and the price mechanism to the activities of manufacturers and entrepreneurs alike. Thus goods and services are produced for which there is an existing demand, and competition among suppliers ensures that scarce resources are used in the most productive way. Planning is carried out by a large number of independent units, and is unco-ordinated, except in the sense that they have in common the need to satisfy the market if they are to operate to maximum profitability.

3.2 Centrally Planned Economies

The alternative system is the centrally planned economy in which economic resources are allocated by a central authority according to a scale of national priorities. Business is transacted by giant state trading and manufacturing corporations, rigidly operating to a series of national plans and performance norms. The indirect disciplines of market demand and the price mechanism are replaced by direct controls that determine the standard of living and the range of merchandise available to the public, as well as the levels of output of the major industries. The choice of the individual is subjugated to the needs of the state. Business enterprise in the capitalist sense is replaced by national planners who try to balance the needs of the population with the resources and production capacity available.

In practice neither system of organization exists purely in the way described here. The USA, regarded as the home of free enterprise, has a measure of central planning and control as well as non-capitalist social services. The USSR on the other hand has diluted the inflexibility of its central planning organization by delegating authority to regional bodies, allowing quasi-free markets in some commodities, and introducing profit-type incentives for managers in basic industries. Most countries employ systems that combine some measure of free enterprise with elements of central planning. Since the end of the Second World War Great Britain has operated a 'mixed economy' in which nationalized industries have worked side by side with private enterprise. Gradually the scope of nationalization has widened until by 1982 the State, in the form of the central government, local authorities, nationalized industries and bodies wholly or mainly dependent on governmental finance employ well over one-half of the working population and account for about 60% of total investment. Indeed some witnesses maintained before the Wilson Committee on Financial Institutions that the size of the public borrowing requirement has inhibited private industry's own investment plans by forcing up interest rates and pre-empting much of the finance available.

3.3 The Public Sector

Differing attitudes to intervention in commerce and industry are perhaps the most important factors distinguishing successive governments as far as business is concerned. Labour cabinets tend to be interventionalist, whilst Conservative ones tend to be less so. The difference is relative rather than absolute; no government can ignore the responsibilities that the growth of the public sector has placed upon it.

The size and influence of the public sector has a profound effect on all types of business. They will find state owned and controlled organizations among their suppliers, customers, and competitors, and perhaps among their shareholders and bankers as well.

Before the Second World War the chief undertakings under national ownership consisted of the postal, telegraph and telephone services, certain Admiralty dockyards, Royal Ordnance factories, HM Stationery Office, and the BBC. Between 1939 and 1951 the railways, London Transport, long distance road haulage, electricity supply, gas supply, coal mining, cables and wireless, the main air services, iron and steel, raw cotton marketing, and the Bank of England had been or were being brought under state ownership. Aerospace and shipbuilding are among those added subsequently. Nationalization has always been politically contentious and in 1981–2 a number of state-owned companies, including British Aerospace, Cable and Wireless, and Amersham International offered shares for sale to the public. Government involvement in business has not been limited to nationalization, however.

3.31 *Regional Policy*

It has long been an aim of government policy to influence the distribution of industry in the United Kingdom. Expansion is strictly controlled in relatively prosperous and well developed areas by the refusal of planning permission for new factories and business premises. There are however an extensive range of grants, allowances, and other incentives to encourage companies to set up in designated Areas for Expansion under the Industry Act 1972 and the Local Employment Act 1972, and there are additional benefits available under the provisions of the Finance Acts.

As can be seen from the map, Figure 3.1, a significant proportion of the United Kingdom qualifies for some form of regional development grant as Special Development, Development, or Intermediate Areas.

The range of assistance currently available includes:

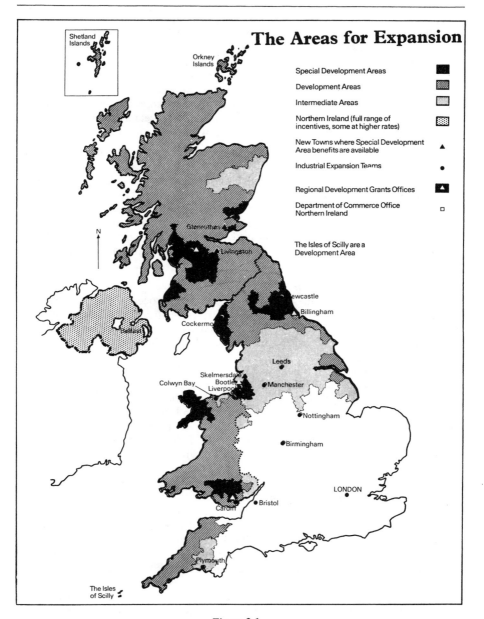

The Areas for Expansion

Special Development Areas	■
Development Areas	▨
Intermediate Areas	▦
Northern Ireland (full range of incentives, some at higher rates)	▩
New Towns where Special Development Area benefits are available	▲
Industrial Expansion Teams	●
Regional Development Grants Offices	◤
Department of Commerce Office Northern Ireland	□

The Isles of Scilly are a Development Area

Shetland Islands

Orkney Islands

N

Glenrothes
Livingston

Newcastle
Billingham
Cockermouth

Leeds

Skelmersdale
Colwyn Bay   Bootle   ●Manchester
              Liverpool

●Nottingham

●Birmingham

LONDON

Cardiff   ● Bristol

Plymouth

The Isles of Scilly

Figure 3.1

Grants for new buildings, works, plant, and machinery.
Selective financial assistance in the form of interest relief grants, removal grants, and service industry grants for projects that provide additional employment on broadly commercial terms.
Government factories for rent or purchase on favourable terms.
Free training services provided by the Training Services Agency.
Settling-in grants and help with travel and removal expenses for transferred workers.
Specially favourable taxation arrangements, such as accelerated depreciation.
Preferential treatment when tendering for government contracts.

The *Small Firms Employment Subsidy* operates on similar lines but in areas that are differently defined.

It is Government policy to help expand employment in manufacturing industry and to aid small firms in the Assisted and Inner City Partnership areas. The Small Firms Employment Subsidy is intended to achieve this by offering to small manufacturing firms in these areas a subsidy for each new job they provide. This currently stands at £20 per week. The Conservative Government, elected in 1979, is reviewing, altering and withdrawing some of these provisions but the basic outlook remains substantially the same.

Industrial Planning and Investment

Planning for investment is one major area where the approach of the private sector contrast radically with that of the public sector. Nevertheless complementary planning is of vital importance, and Britain has been experimenting in recent years with 'indicative planning'. In 1962 the National Economic Development Council was formed for this purpose, representing the Government and nationalized industries; Management, and the Trade Unions, and Economic Development Councils (EDC) have been established for most major industries to participate in planning and to examine the performance of their own industries.

Wool Textiles illustrates the contribution that an EDC can make. The industry's comparative success over recent years in adapting to difficult market conditions is seen at least in part to be due to the efforts of its EDC. The sector as a result of groundwork done by the EDC was the first to be given an aids scheme under the 1973 Industry Act, and over the five years 1973–8 it has re-equipped and moved into new market areas. The EDC has set the industry targets for home and export markets and has monitored progress.

Whilst some of the original EDCs have been retained, for example that for Machine Tools, the post-1974 Labour Government's industrial strategy dissolved some EDCs to make way for 40 Sector Working Parties (SWPs), also with the tripartite membership of Government, Management and Trade Unions, providing a much wider coverage of industry. Both groups of bodies have experienced difficulties in persuading the shop floor, and in many cases management as well, to translate strategy into action. Sometimes there are other more radical reasons for failure. The Petrochemical SWP illustrates the considerable differences that may exist between members. The trade unions insist that the chemical companies should invest heavily in the UK to give Britain a significant lead over the rest of Europe as soon as an upswing in demand occurs. It is however extremely doubtful whether any UK based chemicals major would find it possible to put all its investment eggs in the British basket since experience suggests that it is necessary to have production on the spot to compete effectively in Continental markets. This failure to agree on investment plans for UK petrochemicals highlights some of the problems with the SWP approach.

3.32 *Other Assistance to Industry*

There are a number of other government agencies providing financial assistance to industry. The National Research and Development Corporation (NRDC) was set up with government funds in 1948 to provide finance for developing and exploiting inventions which have failed to obtain backing through normal commercial channels. The Industrial and Commercial Finance Corporation (ICFC) on the other hand provides funds in the £5,000 to £1 million range to companies with a new operation or new management who cannot raise capital on the market for one reason or another but are nevertheless basically sound.

The 1975 Industry Act however greatly increased the emphasis on extending state ownership in the provision of assistance to industry. The National Enterprise Board was set up with initial finance to £1,000 million to assist firms and reorganize industry. A new feature was that it was empowered to extend public ownership not only to companies asking for help, but also into profitable companies. The NEB is required to promote industrial democracy in the undertakings controlled by it and to hold and manage securities and other property in public ownership which is transferred to it. Rolls Royce, Alfred Herbert, and British Leyland are examples. It is expected to earn an 'adequate' return and to make acquisitions exceeding £10 million in a company, or a minimum of 30% of a company's equity.

The NEB has not avoided controversy. During 1978 its action in taking over the Fairey aviation and engineering group, its £40 million investment in the new INMOS micro-electronics company, and its refusal to approve BL's £280 million scheme for doubling production of Land Rovers and Range Rovers without employee agreement on more flexible working practices has shown an agressiveness and toughness of purpose that are unusual in government agencies.

In addition to its activities in assisting the companies in which it has shareholdings, the NEB's role includes organizing company mergers, encouraging product development in key strategic areas of industry such as nuclear equipment, hydraulics, and diesel engines, and helping to expand exports. Many aspects of its current operation may change in the near future, but successive governments have felt the need for an agency to stimulate industrial reorganization, and this is likely to continue in some form or another.

3.4 The Private Sector

Whilst the Public Sector is characterized by giant national boards and corporations, over 90% of enterprises in the Private Sector are small firms employing less than 200 people or having annual turnovers of less than £185,000. Their share of output is less than 25%, and their numbers are declining fast, but their contribution to the nation's economic health is out of proportion to their size. They tend to be labour-intensive and net job creators; they come up with more innovations th‸

large and medium firms; they tend to have better labour relations; and they may
contribute to greater competitiveness in their industries, and hence lower prices.

A strong small-business sector is correlated with economic growth, and Britain,
since the Bolton Report, together with West Germany, Japan and USA, has taken
steps to support small firms.

Table 3.1

Sales

Sales of American-majority affiliates, by country and industry of affiliate
1975, $bn

	Total sales $bn	of which Petroleum $bn	of which Mfg $bn	Total as % of gnp
Britain	45.9	11.1	26.5	20.1
West Germany	38.1	9.7	24.6	9.0
France	26.1	5.1	16.1	7.8
Italy	14.5	4.8	7.4	8.4
Holland	14.2	4.0	7.5	17.5
Switzerland	13.7	1.1	2.5	25.3
Belgium/Luxembourg	13.2	2.4	8.3	20.6
Spain	4.9	0.1	3.6	4.9
Sweden	4.0	1.1	2.0	5.8
EEC	155.8	39.4	91.3	11.5
Europe	186.5	45.1	101.6	10.7

Employment

	No. of US companies	Employees, 000
Britain	1300	800
France	1000	300
Italy	750	200
West Germany	1300	500
Austria	250	?
Belgium/Luxembourg	1100	150
Denmark	200	?
Finland	?	?
Holland	800	125
Ireland	175	25
Norway	?	?
Portugal	100	25
Spain	400	90
Sweden	300	40
Switzerland	500	30

	Employees in Europe, 000	Sales by European units, $bn
ITT	208	6.3
Ford	134	4.7
General Motors	114	5.0
IBM	82	7.0
Chrysler	76	2.5

1976 figures. Intra-group sales excluded where possible. Some sales are
estimated. Source: *The Economist.*

At the other end of the scale is the multi-national company, defined as an enterprise that conducts a substantial manufacturing and marketing operation in a number of different countries. British companies in this category include Imperial Chemical Industries, Unilever, and British Leyland. Although they operate internationally, they tend to take on the nationality of their home countries, and this, combined with the fact that they have not always used their market power responsibly, has often made them the target for hostility in their host countries.

Table 3.1 gives estimates of US multi-nationals' share of business in European countries, the largest but not the only nationality in this category.

In Britain therefore their sales are equivalent to about 20% of the Gross National Product and they employ 4—5% of the working population.

3.5 Forms of Business Undertaking

3.51 *The Sole Trader*

The commonest form of undertaking in Britain is the individual business, the sole trader. The trader himself provides the capital, some of which he may borrow, directs policy, makes his own decisions, does the work, and bears the risks. He is often helped by members of his own family but sometimes also employs paid assistants. His profit has to cover remuneration for his own services and interest on the capital he has invested in the business, either in the form of payments to his source of finance or as a 'notional' return to himself. If he has his own capital in the business, this latter element may never be accounted for, particularly if it is in the form of fixed assets rather than as money balances. In practice the true profit that a sole trader obtains, that is the reward he receives for the risk he assumes does not adequately compensate him. If his business should fail the whole of his private belongings are liable to be taken and sold to satisfy his creditors. He is totally liable for his debts, and has unlimited liability for his business.

In general it is true that an individual is free to go into business on his own account if he wants to. There are of course legal restrictions on this right. Licences may be needed for some forms of enterprise, and local authorities may prohibit some activities in specified areas. The trader may also find that his freedom of action is limited by financial constraints. Nevertheless the individual business is still the most numerous form of undertaking, and predominates in the retail trade, wherever an element of personal service is important, and in the professions.

3.52 *The Partnership*

The first step an individual businessman takes to expand his business may well be to take a partner. This may bring new capital or expertise into the business, or it may be to amalgamate with a competing sole trader and increase the market power of the combined grouping. As defined by the Partnership Act of 1890, a partnership is 'the relation which subsists between persons carrying on a business in common with a view to profit'. Membership is generally restricted to not more than twenty persons, although this restriction does not apply to solicitors, accountants, or members of a recognized stock exchange. Any profit-making association of greater numbers must be formed and registered as a company.

Like the sole trader, the partners provide the capital, run the business, and carry the risk. Their personal liability, like that of the sole trader, is unlimited unless the partnership is registered under the Limited Partnership Act of 1907. In most cases therefore a partner is liable for the debts and obligations of the firm incurred while he is a partner. He is liable both severally and jointly. This means that action may be taken either against an individual partner or against some or all of the partners together for the whole of a debt. A judgment against one however is no bar to a subsequent legal action against others.

A partnership is formed by agreement, and it is usual to commit the agreement to writing in the form of a deed called the Articles of Partnership. This sets out the rights, powers and duties of the partners among themselves. The partners can draft the Articles to meet their own needs, provided of course that they do not break the law.

The Partnership Act of 1890 however includes a model set of articles that are held to apply if a particular question is not covered. Thus in the absence of agreement to the contrary, all partners are entitled to share in the conduct of the business and to an equal share of profits. They are likewise liable to contribute equally towards losses. It is very common however for individual sets of articles to vary the share of profit (and consequently of loss) between the partners according to their share of capital or the amount of effort they contribute. In practice all partners cannot share in the conduct or direction of the business in a managerial sense, and these duties are normally allocated to individuals. The senior partner in an accountancy firm may be directly comparable to the managing director of a company, and of course a partnership may employ numerous additional staff who are not partners.

As mentioned earlier, it is possible to appoint partners with limited liability under the 1907 Act. Their liability is limited to the amount of their agreed capital contribution, they share in the profits of the business, are entitled to inspect the books, and may offer advice, but have no power to limit the firm and may not take part in the management of the business. One important aspect is that there must be at least one general partner liable for all the firm's debts and obligations.

3.53 *The Registered Company*

Neither the sole trader nor the partnership are suitable as forms of organization for major enterprises that might have major needs for capital and be required to grow very fast. Both shareholders and creditors needed assurances that their money was safe that could not be provided by the earlier systems.

The joint stock company therefore developed from the partnership to enable many shareholders to invest their money without, on the one hand, an involvement in the conduct of the business, or on the other an unlimited liability for losses if things went wrong. The earliest joint stock companies followed the scandal of the South Sea Bubble in 1720. These companies were to be either chartered companies operating under Royal Charter, or statutory companies operating under specific Acts of Parliament. Both forms exist today, but the procedures involved were complex and time consuming. The Joint Stock Companies Act of 1844 recognized a third type of organization in the form of the registered company which required only the registration of a memorandum of association and the payment of certain fees. The Act greatly facilitated company formation and was followed by a vast growth in their numbers in the ensuing period. Company Law is currently embodied in the definitive Act of 1948, amended by the Companies Acts of 1967, 1976, and 1980.

3.531 *Legal Entity*. The process of incorporation creates a legal entity that has many of the attributes of an ordinary person. It is able to enter into contracts in its own right and to sue or be sued. But it can only act through its properly constituted agents and only perform these functions permitted by its instrument of incorporation. It exists quite separately from the persons who compose it, and it continues to exist until the correct procedure is followed to terminate it. Its members cannot be held individually responsible for its acts, although its directors and officers may be held liable if they do not conform with the provisions of the Companies Acts. The conditions that regulate the company's relations with outsiders and its own members and define the permitted scope of its activities are included in its Memorandum and Articles of Association, drawn up as part of the formalities of registration.

3.532 *'Ultra Vires'*. If it transacts deals outside this scope it is said to be operating *ultra vires*, it loses its protection from the Companies Acts, and its contracts are void and unenforceable. This doctrine, however, has been restricted by the European Communities Act of 1972. It no longer applies where a person being unaware of limitations imposed by the memorandum contracts with a company in good faith. Thus a company may still be liable on a contract, even if it covers business that is not within the defined limits of its objects clauses. The area of business is decided by the company's promoters themselves prior to incorporation. The principle is that they are obliged to operate consistently with their own stated intentions.

Practically the whole of British manufacturing industry is in the hands of joint stock companies, and large scale private enterprise almost invariably adopts this form. There are over 400,000 companies on the register of the present time of which only 16,000 or 4% are public companies. Nevertheless the combined capital of public companies is vastly greater than that of private companies.

3.54 *Public and Private Companies*

The distinction between private and public companies was redefined by the 1980 Companies Act to meet EEC standards. Previously a private company was defined by the 1948 Act as one that limited its membership to fifty, restricted the right to transfer its shares, and prohibited any invitation to the public to subscribe for them. A public company did not have to meet these conditions, and is clearly a more suitable organization for a large group that needs to raise money from the public.

The 1980 Act made important changes, requiring the public company to conform to a range of minimum standards somewhat wider than those required previously. Thus the new minimum authorized share capital requirement for public companies will be £50,000, and a new company will be required to obtain a registrar's certificate to enable it to do business and exercise borrowing powers. The Act also provides that public companies must include the designation 'public limited company' in their names, instead of the word 'limited'. One other important change is that the minimum number of members needed to form a public company is reduced from seven to two.

The essential characteristic that distinguishes the public from the private company is that the former can offer shares and debentures to the public whilst the latter may not. In future a company that does not satisfy the requirements of a public company will constitute a private company, and the limitations in the 1948 Act relating to private companies will not be retained.

Both private and public companies may elect to be incorporated with limited or unlimited liability, that is to say that a member's liability to contribute towards the company's debts may be limited to the nominal value of the shares for which he subscribes. This is essential if it is hoped to attract small investors with no involvement in the company's management, whilst in small companies the limitation of personal risk may also be critical.

3.55 *Winding-Up*

The process by which the life of a company is ended is termed liquidation or winding-up. The process resembles bankruptcy and follows its rules closely if the company is insolvent, but in other cases is analogous to the administration of a deceased's estate. There are two main types of winding-up; compulsory, where those in control of the company do not want it to be liquidated, and voluntary, where they do not oppose the liquidation.

Any creditor or member may petition the court to wind up the company compulsorily for one of a number of reasons specified by the Acts. The most common are that the company is unable to pay its debts, or that it is just and equitable that it should be wound up. A liquidator is appointed by the Court, and acts under the supervision of a committee of inspection appointed by creditors and members, and of the Department of Trade.

When the directors can make a declaration of solvency, the liquidation proceeds as a Members Voluntary Winding-Up. A special resolution is passed in general meeting, and the members appoint a liquidator who acts under their supervision. In other cases a Creditors' Voluntary Liquidation takes place, with the liquidator supervised by the creditors.

On conclusion of the liquidator's administration the company is dissolved with little ceremony. In a compulsory winding-up the Registrar strikes the company off the register. In a voluntary winding-up the liquidator presents his final accounts to a meeting of members, together with creditors in the case of a Creditors' Voluntary Liquidation, sends to the Registrar of Companies a copy of the accounts and a return of the holding of the meeting, and three months later the company is deemed to be dissolved unless the court orders otherwise.

3.56 *Ownership, Direction and Control*

In principle there is little separation between the ownership, direction and control of a company. The shareholders who provide the money for the business are the owners, and ultimate authority is vested in a shareholders meeting at which they alone have the power to vote. The Companies Acts provide a structure of extraordinary, special, and annual general meetings that alone can make certain decisions. These are subject to legally defined periods of notice and other conditions. Thus auditors can only be appointed at the annual general meeting and a stock option scheme for senior executives requires the approval of shareholders at an extraordinary general meeting. The Acts also provide a number of other safeguards that enable shareholders to influence the actions of the company, usually dependent on obtaining a stated proportion of all shareholders or of the total equity capital to support the move. In practice it is extremely difficult for individual shareholders to play an active part in the management of their companies.

Usually shareholdings are too widely spread to allow shareholders to exert pressure. Tesco Stores for example had 59,263 shareholders in 1981 of whom none, with the exception of a handful of directors and closely related family groups, were beneficially interested in 5% or more of the share capital of the company. In the circumstances an effective shareholders meeting is impossible, although the Acts provide for proxy voting if members cannot attend.

A shareholder may however be unable to contribute sensibly because of age, ignorance of business, or simple apathy. It may be maintained that the small shareholder deliberately abdicates control to the Board to operate in his interest, and, in the case of Tesco at least, this policy might pay him handsomely. If he disapproves of the actions of management he has the option of selling his shares.

The institutional shareholder presents a different case. Insurance companies, investment and unit trusts, and pension funds invest a proportion of the funds at their disposal in public companies. In 1975 the institutions accounted for 65% of all purchases of equity capital, but have traditionally not taken part in the management of the companies concerned. There is however a tendency for them to take a more active part, both because of the size of their influence and as a protection for less expert shareholders. Organizations like Equity Capital for Industry make it a condition of investment that they should appoint a nominee director, a reasonable demand in support of a holding that might well be as high as 30% in some cases. Often an institution will restrict its holding to under 5% to avoid the current legal requirement for disclosure in the annual report.

Once they are appointed, a high degree of trust must be placed in the directors of a company. The Companies Acts prescribe certain of the directors' duties, but these provide only the most obvious safeguards. As described in Chapter 2, it is not possible to codify the manager's role in a legal sense. Its essence is in successful performance by the company, and it is sometimes argued that a shareholder's real interest is confined to receipt of his annual dividend.

3.57 *Recent Developments*

In recent years a broader view of the constitution of the company has been put forward. Other claims than those of the shareholders need to be taken into account.

Customers come first for if they are not satisfied there is nothing to deal with. Governments need to be satisfied if the industry is one that depends on government support in any major way. Employees have an obvious claim, and interests of the general public need to be taken into account. Those who provide the funds, although not necessarily shareholders, need to be satisfied, and managers need to be recognized as a special group of employees with distinct skills and aspirations.

In particular the right of the employee to participate in the running of the business has been recognized. Initially this took the form of joint consultation between staff and management on conditions of employment and the provision of facilities. Some nationalized industries now have worker-directors who are elected by employees, but operate in every other way as a normal director. The White Paper of May 1978 on Industrial Democracy proposed a system of two-tiered boards designed to enable employees to participate directly in the management of their company. A policy board of directors, trade unionists, and shareholders would set corporate objectives and monitor the performance of a management board responsible for the day-to-day running of the company.

These trends represent a very profound charge in the balance of power in the company and have caused serious concern among representatives of management and shareholders. A detailed review of Industrial Democracy is postponed to Chapter 12.

3.6 Development of Organization Structures

The organization structure of the individual business is one of the most critical elements in its success or failure. If structural deficiencies exist, then, as described in Chapter 2:

motivation and morale may be depressed;
decision-making may be delayed and lack quality;
co-ordination between planning and operating may weaken;
liaison between managers may deteriorate;
the company's ability to respond to outside threats may be reduced;
costs may rise as additional co-ordinators and inter-unit meetings are required.

At any given time a company is faced with the *fait accompli* of its existing organization. It has however a wide range of discretion in selecting a structure to meet its needs, and should not regard its current model as immutable. A structure is a means of attaining the company's goals and objectives. These change over time, and development of the organization should keep in step. It follows that there is no one best structure of universal application, and there is little correlation between business success and one particular form of structure.

Joan Woodward in her study of the organizational effectiveness of some 200 manufacturing firms in South Essex found that the 5 most successful unit production firms had organizational characteristics in common, as had the large batch, mass production, and process production firms studied. In unit production for example, short and broadly based pyramids seemed to ensure success, whilst in process production taller and more narrowly based pyramids appeared to be required. Thus the system of production is often an important variable in the determination of organizational structure. But it is not the only one. All the components of organizational structure can be designed to take a number of forms, and a company should give high priority to designing those most appropriate to itself.

Size has very important implications for organizational design. The environment in which it operates, the character of its activities, the degree of uncertainty and risk it faces, its degree of dependence on other organizations, the nature of demand for its products, the strength of competition, its channels of distribution, its product range and development policies, and of course the margin of profit attainable, will be among the factors influencing this selection, whether the company produces consumer or industrial goods or is a finance or professional service company.

In practice there are six areas where organizational choices have to be made.

1 *The nature of work to be done.* This will determine the degree of specialization that is desirable, and the size and structure of operating departments. It will also determine how closely jobs should be defined and the degree of discretion that should be left to individuals.

In turn these factors will condition the amount of supervision required and the character of basic managerial functions.

2 *The shape of the hierarchy.* A balance between the number of hierarchical levels in an organization and the spans of control of managerial and supervisory staff needs to be reached. An extended hierarchy brings increased administrative overheads, communication failures and low motivation of staff at the periphery. A vertical hierarchy based on very narrow spans of control may reduce opportunities for personal discretion and initiative, and reduce momentum as a result.

3 *The grouping of activities.* Activities in an organization may be grouped in a number of ways:

a functional grouping comprises people employing a similar expertise;
a grouping based on processes emphasizes common factors in plant and technology;
a product division grouping centres on a product or service;
a geographical grouping organizes activities by location;
a project grouping would associate all staff involved in a particular project.

In a matrix structure staff and line relationships are combined to get the best from functional and product division groupings. These advantages must be balanced against loss of unity of command and potential conflicts between staff and line management.

4 *Problems of integration.* Inadequate co-ordination between the different departments and the specialist staff of an organization is often a cause of poor performance. The relation between production and sales is one frequent example. The degree of integration required will differ from business to business. Thus where control over the successive stages of an operation is desirable, as in a case like Courtaulds in the cotton industry, a high degree of vertical integration may emerge. Where economies of scale in one stage of distribution are significant, a degree of horizontal integration may be more desirable.

5 *Management control.* The main organizational design decisions concerned with control are:

how far to delegate decision-making;
the extent to which formal procedures and work practices can aid control;
what emphasis to place on direct supervision.

The production of management information and the development of effective
two-way channels of communication are also central to effective control.
6 *Problems of growth.*   A company that decides to expand the scale of its
operations has two basic choices:

> it can grow organically by increasing its working capital and fixed investment,
> producing more of its current or internally developed product ranges, and
> taking a larger share of the markets in which it operates;
> it can grow by acquisition, taking over or merging with other, outside,
> companies.

Organic growth can be a slow and painful course, and there is evidence that it is
easier to raise finance for an acquisition bid than to obtain capital for internal
expansion, in spite of the degree of government assistance often available.

3.7 Acquisitions and Mergers

A merger or takeover is often a much faster way of increasing profits. Market share
may be extended by buying new complementary products, and it is also possible to
buy management and technology as well as fixed assets. A takeover may on the
other hand be defensive, designed to weaken or eliminate competition, safeguard
a market, or secure a source of supply. Yet growth in itself will not necessarily
increase profitability. Size may bring difficulties in management control, extended
communications, and organizational strain. Economies of scale will not be realized
automatically.
  A recent study by Geoffrey Meeks examining 233 mergers between 1964 and
1977 found that in most cases merged companies have been significantly less profitable in the years after a merger than would have been expected on the basis of their
industries' performance if they had continued separately. The costs of increasing
size have often been larger than the savings. This evidence is not conclusive and
there are many exceptions. The GEC-AEI—English Electric merger is certainly one
of the success stories of post-war British industry.
  It is however clear that the search for increased profits through takeovers needs
to be planned with particular care if the expected benefits are to accrue. Synergy,
the condition in which two units earn more together than they can as separate
entities, requires a careful selection of partners based on a realistic view of the
complementary nature of the businesses concerned and the part each will play in
the combined corporate strategy. Thus the merger in late 1978 between luxury
knitwear group Dawson International and John Haggas, the yarn spinner from
Yorkshire will solve a number of problems. The merger will enable Dawson to
diversify down market into worsted yarns. Its knitwear accounts for only 40% of
turnover, whilst the bulk of revenue comes from yarn. Dawson also gets a less
erratic pre-tax profit pattern and the injection of management talent from Haggas.
There is the opportunity for an increased dividend payment from the new holding
company, and Haggas will be able to give shareholders a partial return of its substantial surplus funds through a cash payment, as well as shares in the new holding
company in consideration for their holdings.

The merger between the Anglia and Hastings building soceties illustrates other benefits. The combined group with deposits of £1.2 billion will be able to compete with the giants of the movement through improved economy of management, overall efficiency, the rationalization of branch and agency networks, and an improved national coverage. Compatible lending and investing policies are other plus factors.

3.71 *Vertical Integration*

A company may reduce competition in its markets by extending its control over raw material suppliers on one hand and distribution channels on the other. This process is known as vertical integration, and the Unilever organization provides a good illustration, shown in Figure 3.2.

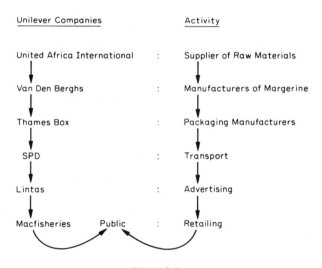

Figure 3.2

3.72 *Diversification*

Diversification is the planned attempt by companies to move into a broader range of activities than they currently encompass. It can be achieved by acquisition and merger or by developing resources that the company already possesses. Motives for this type of strategy are numerous.

Diversification can strengthen a company's hold on its markets through vertical or lateral integration. Thus in the period 1960–70 Reed International, the paper group, bought Field Sons and Co. Carton manufacturers, Wall Paper Manufacturers and Polycell Holdings, also taking over International Publishing Corporation, the parent of the Mirror Newspaper Group.

Sometimes diversification can provide benefits even when common interests are not obvious. This was the case when Allied Breweries, the Skol, Double Diamond and Long Life group, merged with J. Lyons, the tea and foods combine.

Although there was some overlap in soft drinks, a major attraction for Allied was that Lyons has more than half its business outside the UK.

Diversification may be virtually forced on a company by the collapse or sudden decline of a traditional product. The collapse of the transformer market in the UK which followed the oil crisis in 1975 seemed to signal the end for Ferranti's custom-built transformer factory at Chadderton near Manchester. Ferranti diversified into materials handling and its new subsidiary, Ferranti Engineering Ltd, is now making straddle carriers, the large £150,000 machines which shift containers around the docks by moving over them on extended 'legs' and clutching them to their 'bellies'. Transformers now account for only one-third of the plant's output, but the carriers have achieved about one-third of the world market.

Diversification can provide protection against either a downturn in the case of a company overly dependent on a limited range of products, or against a disruption at an individual major customer. In 1973 Midland Engineering had around 40% of its turnover in castings sold to the car industry. By 1977 its dependence on the car industry had been reduced to about 10% of turnover. The tractor industry had replaced it as the group's major source of business, but castings from the group's foundries now supply diesel engines, industrial heating equipment, and Ministry of Defence requirements.

Government policies are sometimes a spur to diversification. The efforts of the tobacco companies to diversify into food, toiletries, cosmetics, and other products not affected by the expected controls on smoking are well known. More recently asbestos has been recognized as a health risk, and Turner and Newall have followed a positive policy of diversification that included eleven acquisitions in 1977. In that year asbestos mining and fibre distribution represented under 10% of sales and only 4% of capital employed.

The Economist commented in May 1978, 'A company that makes a takeover is more often than not doing its shareholders and employees positive harm. And one that diversifies, whether by takeover or internally is usually doing nobody any positive good'. Yet time and time again diversification has provided a new start and fresh opportunities for growth and increased profitability. It is however necessary to investigate a prospect thoroughly before acting and to make sure that management are aware of the conditions for achieving synergy and the steps that must be taken. Often these steps include organization re-structuring on the lines discussed in this chapter.

3.8 Mergers and Organization Structures

Midland Engineering provides an example of a small company that survived an almost disastrous merger in 1969 to grow into a medium-sized group with a turnover of £29.5 million in 1977. Mr Arnold Goldsborough, Group Vice Chairman, explained the approach adopted as follows:

 ' "Following the merger we had become top heavy with head office management. The chain of command was ridiculously long and inefficient; too much time was being wasted on empire building, office politics, meaningless paperwork and administration and not enough time was being spent on running the business.

"The management structure had taken on the appearance of the classic inverted pyramid and the year when we made our loss was when all our chickens came home to roost.

"I have always believed that it is important for management to be where the action is and not sit in some kind of ivory tower, miles away from where the real decisions have to be made," says Mr Goldsborough.

"We have tried to aim at a kind of loose federation within the group with as much local autonomy as possible — so that the man on the spot is not frightened of taking decisions, and if necessary, corrective action can be taken immediately without going through a convoluted chain of command.

"All the managers here are salesmen," says Mr Goldsborough. "We can all go out and get orders and if there are any problems then I expect customers to ring straight through to me or any of the senior managers so that there is no time lag (while memos are written) before action is taken."

Mr Goldsborough does not see the group trying to extend castings output beyond 100,000 tonnes a week. "It's a sensible ceiling for a group this size. Once you go beyond this kind of target then you start to get all the old management problems that size brings with it; while you would probably have to grow much larger before the economies of scale start to work through.

"I believe that once we have reached this target then we will have reached a sensible limit for organic growth — without losing management efficiency — and so we will start looking around for other fields to invest in." '

Source: *Financial Times*

Turner and Newall with 1980 sales of £635 million is in a substantially larger league. As concern over the health hazards associated with asbestos has mounted, the group has pursued acquisitions as part of a long range growth and diversification plan. Many of the same organizational principles apply however.

The group is divided into five worldwide divisions, and the three largest manufacturing divisions are each headed by a chief executive who is also a director of Turner and Newall. Since these divisional chief executives are also chairmen of the individual operating companies within each division, there is close co-ordination and liaison between managers that speeds the flow of decisions through the group and assists the implementation of group policies.

Substantial authority is delegated to operating management, but at the same time tight control is maintained at the centre over profit, planning, capital budgets, and cash flow. A number of essential services are also provided centrally from Turner and Newall's headquarters in Manchester. These include financial, legal, corporate planning, personnel, public relations, and medical services. Figure 3.3 gives an outline of this structure.

The multi-national company often adds great complexity, huge geographical coverage, and sometimes political hostility to the straightforward organizational problems of size.

Many multi-nationals organize their activities on divisional lines, according divisional chief executives a high degree of autonomy subject to certain constraints, very much in the way already discussed for smaller companies. Thus Arnold Weinstock of GEC wrote to English Electric managers after the merger in 1968,

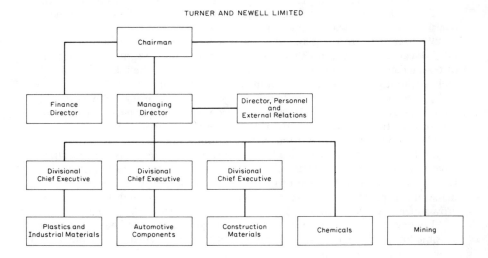

Figure 3.3

'Real success depends on the individual managing directors of our many product units. Our help from HQ does not relieve you in the least of the responsibility for that part of the business which is in your charge. You will of course see that your sub-managers are given well-defined, specific tasks and objectives and discharge their duties effectively . . . The managing director of every operating unit is responsible to me . . . You will have a considerable autonomy for the running of your unit, subject to certain controls . . . ; these are largely financial, but monthly reports should cover everything of consequence concerning the business.'

On the other hand the largest multi-national of all, ITT, has one of the most centralized systems of control ever imposed on a company of comparable size and diversity. Thus more than 100 managers are required to supply weekly reports on their sphere of responsibility and to supplement these with more detailed monthly data. The chief executive holds in his hands effective control over every aspect of the company's operations. Whether it will be possible to retain such iron control over such a disparate number of entities is often asked in the Press. Its record to date is extremely impressive; until it became involved in anti-trust actions in 1973, ITT had achieved 58 consecutive quarters of increased earnings, and its 1980 sales total of $23.8 billion places it on a par with governments rather than companies.

It is pertinent therefore to close this chapter with the question how far multi-nationals are a danger to the countries in which they operate and whether they should be subject to special control. The activities of ITT in de-stabilizing Latin American governments in the early 1970s and the unsavoury revelations about Lockheed's sales promotion practices immediately come to mind.

Multi-nationals are generally attacked because of the peculiar advantages they enjoy in their relationships with the national state. Their size gives them very real power and their international status may enable them to exert political pressures that the large national company cannot. The threat not to invest in a particular country, the temptation to indulge in currency speculation, and the ability to avoid taxation through biassed inter-country pricing policies are some examples.

In practice modern marketing methods demand the existence of multi-national organizations, or something very like them. The sheer scale of the investment in technologically advanced products like computers mean that even the widest national boundaries are too small to justify the costs incurred. Similarly national markets may be too small to be viable, as in the case of tractors and earth-moving equipment for example. The multi-national corporation comes into existence when international trade consists of modern technical, specialized, or uniquely designed products. As such it can claim to contribute to efficiency in marketing and production, to raise living standards through the employment it provides, and to develop exports both through its own efforts and through reciprocal opportunities for the products of the host country overseas.

Their power certainly exists, but the foreign-based company generally brings it to bear more tactfully than equivalent domestic companies. It is up to individual governments to make sure that it is exercised with restraint and that proper guidelines are given. The existence of an internationally administered scheme for the registration and regulation of movements of funds by multi-nationals could contribute here.

4. Channels of Communication

A frequently voiced platitude is that today's major problem in business and industry is lack of communication. Communications have been at the centre of managerial attention at least since the end of the Second World War, and yet Drucker can still maintain that 'Communications are by and large just as poor today as they were twenty or thirty years ago when we first became aware of the need for, and lack of, adequate communications in the modern organization'.

Communication may be simply defined as: 'the act or any natural or artificial means of conveying information or giving instruction'. Good or bad performance in this task has an impact on business results that is quite out of proportion to its apparent simplicity. In his report on a recent series of factory visits, Prince Charles concluded that communication could be an alternative to confrontation in the field of human relationships at the workplace. If the cost of industrial unrest is taken into account, the value of good communications can be seen in its true perspective.

4.1 Communications and the Manager

Most managers are primarily engaged in activities that can be classed as 'communications'. The author's study quoted in Chapter 3 showed that his sample of managers typically spent between 50% and 75% of their time in meetings, in face-to-face discussion, or on the telephone, and this finding is supported by many other studies. The dominance of this aspect of the job is apparent if communications are broken down into their three basic tasks, which are to:

convey facts;
influence opinions;
cause action to be taken.

In this guise communications clearly relate closely to motivation which is at the heart of the manager's function. The manager must be a skilled communicator if he is to achieve his planned results through the efforts of other people via these three steps. This is a social skill that depends on the nature of his interaction with the people under his command and many of the difficulties in good communications relate to the infinite complexity of the individual human being. This is particularly true of the marketing manager, whose activities take him into many departments; his ability to communicate across a broad front is at a premium.

Here it is assumed that the manager has the will to communicate. Sometimes this is not so; he may play things close to his chest for reasons that may range from defensiveness to a genuine regard for security.

4.2 Communications and the Organization

Good communications are also central to organization structure design. An organization depends on a network of communications to co-ordinate its activities and provide forward momentum, and the length of each channel can influence the effectiveness of its operation. In Figure 4.1, chart A, channels between top management and shop floor are relatively direct, and serious distortion would be relatively unlikely. In chart B however a message has further to go, and this organization could be expected to be clumsier and slower in reacting to events, although there might be other reasons, like perhaps the need for highly ranked functional experts,

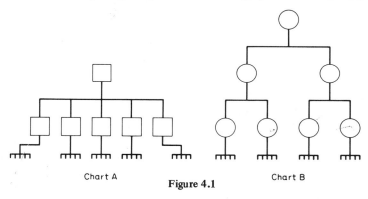

Chart A   Chart B

Figure 4.1

that would justify it. As an organization grows, communication problems increase. Extra co-ordination and supervision are needed to help it to function, and there is a tendency for it to become bureaucratic and paper-logged. There may be a much smaller amount of communication between members who may feel remote from the centre and reduce their participation as a result. Delegation is often an effective counter to this tendency. Thus Britain's largest private employer, GEC, with 191,000 people, is organized into six broad sectors covering networks of related businesses, each of which has a large degree of autonomy and direct responsibility for its results. The Consumer Products sector includes Osram, Xpelair, Hotpoint, GEC (Radio and Television), and GEC-Schreiber, manufacturing lamps and lighting, electric fans, domestic appliances, radio and television, and furniture respectively. Each is organized as a profit-accountable medium sized company and many of the communications problems in a very large organization are reduced. As a principle, minimum interference but maximum communication should be the aim of a central management controlling decentralized units.

Levels of activity in business fluctuate in a broadly cyclical pattern and change in companies tends to be dynamic, either accelerating or decelerating with the trade cycle or in response to some other influence, like new management. It is at times of change that communications become vital since response to management needs to be fast and automatic. If the organization structure inhibits the communication flows between top management, managers, and subordinates, that are necessary to put any plan into action, the company may well share the fate of the dinosaur that became extinct because it could not react quickly enough to outside stimuli.

The lines or channels of communication in an organization flow in all directions. Downward flows are the passing of instructions from senior to subordinate, whilst upward flows are from the workers to management by way of complaints, suggestions, the formal channels of industrial relations, or official reports on results or working conditions. Horizontal flows comprise contacts between functional areas in the normal course of work, between members of technical committees or other groups of members of broadly equal status, like shop stewards' committees.

It is now recognized that informal flows can be both influential and disruptive. The 'grape vine' exists in most, if not all, companies and can seriously distort the facts of a situation if management is slow with a definitive and authoritative version. Informal work groups often exist with their own values and objectives that may differ from those of the organization itself. Communication within such groups will be fast but selective, and a particular distorted view may well be disseminated among members only. Again, management needs to be aware of this situation and to take suitable steps to counter it.

4.3   Channels Available to the Manager

The channels or flows of communication available to a manager within a business are many and varied. The following list is far from comprehensive, but it includes many of the most important means by which a manager can affect opinion, convey information or give instruction. Effective channels should be open in both directions, and the same media are available for the employee needing to contact management.

Oral communication includes:

meetings and conferences	joint consultation
telephone and tannoy systems	trade unions
personal interviews	personnel department
training courses	committees

Oral communication is not necessarily face-to-face, but the degree of personal interaction between the parties is high, impact is immediate, and the temptation to speak without adequate preparation is greater than with the more permanent media. The hasty word is the bane of industrial relations.

Written communication consists of the following:

memoranda and correspondence	house magazines
teleprinters and telex	annual reports
bulletins and notices	organization, policy, and
suggestion schemes	procedure manuals
meeting agendas and minutes	operating reports and proposals

Written communications are in permanent or semi-permanent form and tend to carry more weight than the spoken word. They therefore merit more careful preparation and each should be written in clear and simple language for readability, in a style and layout that is likely to be understood by these for whom it is intended.

Visual means of communication may include:

notice boards	mechanical or electrical signals
wall charts	statistical graphs
posters	visual aids
films and slides	closed circuit television
microfilm	visits to other departments or centres
photographs	organization charts

Generally visual media are less direct than either oral or written communications. The target audience has more freedom to ignore the message, or may simply not notice or understand the display. Visual communications are passive, depending on the subjects' willingness to make the effort to interpret and digest the message. Consequently they do not normally stand alone but are ancillary to the other forms of communications.

Two of these methods stand out as being of major interest to the practising manager. They occur frequently in his work, ahd he is usually able to improve his own skills in using them to a significant extent by practising the principles outlined in this chapter.

4.31 *Committees*

Effective use of time in committees and meetings is of particular importance both because it occupies a large proportion of the manager's working day and because a number of people are involved. Thus half-an-hour wasted by a meeting of sixteen people grosses up to the loss of a whole man-day.

Meetings and committees fall into many categories, ranging from the Board meeting which has statutory functions and responsibility, to the informal meeting of two managers to discuss a particular operating question. The ability to control a meeting and to participate in it effectively are pivotal skills for the manager. He may use a regular work session to co-ordinate the efforts of the staff of a number of departments in a project like the development of a new product; he may use *ad hoc* meetings to hear reports on progress by outside staff; or he may have to present action plans to an executive committee of his superiors. In each case his degree of success in achieving his overall goals will directly relate to the communication skills that he exercises in the meeting.

The chairman's role in controlling discussion, maintaining order, and ensuring that those able to contribute are given the chance to do so, needs to be exercised both firmly and fairly. If he gives the impression that he is using the meeting to railroad his own ideas through he may generate counter-productive hostility among the members. The rules of procedure of the meeting should be understood and consistently enforced. The chairman has to be something of a diplomat as well as being sufficiently sensitive to the tenor of the meeting to know when debate should be curtailed to save valuable executive time.

An agenda distributed in sufficient time before the meeting to allow members to prepare their contributions on each subject in advance can increase the productivity of the group to a great extent. Similarly minutes that record agreed action, responsibilities for taking it, and time scales for its completion can contribute positively to the value of the meeting and provide a means of monitoring progress between meetings.

Meetings can often be a serious waste of time. Peter Drucker in 'The Effective Executive' regards meetings as 'by definition a concession to deficient organization. For one either meets or one works. One cannot do both at the same time'. Meetings need to have clearly defined goals and to be run in a purposeful way towards those ends if they are to justify their existence. A manager needs to be selective in his attendance, asking whether his presence is really needed. He should also be aware that his attention span is unlikely to exceed an hour by a great deal, and he should plan to conclude the meeting within this time-span if possible. A simple mechanism for this is to summarize the progress made and obtain agreement to the next steps to be taken.

4.32 *Interviews*

An increasing amount of attention has been given to development of interviewing skills in recent years, and many leading companies like Barclays Bank, Abbey Life, ICI, and Unilever have provided training for their staffs. Face-to-face interviewing is the most direct form of communication, and one in which manager and employee are at their most exposed and vulnerable.

The *Selection Interview* for new entrants to a company is today usually supplemented with psychological and aptitude tests designed to provide some objective measurement of the applicant's abilities and traits of character. It is always wise to take up references also, but this is seldom possible before at least a provisional decision is reached on whether to engage him or not.

The interview alone will seldom be the sole criterion for selection, but it may nonetheless be a very tense experience.

The interviewer needs to reach a definite decision in a very short time, whilst the applicant is aware that the much desired career may well depend on the impression he gives in the next few minutes. If he is to be given a fair chance to present himself, the interviewer must put him at his ease. The interviewer should also have planned the ground he wishes to cover to enable him to complete an analysis sheet after the interview as a basis for subsequent comparison between candidates. His skill in listening is of critical importance, and he must say only enough to encourage the applicant to supply truthful but comprehensive details of himself and his aspirations. Non-verbal clues (to be discussed in the next section) may provide valuable evidence of the real person behind the facade.

The *Appraisal Interview* employs many of the same skills, yet may have even greater impact on the performance of the individual. Usually held annually, this interview provides for discussion and feedback between an employee and his manager on performance during the year, planned activities for the next year, and a rating or assessment of the individual's work and his prospects of promotion.

Unless handled carefully, this interview may prove an ordeal for both participants. If, however, the interview is properly prepared, if performance is monitored fairly against objectives formulated by the employee himself, and if emotional issues are dealt with in a commonsense way, an appraisal interview can be a very effective means of motivation. Again the manager has to be aware of the interviewee's reaction to what is being said, because the very importance of the topics under discussion can be a barrier to effective communication. The interviewer must ensure that his message is being received without distortion, by maintaining a balanced two-way flow during the interview.

In both types of interview the manager must be constantly aware of the impression he is creating. This is often difficult, but a form of training known as Sensitivity Training can sometimes help. In it a group feeds back to the individual the aspects of his personality and mode of behaviour that seem most striking with an evaluation of his impact on them personally. This process may help in the formation of personal insight that is a good basis for development of communication skills.

4.4 Non-Verbal Communication

The effective exercise of these skills in any form of communication may depend to a very large degree on factors that have little to do with the message itself. Personal likes and dislikes, the popularity and standing of the communicator, pre-held prejudice and bias, and a host of other factors in the environment can intervene between the communicator and his audience, distorting the message to a serious degree. People at work interact with each other continuously, and managers in particular spend a major part of their time interacting with other people. Part of this may be in specific terms, expressed verbally or in one of the ways already discussed. It happens on the surface for all to see, and the manager is in fact saying, 'please listen to me as I have something to tell you'.

At the same time ideas and attitudes are being expressed in a less obvious way without the use of words or the other recognized means. There are many familiar examples of non-verbal communications. Thus in a boy-meets-girl situation a widening of the eyes or a movement of the eyebrows can communicate an invitation as effectively as any words. Sometimes this 'body language' is ritualized as in the handshake that traditionally meant, 'Look, I come in peace, I have no weapon'.

Non-verbal cues are important to understanding the interaction between communicator and audience that determines how efficiently his ideas are transferred. These non-verbal elements fall into the following categories:

(a) Body contacts vary enormously from culture to culture. A Bengali may communicate empathy during a conversation by holding a friend's hand. Stroking or caressing are obvious examples of warmth of feeling. A hand on the arm can express hostility, a desire to attract attention, or a peremptory demand to stop a particular action.

(b) Posture may reflect the attitude of the audience. Slumping may indicate lack of interest or rejection; a rigid posture may reveal unease or a recognition of status; leaning forward towards the speaker may represent aggressive rejection or apt attention, depending on other non-verbal signals.

(c) Proximity and positioning can vary with different situations and the distance at which people sit or stand in relation to each other can give clues to their attitudes to the details that are being communicated. Thus in a round table meeting a member who leans back in his chair may be expressing doubt or dissociating himself with what is being said.

(d) Physical appearance usually remains fairly constant during a meeting, but taking one's coat off can be a sign of relaxation for example, or rumpled hair may indicate pressure or tension.

(e)   Facial movements or gestures are easier to interpret. Facial expressions can monitor for a speaker how he is getting on. Nervous hand movements, a clenched fist, or bitten nails indicate some element of worry, rejection or plain boredom. Folded arms or hands held in front of the body or face sometimes reveal a defensive attitude.

(f)   Gaze direction is one of the most important aspects of non-verbal communication. It can establish on intimate relationship, or a questioning gaze can express doubt or a lack of understanding. By directing his gaze to individuals a speaker can do much to retain their attention. A gaze directed to maintain continuing eye-contact can add dimensions of hostility, dominance, determination, or deep concern to an apparently innocuous spoken message.

Non-verbal communication is one aspect of Interaction Analysis — a technique designed to improve social skills in working with people. Its importance for the manager is that it provides both insights into the quality of his performance as he tries to communicate and a basis for improving his skills in training.

4.5 Obstacles to Effective Communication

The existence of numerous channels is not alone sufficient to ensure effective communications. A medium of communication is a tool that will perform well in the skilled hand, but badly in the hand of an unskilled or clumsy operator. The fact that the skills concerned are personal and social as well as technical adds to the difficulties encountered.

Figure 4.2 presents a 'snapshot' of the process of transfering an idea from one mind to another and receiving another idea in exchange.

It is not difficult to see where the idea may become distorted. The original image has to be couched in words appropriate both to the idea and to B. They then have to be expressed by A who may have personality or speech traits that intrude. As far as B is concerned the similarity of the image received by him to that transmitted by A will depend on the physical act of hearing, the degree of attention that is being paid, and all the subjective elements involved in interpreting and evaluating what is heard. 'Noise' of this kind can reduce the quality of communication anywhere in the system on the return journey between A and B.

4.51 *Inadequacy of the Communicator*

Probably the most frequent examples of 'noise' stem from the shortcomings of the communicator himself. The necessary skills include choice of words that both expresses the message accurately and is understood by the listener. Words mean different things to different people and can change as situations change, so understanding must never be taken for granted. Most evaluative words like 'good', 'acceptable' and 'satisfactory' depend on agreed common objectives and may be meaningless out of this context.

The manager needs what Wilfred Brown refers to as 'a clear language in which all of us can communicate with each other so that we share the same mental models

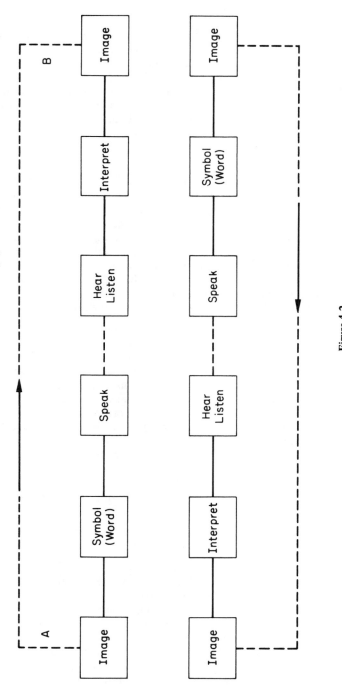

Figure 4.2
(Source: Sundridge Park Management Centre)

of the many social institutions within which we take up different roles (at work)'. Thus a word like 'profit' with its overtones of success on one side and worker exploitation on the other may not only contribute to misunderstanding, but may also generate actual hostility.

Poorly laid-out written communications, and ones that are vaguely-worded or ambiguous are another common weakness. Similarly a poor speaker can materially reduce the level of communication through personal failings in expressing himself.

4.52 *Existing Attitudes*

A communication may be almost totally misconstrued because of pre-existing attitudes between the parties. A recipient may tend to read additional features into a message if he has strong feelings either about the sender or the content. Particularly if he feels threatened, he may reject it consciously or unconsciously, interpreting it in a way favourable to himself. Where industrial relations are bad, the most innocent statement by management may produce a totally unwarranted reaction. Past, bad experiences in communication can lead to rejection of subsequent messages. Where a manager has made a number of statements that are construed by his staff as promises and which do not subsequently mature, distrust may be generated that will hinder future communications of the same type.

4.53 *Status*

Status in the business hierarchy is another barrier to good communications. A wide gap in status between communicator and audience can lead to embellishment of the information communicated beyond its intended meaning. A junior manager may read more into the chance social remarks of the managing director than are really there, perhaps desiring to believe that he has been especially selected to receive an important message. Another employee may become so tense in the presence of a senior manager that his faculty of listening becomes seriously impaired.

Transactional Analysis is a psychological technique that has relevance to business communications. People are seen to react to others in one of three modes or 'ego states':

as a Parent, in an instinctively dominant style like a teacher to a pupil;
as a Child, in an emotional and immature manner, emphasizing personal feelings;
as an Adult, in a rational and logical way characterized by balanced thinking.

An individual may adopt different ego states in different situations, but it is only when an Adult 'transacts' with another Adult that communication flows more freely in each direction. Thus a clerk, experiencing Child reactions on the appearance of a senior director, may be unable to do himself justice in the answers that he gives, particularly if criticism is stated or implied.

It is desirable that nothing should inhibit individuals from applying to others for information, advice, or general help. Status and technical prestige that are based on functions, seniority, privileges, or personal kudos are now recognized to be among the most serious barriers to effective communications.

4.54 *Organizational Weaknesses*

Poorly designed channels of communication can also be a danger. If information does not reach all these who should receive it, its planned objective will not be achieved. Similarly if written communications proliferate, their value will be debased, the system becomes clogged with paper, and managers' attention is diverted from their priority tasks.

As indicated earlier, channels may become over-long and the flow of information may slow down. Quick and continuing access of workers to management is a priority in any business organizations with a labour force of any size.

4.6 Symptoms of Inadequate Communications

The behavioural scientist has shown an increasing interest in business communications in recent years. Yet a manager does not need to be a trained psychologist to delegate work and motivate his staff in their day-to-day contact. Awareness of the symptoms of inadequate communications and their causes can give him the insight to improve his own performance and often to increase the job satisfaction of his subordinates to the benefit of the organization as a whole. The following checklist provides a practical start:

4.61 *Symptoms of Inadequate Communication*

1   An increase in apathy and withdrawal by subordinate staff
2   An increase in rumours and grape-vine activity
3   An unaccountable increase in mistakes and misunderstandings
4   Confusion in the implementation of decisions
5   A tendency for staff to become aggressive and hostile
6   An increase in the general anxiety level
7   Increasing demands by staff on management
8   Frequent demands from subordinates for reassurance of their personal worth
9   Need for repeat communications at a subsequent time
10 Reluctance of managers to make decisions on their own authority.

There are of course many more, and they may also often be the sign of other management weaknesses, such as poor supervision or inadequate training. It is surprising how often weaknesses in communication lie at the root of other management failings. The manager can in practice examine each of the stages of communication listed below in his own area of responsibility and reach his own conclusions:

(a)   Framing a message for transmission
(b)   Selecting the medium
(c)   Transmitting the message
(d)   Receiving the message
(e)   Enquiring whether the message has arrived
(f)   Checking that the planned action has been implemented.

4.62 *An Example from the Mass Media*

The disciplines of the mass advertising media demonstrate an extremely professional approach to communication effectiveness. Framing the message may well involve
extensive market research, many hours of client-agency debate, and the services of
highly-paid creative departments. The effectiveness of the creative approach is
likely to be pre-tested by consumer research prior to transmission. In most major
companies media selection is itself a highly skilled exercise. Media planners will
take meticulous pains to indicate the combination of media that will give the most
economic yield in opportunities to be seen by the target market, which will have
been defined in detailed socio-economic terms. The quality of transmission or
publication will be carefully monitored and post-exposure research will be used to
check on the impact of the message, whilst the mechanical details of 'delivery' will
be registered by the JICTAR or other appropriate media research body. Finally
retail audits will reveal whether the planned consumer action actually occurred.

4.7 Good Business Communications in Practice

Obviously this depth of research and monitoring is not applicable to day-to-day
business communications, but many of the same principles apply and should be
borne in mind by the practising manager as he decides how best to implement his
plans.

Firstly he should frame his message with the recipient clearly in mind. Words,
phrasing, and style need to be tailored to the target audience. Although a clear,
concise, all-purpose style is desirable, there may be occasions when a note to the
chief accountant should differ in style from an announcement to the shop floor.
Reference points, behavioural patterns, and other characteristics will provide a
guide. Choice of medium is equally important. A two-line memo will only convey
the simplest message or confirm action already agreed. If additional explanation is
necessary a face-to-face occasion may be better. Where a favourable reception is
important, a meeting may be necessary to canvass support. Personal presentation
of a proposal to senior management may be more effective than an elaborate report
in achieving this.

An impact may often be reinforced by using additional media to appeal to the
other senses. Thus a product manager presenting a new fabric might well support
his speech (oral) with colour slides (visual) and product samples (touch and smell).

A recent political example illustrates these two points. Bangladesh held its first
general election in February 1979 and immediately encountered the problem of
communicating the details of 55 political parties to a largely rural population, over
75% illiterate, with no national media. The chosen solution lay in a selection of
symbols that soon appeared over every available surface, as shown in Figure 4.3.

Transmitting the message is of vital importance and calls for all the manager's
skills of presentation and self expression. This is the central act of communication,
but the wise manager will also be watching for the first reactions of his audience,
and making appropriate adjustments as he goes along. Listening is one of the major
skills in communications. It is the active side of hearing, consisting of a positive
attempt to understand not only the words but the meaning of the speaker and

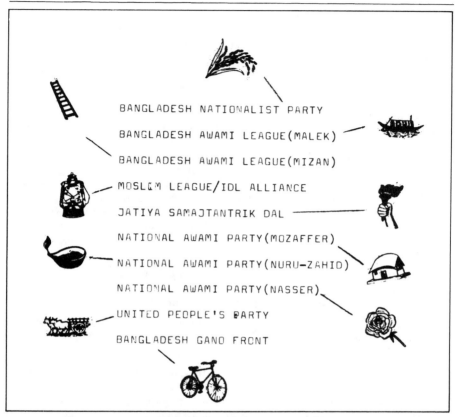

BANGLADESH NATIONALIST PARTY

BANGLADESH AWAMI LEAGUE(MALEK)

BANGLADESH AWAMI LEAGUE(MIZAN)

MOSLEM LEAGUE/IDL ALLIANCE

JATIYA SAMAJTANTRIK DAL

NATIONAL AWAMI PARTY(MOZAFFER)

NATIONAL AWAMI PARTY(NURU-ZAHID)

NATIONAL AWAMI PARTY(NASSER)

UNITED PEOPLE'S PARTY

BANGLADESH GANO FRONT

Figure 4.3   Electoral Symbols of the Main Bangladeshi Political Parties

evaluate his message.

The manager can check whether his message has been received in a number of ways, depending on its nature and the media used. He can:

use a playback device like, 'let's summarize what we have agreed to do';
provide an element of two-way communications by either asking for comment or requiring an answer to a memo;
hold feedback sessions with subordinates;
telephone a sample of those involved;
hold a series of meetings representing all management groups to discuss the proposal.

In many cases of course the effort involved in this procedure is too great for the benefit obtained. Whether a single telephone-call or a major presentation is involved however, the principles of planning message and medium specifically for the target audience, establishing two-way communications, concluding with a summary of the points agreed, and obtaining some feedback of the results, apply to some degree, and are the essence of effective communications.

4.8 Employee Financial Reports

The trend towards more participative management has involved a major effort to communicate financial information about their company to employees, and many companies have began to produce a special annual report for them, avoiding many of the complications of statutory reports. Figure 4.4 from the Brockhouse group of engineering companies shows how dull, financial facts can be given impact and meaning for the layman.

Some benefits of this approach are already clear. A recent study indicates that employees welcome these reports as a sign that management is at last adopting a more consultative approach, and that the report is a positive aid to breaking down the 'them and us' attitude prevalent in much of British industry. Although employees may not have understood the financial information presented and may take little interest in it, they nevertheless want the exercise to continue.

All comment on the new reports has not been as favourable. To some they have appeared patronizing, and it must be admitted that a colourful cartoon approach does not necessarily mean good communications. Another survey among recipients concluded that:

> less than one-quarter of respondents wanted more financial information;
> only one-fifth found the reports 'very interesting';
> 44% regarded them as of little importance to their job.

Some reports are clearly doing only a partially effective job. A manager who wished to improve their quality might well start with the following checklist of questions:

> Do the true objectives concern communication, or simply a gesture to current opinion?
> Is the report a suitable medium for communicating this type of information?
> Does it conform to the expected pattern of company communications, or is it a 'one-off' that will cause suspicions about its motives?
> Is twelve months the optimum period between reports for staff to retain details in mind?
> What steps have been taken to ensure that employees will respond favourably to the report's style and content?
> Can the report be made more relevant to the employees' own job and immediate future?
> How will the impact of the report be monitored?
> How can the two-way principle of communication be introduced?

4.9 The Communications Audit

A working manager seldom has the time or resources to sit down and analyse his communications problems in detail. One answer is to employ outside management consultants to conduct a communications audit.

Stone-Platt is an engineering group with twenty plants in the UK employing between 50 and 1,500 people. Although most manual workers were unionized

Where the money goes . . . .

wealth we have created

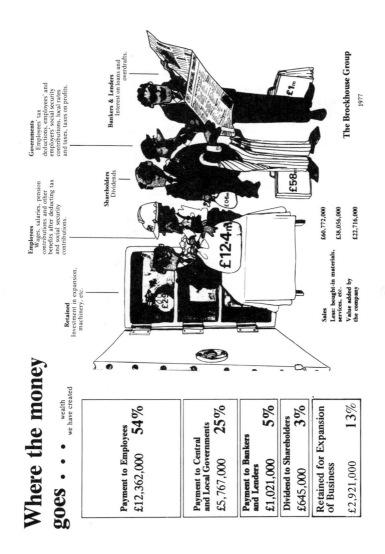

Payment to Employees	£12,362,000	**54%**
Payment to Central and Local Governments	£5,767,000	**25%**
Payment to Bankers and Lenders	£1,021,000	**5%**
Dividend to Shareholders	£645,000	**3%**
Retained for Expansion of Business	£2,921,000	**13%**

Retained Investment in expansion, machinery, etc.

Employees Wages, salaries, pension contributions and other benefits after deducting tax and social security contributions.

Shareholders Dividends

Governments Employees' tax deductions, employees' and employers' social security contributions, local rates and taxes, taxes on profits.

Bankers & Lenders Interest on loans and overdrafts.

Sales	£60,772,000
Less: bought-in materials, services, etc.	£38,056,000
Value added by the company	£22,716,000

The Brockhouse Group
1977

Figure 4.4

there was no central bargaining at the time, and among white collar workers there were varying degrees of unionization. The chief executive wanted to know 'whether we were telling people the right things; whether we were telling people the things they wanted and needed to know; whether there was a free flow of information in both directions; and whether our arrangements were consistent with good industrial practice and making the practice match the theory'.

The major conclusions of the consultants were that:

1　A major gap in communications existed between junior management and supervisors.
2　People tended to learn about new orders, and hence the prospects of the company, from the Press rather than from management.
3　There was scope for improving communications between marketing, engineering and manufacturing.
4　The company tended to communicate bad news rather than good news.
5　Although communications between the centre and the divisions was good, decisions often did not percolate downwards within these divisions.
6　Organization structure, described as a 'three headed monster', was a serious barrier to good communications.

The reorganization has put the lines of command into a readily recognizable form. The pump division was divided into three businesses in the UK, each headed by a general manager running 'profit responsible' management teams. The businesses produce different products and are based at different locations, although certain functions such as technical quality, design, and new products remain partially centralized at divisional level.

A number of direct efforts were made to improve the standard of communication between top management and the rest of the company. These included:

formal communications meetings held regularly for groups of employees;
regular meetings held with foremen;
a house magazine mailed every two months to each employee's home.

In addition a semi-social club for senior and middle managers now receives a 'state of the nation' address from the Chairman at regular intervals.

These are essentially first steps, and a continuing gradual improvement is expected rather than a dramatic leap forward. Management is conscious that there is plenty of room for improvement and that the process of changing attitudes is a slow one. The need to get more instantaneous feedback of the sort of things employees are worrying about at the lower levels is regarded as a major objective for the future.

5. *Planning and Control*

'Plan' is probably the most overworked and misunderstood word in the vocabulary of business. On one hand it has connotations of government bureaucracy and red tape; on the other it smacks of irresponsible crystal ball gazing. In many multi-national companies it is a continuous practice that goes on throughout the year to a formal and rigid schedule, and the plan may sometimes appear more important than the business itself to the harrassed executive faced by its demands. Yet without some basic method of planning the problems of the future seem much more intractable than they really are; the problems of co-ordination between management functions become much more complex; and the task of controlling the progress of the organization much more difficult.

The business plan for a major international company can be incredibly complicated and detailed. The case of ITT is a good example. Through its planning procedures it has developed from a holding company type of operation to become an integrated, multi-national, multi-product and multi-service business including internationally known names like Avis in car rentals, Sheraton in hotels, Abbey Life in life assurance, as well as STC in its 'home' area of telecommunications. More than 200 days a year are devoted to management meetings at various organizational levels throughout the world. The company describes its decision making in the following way:

'... decisions are based on logic — the business logic that results in making decisions which are almost inevitable because all of the facts on which the decisions must be based are available. The function of the planning and the meetings is to force that logic out into the open where its value and need are seen by all'.

Each unit prepares its detailed five year business plan annually. These plans are analysed, reviewed and tested on a continuing basis to ensure that they are responsive to the needs of the market place, the company, and the community.

Whilst planning is one of ITT's major strengths, procedures of this complexity could stifle initiative and entrepreneurial drive in other environments. There is no correct approach. It is partly a question of management style and partly of organization structure concerning the degree of central control exercised and the amount of responsibility delegated to management on the spot. The ITT structure would be totally inappropriate for the Lonrho of Tiny Rowland for example. Nevertheless both types of organization need to plan and both are extremely successful in their different styles.

65

5.1 The Planning Concept

Planning itself is extremely simple in concept. It consists basically of a decision today on where the company wants to be tomorrow and the selection of means and actions that will get it there. A firm has two basic postures that it can adopt towards its future:

> it can react to external changes as they occur, acting opportunistically to good and bad developments; or
> it can follow a pre-determined course of action designed to influence future events in its own favour as far as possible.

Most companies claim to follow the second, but in practice have more in common with the former. A major reason is that the pressure of events can force any but the most well-founded plan off track, and so flexibility to adjust to unforeseen developments must be part of the planning process.

Planning is not a technique in itself, although it may use all or any management techniques. It is rather an approach to business, a philosophy that commits the company to taking its future into its own hands. It is a guide and a method of charting the progress of a firm, but it is not a substitute for risk-taking, entrepreneurial flair or management decision-making, all of which have important roles within the planning framework. It may not be possible to plan the genius of a Ford, Einstein or Edison, but it is possible to plan the environment in which their efforts can flourish.

There is often a temptation to emphasize the strategic or tactical aspects of a plan to the detriment of the other components which may be more or equally influential in causing its success or failure. A similar mix of elements is required in a plan regardless of the product it features, its scale or its aims. These may be summarized in four questions:

1 Where are we now?   — Situation audit
2 Where do we want to go? — Determination of objectives
3 What do we have to do?   — Strategic or tactical action plans
4 How are we getting on?   — Monitoring and control

The emphasis is on a sense of direction and some sort of corporate scanning device to make sure that the destination is reached. Theodore Levitt summed up the basic idea: 'If you do not know where you are going, all roads lead there'. Lack of planning is the most direct route to nowhere.

The corporate plan is an amalgamation of all the individual functional plans of the organization. Activities in each section affect the efforts of other sections, and the corporate plan must cover every facet of the business. If marketing, production, personnel, finance and research plans were drawn up independently the result would compare with a team of horses pulling in different directions, and liaison and co-operation between the managers concerned is of vital importance. This indeed is one of the major 'spin-off' benefits of effective planning. Managers have a clearer knowledge of the opportunities, frustrations and aims of their colleagues in other parts of the business and can take a broader view of their own responsibilities as a result. Moreover a formal plan provides the opportunity not only to understand the framework of thinking within which corporate management operates, but also to judge the quality of its logic, the credibility of its solutions and the value of its contribution to the company as a whole. At this stage it is worth restating the basic reasons why a planning process is both desirable and necessary.

1 Construction of a plan involves the revision of all relevant facts in the current situation that affect the company, the consideration of new developments and the elimination of those hunches, hypotheses or assumptions that have been invalidated since the last revision.
2 It brings together all available information and thinking and co-ordinates them into a self-contained and completely documented charter of the product or service concerned.
3 The plan makes available to all members of the management details of the product's *status quo*, its problems and where the planner intends that it should go. It raises the veil of mystery and enables any manager with appropriate responsibility, authority and determination to appraise the operation in the context of his own function.
4 In this way it places the spotlight on every element in the business plan. Every aspect of production, research, promotional strategy, distribution planning, pricing and product development is open to challenge and informed criticism. The possibility of a strategy continuing from year to year just because nothing better has been proposed is notably reduced.
5 Most important of all, the existence of a corporate plan helps to integrate the different elements of the company. The departments of the company are not a series of independent functions that by quirk of fate or corporate organization are thrown together under one umbrella. Each interacts with the next and all must be considered in relation to each other. Each contributes technical expertise, muscle, creativity and enterprise to differing degrees, but without the structure and discipline of a corporate plan they may burn themselves out unproductively and never make their full contribution to the company's well being.

Newcomers to planning often raise the objection that since it is impossible to foresee the future, it is impossible to plan for it in other than very general terms. There is, of course, an element of truth in this as all forecasts, however soundly based, involve some degree of uncertainty. Here the marketing manager has a critically important part to play. In most businesses the limiting factor is the availability of sales at an acceptable cost, and planning for the company is geared to the estimate of revenue included in the sales forecast. Its accuracy is therefore a key element in the corporate planning process.

Planning involves forecasting all significant developments to a business, but it also includes the element of management intention. Pure forecasting is passive, concerning things that may 'happen'. Planning on the contrary is a positive attempt by management to control and influence its future.

5.2 Situation Audit

The first step is to stop and take stock of where the company and its products are. The temptation is to skimp this stage or to restrict it to a formal exercise. But markets are dynamic and nothing stands still. A well-run company will regularly monitor all significant aspects of its operation as conditions change. Just as machinery inexorably wears out, so technologies change, new materials are developed and competitors gain or lose ground.

Painstaking review of each sector of a company is part of the valuable discipline of planning. If nothing remarkable emerges this year, then at least everyone will sleep that much easier in their beds. But change is endemic, as the table below illustrates. It summarizes a study by the A. C. Nielsen Company covering forty-seven consumer product classes over six years.

Table 5.1

Trend	*Description*	*Proportion* %
↑	Markets in which leader's position improved at the expense of other manufacturers	30
→	Markets in which leader's position showed no significant change	9
↘	Markets in which the leader lost share	42
↓	Markets in which the leader lost leadership	19

It would be interesting to know how many unpleasant and expensive surprises could have been avoided by the simple inclusion of a systematic company situation audit in the annual planning process.

The actual scope of the audit will depend on the amount of information available, the intensity of competition, and the product category in which the company operates. Questions that need to be asked will also vary from situation to situation, but the following outline has a wide application. It has five component parts:

5.21 *The Performance Analysis*

This stage consists of a systematic appraisal of how each part of the company has performed in the previous period. In particular it is designed to define the reasons for present success and failure and to identify the key profit-making factors, that is those that have a disproportionate influence on the final results achieved. Assessment of strengths and weaknesses is fundamental to planning, and many corporate plans come to grief because management is unable to make realistic judgements on its own relative abilities.

In most companies this analysis will cover:

Management	Marketing	Physical Assets	R & D
Labour	Distribution	Systems	Capital Structure
Products	Financial Reviews	Plans	Taxation

5.22 *The Environment Audit*

Whilst the Performance Analysis looks at what has been going on inside the company, the Environment Audit considers developments outside, over which it normally has little control. Economic Factors, like taxation, tariffs, and investment incentives can have important effects on the company's operation. The level of demand facing most companies is closely related to levels of employment and national expenditure patterns for example. Technological changes can very quickly cut the ground from the best established product, and political or legal factors can also be influential. Tobacco and asbestos are two industries that have suffered in this way. Society, industry, and the businesses that serve them are continuously evolving and developing. No individual group can hope to ignore these movements and prosper.

The problems of the nationalized industries are particularly complex because of their vulnerability to changes in government policies. According to a recent survey by the National Institute of Economic and Social Research, British Gas and British Rail make assumptions about 17 economic variables in drawing up their medium range plans, whilst the National Bus Company concentrates on just five. The objective of the Environment Audit is to ensure that all relevant factors are evaluated and taken into consideration. Their number will depend on the facts of the situation.

5.23 *The Market Review*

The market review also concerns factors over which the company has usually little control. Product by product, all the markets in which the company is active or potentially could be active are analysed in terms of:

Market share held over past five years
Growth trends of the whole market and each relevant sector
Product performance in each area
Distribution trends
Price and margin developments
Competitive activity
Usage patterns and trends
Customer profile

The temptation to 'number-crunch' for its own sake must be studiously avoided. The aim is to identify developments that are significant to the company. There is often an inverse relationship between quantity and quality at this stage and a high degree of astuteness and insight are required to get the best out of this review.

5.24 *Assessment of Threats and Opportunities*

This is the first truly creative input to the plan. The facts developed in the survey of market developments provide the basis for this section. Review of these facts should indicate specific threats or opportunities. It would be idle to pretend that this can always be achieved without personal and emotional involvement. Just as every man believes in his heart of hearts that he is a better-than-average driver, so every manager prides himself on his ability to read the signs in the market place.

It is the expertise of management at this stage that will provide the dynamic for the company's progress during the period of the plan.

The threats and opportunities concerned are as wide as the company's area of operations itself:

The Purchasing Manager may identify new materials or suppliers
The Factory Manager may foresee obsolescence for a particular process
The Administrator may see potential cost savings in invoicing procedures
The Sales Director may recognize a new category of customer
The Corporate Lawyer may see a particular threat in product liability

The list is endless, but anything that impacts significantly on the company's business is grist to the planner's mill at this stage.

5.25 *Profit Improvement Programme*

The danger that planning will become bureaucratic and over-academic is a serious one that can discredit the whole process if not kept in check. At this stage the ideas that have evolved for immediate short-term cost savings and improvements should be co-ordinated into a programme of profit improvement projects to take effect immediately. Material benefit can be obtained in this way from the analysis performed so far while the central planning process continues.

5.3 Setting Objectives

In terms of the four basic questions referred to on page 66, the corporate planner now knows where he is. He can now proceed to ask, 'Where do we want to go?'

Objectives should be statements that clearly indicate what it is intended to happen and when. They should be specific, and responsibility for the achievement of each should be attributed to one manager who will be accountable for success or failure. Wherever possible objectives should be quantified and refer to a scheduled time span.

In recent years it has been fashionable to maintain that there is really only one real corporate objective, the improvement of profitability as expressed by the ratio Return on Capital Employed (ROCE). In a long term sense this is clearly true, but in the shorter term this may not be the most effective approach to performance optimisation. A structure of sub-objectives is needed to direct the efforts of all responsible managers in the organization. Peter Drucker in fact defines eight areas that are appropriate for corporate objective setting. They are:

Profitability
Market Standing
Productivity
Use of Financial and Physical Resources
Innovation
Manager Performance and Development
Worker Performance and Attitude
Public Responsibility

The important point is to make objectives action-oriented. There are few prizes for theoretical purity. The aim is to define objectives that will provide the basis for the action that will take the company to its goals at the end of the planning period. At corporate level these may be expressed as desired results, for example, 'To achieve a Net Profit of 15% before tax on net assets at written down value' or perhaps 'To increase our share of the market from 30 to 45%'. These in turn provide the objectives for the activity of each subordinate unit which will produce its own tactical plans to insure that its share of the activity envisaged in the corporate plan is achieved. This multi-tier aspect of planning is illustrated in the following table by the example of a new product:

Table 5.2

Organizational Level	*Appropriate Objective within 12 Months*
1 *Corporate*	To produce an extension to the XY range designed to appeal to the growing pensioner sector for launch in September at a volume rate of 50,000 units in the first 15 months
2 *Department*	
Manufacturing	To achieve a production rate of 500 units of XY/Z per week from 15 July, i.e. immediately before factory shut-down
3 *Section*	
Design Office	To complete design studies for XY/Z not later than 31 March
Drawing Office	To complete drawings for XY/Z not later than 31 May
Purchasing	To finalize the materials specification for XY/Z by end February
Tool Room	To complete tooling for XY/Z by 14 June

Obviously many other departments and sections would be involved, but the method is clear. Each unit knows what is expected of it, and can begin to decide how to go about achieving it.

5.4 Strategic Planning

The heart of the plan lies in the question, 'What do we have to do to get where we have decided we want to go?' This is the strategic element in planning.

Strategy is the package of specific methods that the company chooses to employ to attack the opportunities before it. This is the core of the plan and is the part that enjoys the most glamour and attention. The analogy with military operations is apt. Developing strategy requires ideas, creativity and imagination within the discipline of the objectives that have been set. The competitor is the enemy to be harassed and caught unawares if possible.

Strategy is the grand design that may cover a number of years. Tactics on the other hand are the methods used to meet short-term situations. Thus, as far as the sales force for example is concerned, strategy covers the size of the team, how its activity is spread regionally, its hard or soft sell orientation, its seasonal activity pattern and the channels through which it will work.

Tactics cover such operational considerations as who the salesman will call on, the details of the current promotion, sales literature requirements, what the advertising will say, how sales management will motivate the salesmen, and how to plan, co-ordinate, and integrate all these efforts so that the whole marketing effort moves forward harmoniously in the same direction at the same time.

The process of strategic planning has two phases. Firstly as many ideas as possible that can reasonably be expected to meet the objectives need to be identified and recorded. This process should be as free and open as possible, and managers are encouraged to produce ideas even if they do not at first seem realistic. There are a number of techniques such as 'brainstorming' to facilitate this process. A free flow of ideas can spark off a genuinely original approach to a problem.

Most people have habits of thought that inhibit original thinking. The successful innovator is often distinguished by his methods of thought rather than the inherent quality of his mind. Two types of thinking have been identified:

Vertical or convergent thinking tends to take the most direct logical route to a solution, be content with the first explanation and move on to the next problem. Children of high IQ tend to be vertical thinkers.

Lateral or divergent thinking tends to examine a number of alternatives before deciding which will be the most appropriate. Highly creative children are often lateral thinkers, challenging conventional ideas and seeking new ways of studying situations.

Secondly, the ideas are developed into a number of alternative strategies or planning cases. Each is evaluated in depth and one or two are selected that are judged to be most capable of being developed to meet the objective.

The National Enterprise Board provided a good example of this process in its review of British Leyland's car operations prior to the announcement of the chosen strategy.

Four possible strategies were analysed in depth.

Option 1 would give the company a full range of vehicles ranging from the new replacement Mini to the luxury specialist saloon and sports cars. Sales would be directed to a worldwide market with a target of 1.2 million vehicles by 1986, and the whole of the existing workforce would be employed.

Option 2 involved a controlled withdrawal from the lower end of the market, abandoning both the Mini replacement programme and the proposed middle range car. This would leave a restricted medium-sized range with the emphasis on specialist Jaguar and Rover vehicles. This strategy would result in up to 30,000 redundancies by the early 1980s and total sales declining to less than 700,000 vehicles a year.

Option 3 provided for an immediate withdrawal from the volume car market with concentration on specialist cars. Models would be restricted to the Princess upwards. About 50,000 redundancies would result, with the closure of most of Longbridge, Cowley South, Castle Bromwich, Tile Hill, Liverpool and Seneffe works. Output could be expected to stabilize at about 450,000 vehicles by 1986.

Option 4 again favoured the specialist cars and involved a curtailment of investment on vehicles in the lower ranges. The Mini replacement programme would go ahead, but with lower capacity and less investment. Sales of about 900,000 vehicles could be expected, but the company could expect to be very vulnerable in the medium car range by the late 1980s.

After rigorous analysis Option 1 was chosen on the grounds that it would give a competitive model range with wide market coverage. This would offer flexibility to respond to market changes and also support the present extensive distribution network.

There are, of course, as many strategies as there are companies and market situations. Whatever its business, a company must decide what opportunities it wants to pursue and what risks it is willing and able to accept. Having expressed these general aspirations in terms of specific objectives, its management must define the strategies and tactics to achieve them. This is probably the most stringent acid test of its ability that it will have to undergo.

5.5 The Structure of the Plan

The 'Master Plan' from which all others will be derived can now be drafted. It should include the following information to cover the whole organization throughout the planning period:

1 Statement of purpose and objectives
2 Projected Balance Sheet
3 Forecast Profit and Loss, with volume and margin assumptions
4 Major requirements of finance and facilities
5 Product Development Plans
6 Anticipated staff and labour needs
7 Information on competitors
8 Assumptions on which the plans were based

Long- and short-term operating plans will be drawn up setting out in detail the goals for each sub-unit of the organization both as a statement of direction to the management concerned and as a basis for controlling the progress of the organization towards meeting its objectives. A convenient form for this part of the exercise is to decide on the 'milestones' that have to be passed on the way to the final objective. Thus in the case of Purchasing Department's objective mentioned on page 71, 'To finalize the materials specification for XY/Z by the end of February', milestones might be:

(a)   Initial discussions with suppliers complete by 31 October
(b)   Material performance trials complete by 31 December
(c)   Preliminary cost estimates made by 31 January

(d)   Management approval by 14 February
(e)   Specification finalized by 28 February

5.6 Evaluating the Plan

The completion of the plan is itself a milestone in the company's calendar, but its quality can be no better than the management judgements on which it is based. Prior to implementation it should be analysed in detail and critical faculties brought fully to bear on it. It is helpful to apply three groups of criteria:

5.61 *General Credibility*

Such questions as the following can establish that the plan has sound foundations:

Do the expected results match up to the stated objectives?
Are the resources allocated adequate for the tasks?
Are the underlying assumptions of the plan valid?
Is the proposed activity capable of reaching the plan's goals?
By what mechanism does the proposed action take effect?

The simple direct question is the best analytical tool, particularly as the chain of cause and effect is often not totally understood, even by professionals.

5.62 *Comparison with the Past*

Just as the roots of the future lie buried in the past, so what is achievable in the coming year will bear some relation to what happened last year. Forecasting techniques are still imperfect, but the results included in the plan need to be compared in detail with the latest actual results to ensure that the proposed action is capable of making these changes take place.

Growth patterns in sales volume, sales revenue and market share need to be considered and changes in the components of the product mix and the contribution that each makes towards company profit should be traced. Changes in the basic ratios should be calculated including:

Gross margin	:	sales revenue
Sales revenue	:	sales expense
Sales revenue	:	media advertising
Sales of individual products	:	total sales revenue
Contribution of individual products	:	total contribution

These may be expressed as percentages and may be developed to cover any significant aspect of the plan.

5.63 *Performance Standards*

Unless positive action is envisaged or a change in circumstances expected, the plan should incorporate performance standards that are consistent with those actually achieved in the past, or include an explanation for the improvement. Such standards include:

Average sales revenue per salesman
Average number of sales calls per day
Total marketing expenditure: Total Sales Revenue
Usage per target customer

A dramatic change does not necessarily throw doubt on the credibility of the plan, but it does identify an area where some major action or change in circumstances is making the past significantly different from the future and the reasons need to be understood. The temptation for a 'new broom' manager to assume major increases in productivity without detailed planning is often hard to resist.

5.7 Implementing the Plan

The implementation of the corporate plan is the day-to-day running of the business, but the planning process itself is not complete on the day that systems go live for the first time. Further procedures have to be established before the planner can feel that his task is complete.

The existence of a plan is not sufficient to ensure the results that it envisages. Positive action is needed to control progress and keep the plan updated if circumstances demand a change of course.

5.71 *Overall Co-ordination*

It is usual to appoint an overall co-ordinator to keep in touch with progress and to sound the alarm if significant shortfalls occur. The overall corporate plan of a major group can be very complicated and a critical path network (e.g. PERT) is often advisable to chart the impact that a development can have on the plan as a whole. In many cases this will be a full-time job for the corporate planner concerned.

5.72 *Allocation of Responsibility*

Responsibility for each aspect of the plan needs to be allocated to an executive who can be personally held to account for its success. For each section of the plan therefore there will be a network of subsidiary action plans, each outlining the required activity and when it should be complete, needing to be kept in phase.

5.73 *Plan Review*

The plan needs to be reviewed at regular intervals to ensure that it is still relevant. A plan is not a crystal ball, and circumstances change. It is in no sense a failure to have to up-date the plan from time to time. This should be a routine and regular process carried out monthly in most companies. Only a miracle will result in sales volumes that are exactly 100% of plan, and the impact of even minor variations will be felt in the plans of many other functions of the company.

5.74 *Budgetary Control*

The basic planning control mechanism is the identification of variances from plan and their analysis to reveal what happened differently from what was expected.

A procedure of controls and reporting is required to ensure that planned action is taken when due. A series of monthly meetings is the usual mechanism for assessing progress and ensuring that those responsible take the appropriate action. The most important of these procedures is Budgetary Control.

A budget can be defined as a financial or quantitative statement, prepared in advance of a defined period of time, outlining the policy to be pursued for the purpose of achieving a given objective. It may be regarded as a re-statement of the plan in financial terms.

The first budget to be presented is usually the Sales Budget because in most businesses sales are the limiting factor that will determine the scale of activity in the coming period and other departmental budgets will accordingly be geared to it. It is vital that responsibility for its achievement should be allocated to a named individual who should play a central part in drafting it. Once it has been confirmed that the factory has adequate production resources to make the budgeted volume, the budgeted sales quantities are evaluated at net selling prices and incorporated in the overall Master Budget. The Master Budget is then broken down into a number of budget centres that correspond to the area controlled by each individual manager. Thus separate budgets are prepared wherever there is defined managerial responsibility for an operation or activity. This process is carried out throughout the organization. Most departments have expense budgets covering the level of cost allocated by the plan to their activities. The Sales Budget, however, has two aspects, a sales revenue budget as well as a sales expense budget.

5.8 Variance Analysis

The control element in budgetary control is the determination of variances from the budget. If the budget and the standards on which it is based are in sufficient detail, the magnitude of these variances and the area in which they occur provide the key to management action.

Although profit is not a 'cost' as such, it can be budgeted and the first comparison that should be made is between planned or budgeted profit and actual profit. Having measured this variance it is necessary for the manager to know what factors caused the variance to arise and the extent to which each affected profit. He needs to differentiate between elements of variance due to departures from budgeted quantity, net sales value achieved, unit cost, and sales product mix, so that he can explain why income or profit has exceeded or fallen below budget. In the following example two products, chucks and saws, are sold, and details of budgeted and actual sales performance are shown in Table 5.3.

Sales revenue has fallen seriously below budget and it is clear that three factors have been at work:

the total quantity sold is below budget
the sales mix has altered
the sales prices have changed.

(a)   *The Total Sales variance* represents the difference between total budgeted and total actual sales. In this case it is an adverse variance of

$$£1,380 - £1,160 = £220$$

Table 5.3

	Quantity (units)		Sales Mix (%)	Sales Price (£)	Sales Revenue (£)	
1 *Budget*						
Chucks	60		25	5	300	
Saws	180	240	75	6	1,080	1,380
2 *Actual Sales*						
Chucks	80		40	4	320	
Saws	120	200	60	7	840	1,160

(b) *The Volume or Quantity Variance.* The total quantity sold is 40 units below budget. Taken in isolation, this results in an adverse variance of £230.

As Budgeted:
Chucks   240 x 25% x £5 =   300
Saws   240 x 75% x £6 = 1,080   1,380

Actual Quantity 200 : Budget Price and Mix
Chucks   200 x 25% x £5 =   250
Saws   200 x 75% x £6 =   900   1,150

                                                              230

(c) *Product Mix Variance* results from products being sold in a proportion different from that planned. Here it represents an adverse variance of £30.

Actual Mix : Actual Volume : Budget Price
Chucks   200 x 40% x £5 =   400
Saws   200 x 60% x £6 =   720   1,120
Actual Quantity : Budget Price and Mix (above)   1,150

                                                                30

(d) *Sales Price Variance* isolates the further effect of a change in sales prices, showing a favourable variance of £40.

Actual Price : Actual Quantity : Actual Mix
Chucks   200 x 40% x 4   =   320
Saws   200 x 60% x 7   =   840   1,160
Actual Mix : Actual Quantity : Budget Price (above)   1,120

                                                                40

We can now pull all these variables together to explain the original Total Sales Variance of £220:

	£	
Quantity Variance	230	(Adverse)
Mix Variance	30	(Adverse)
Price Variance	40	(Favourable)
Sales Variance	220	(Adverse)

Other departments will analyse their different variances. Thus most variances from the Production budgets can be traced to variations in one or other of the following:

1 Efficiency
2 Shortages or bottlenecks
3 Sales Pattern
4 Unforeseen circumstances

The reasons for any shortfall from budget can be determined, and action concentrated on finding appropriate remedies. This process is termed 'management by exception'.

5.9 Conclusion

Our guinea-pig company, Consumer & Electrical, follows the pattern of business planning set out in this chapter with some care. The corporate planning process is one of the few functions remaining centralized after the re-organization described in Chapter 2. There is a Director of Planning with a seat on the Board and a highly qualified and experienced staff. There are in fact three plans, a short-term one year plan, a medium-term five year plan, and a rather shadowy long-term ten year plan. The shorter the time scale of the plan, the greater the detail it contains and the more serious is the commitment of the manager concerned to achieving it. The process starts with the Situation Audit described on page 67. Group Divisional Objectives are then defined in discussions between the Chief Executives of the Divisions and the other directors. Divisional objectives are then broken down into objectives for each responsible manager who will contribute to the final result. At each level in the organization these managers outline their own plans for achieving their part of the overall objectives.

Gradually the plan for the whole group takes shape. It may be necessary to revise objectives up or down before the plan is finalized. The activities of the divisions are very different and their plans will provide for these variations.

Planning at Consumer & Electrical is a continuous process, with careful revisions made at regular intervals. It also provides the Managing Director with the tools to control the activities of the Divisional Chief Executives. Actual performance is closely monitored against that called for in the plan, and monthly reporting meetings consider variances from plan and the action proposed to remedy them. Planning in this form is demonstrably result-oriented, and enables the company to react quickly when performance falls short. Divisional Management is not expected to wait for the next meeting before it flags a situation that calls for action and makes its proposals.

At this stage it will be apparent that there are a number of constraints on the company as it plans and controls its operations. One of the most important of these is the Law, and this factor is considered in the next chapter.

6. *Business and the Law*

Today's manager cannot afford to regard 'the law' in Gilbert and Sullivan terms as a bumbling if jovial and well-meaning ass. Nor is it safe to dismiss it as the exclusive province of learned and experienced barristers or solicitors. Whichever way he turns the manager will find his freedom of movement constrained and his interests either threatened or protected by 'the law' in one of its many forms. They represent the 'rules of the game' that he has to play and are a critical aspect of any environment in which he wishes to operate. Whether he is dealing with his staff, paying his taxes, competing in the market place, publishing his accounts, installing office heating, promoting his product, negotiating to buy another company, or undertaking any one of a thousand day-to-day business activities, he will be ignorant of the law at his peril. Successive governments intervene in industry and commerce to differing degrees, but the law remains at the centre of the business process whatever the political colour of the party in power.

The law governing the conduct of business is not an homogeneous body of principles and rules. A manager may well be affected by three distinct orders of law.

6.1 National Law

Almost all countries have their own systems of law regulating business within their national boundaries. In most cases these are either based on a formal constitution and written code (as in the case of France and USA), or combine a number of elements into the judicial system (as in Great Britain). Thus British law consists of:

Common law, based on customs and usages, some of which are very ancient, that are recognized by the Courts.
Case law, the principles of law laid down in cases heard in the Higher Courts.
Statute law, the Acts passed by the Houses of Parliament and the statutory instruments which have been made under them.

In addition the manager must take cognizance of a wide range of regulations passed by such bodies as local authorities as well as a number of codes of practice that may have quasi-legal status.

6.2 International Law

Every export transaction inevitably contains an international element. This raises problems of which the exporter should be aware and which he would disregard at his cost. There are three categories of international law:

6.21 *Public International Law*

Public international law, sometimes called the law of nations, is the body of international custom prevailing between the nations of the world and also between a sovereign state and the citizens of another state.

The exporter may come into contact with public international law through the doctrine of sovereign immunity. When he asks for payment or wishes to pursue a claim for damages under a contract with a foreign government, it may refuse to pay, pleading immunity to private suit. Even where a court makes judgement against the foreign sovereign, the latter may plead sovereign immunity.

6.22 *Private International Law*

When there is a question about which country's laws should govern a particular transaction, a series of rules known as private international law or 'conflict of laws' apply. Thus the capacity of a party to contract is governed by the law of his domicile, the country where he makes his home. The formalities of the contract however are governed by the law of the country where the contract is made. The essential validity, interpretation and discharge of the contract is governed by the law which the parties either explicitly or implicitly intend shall apply. A contract will not be enforced in England if it is illegal in the country applicable to the contract, in the country in which it is to be performed, or under English law.

6.23 *European Community Law*

European Community Law is based on the three Treaties of Rome. They do not contain detailed provisions to regulate the matters to which they apply, but provide a body of general principles and basic rules for the institutions set up to implement the treaties. These institutions are quasi-government bodies clearly distinct from the authorities of the member states and exercise legislative, administrative and judicial rights that member states have conferred on them. Their regulations have general application throughout the Community and are binding in their entirety on member states, being applicable without intervention or interference by national authorities.

Community Law, which is implemented through the European Court of Justice, consists of:

1 the European Treaties establishing the Community
2 the regulations, directives, decisions, and international agreements of the institutions of the Communities
3 the general principles common to the laws of Member States, determined by comparative study and other means
4 the fundamental rights common to the constitutions of Member States, for example the Convention on Human Rights
5 the body of case law and precedent established by the Court of Justice in interpreting and applying the provisions of the treaties
6 the international agreements conducted by the Community with third countries.

The establishment of the Common Market and the gradual approximation of the economic policies of the Member States will have a progressively greater impact on business operations and it is already impossible for any organization to stand aloof from these developments. The following list of community objectives for the main areas of activity indicates how profoundly EEC Law will influence business in each individual country:

Elimination of customs duties and quotas and the introduction of common customs and commercial policies.

Free movement of persons, services, and capital in the Community, including the right to establish businesses and the harmonization of company law.

A common agricultural policy, including the free movement of agricultural products within the Community and a high degree of self-sufficiency in temperate foodstuffs.

A common transport policy, including the integration of road, rail, air and sea facilities.

Regional policies for the correction of structural and regional imbalances.

A Social Fund designed to increase geographical and occupational mobility of labour within the Community.

A common industrial policy, providing a single industrial base for the Community as a whole.

Harmonization of economic and monetary policies, with the final objective of achieving economic and monetary union.

6.3 Civil and Criminal Law

A further distinction has to be made before the content of the law itself can be considered, that between civil and criminal law. The object of civil law is to resolve disputes and to give a remedy to the parties that have been wronged. It may not be necessary to proceed as far as the award of damages if the parties concerned are satisfied by an intermediate outcome. Action is begun by a private individual or firm who has the right to determine how far it shall continue. The object of the criminal law however is to punish the wrong-doer, and is seldom concerned with compensation of the victim. A criminal prosecution is usually begun in the name of the Crown by the police, and its process is not the concern of the victim.

Generally the manager will be more concerned with civil cases, but there are many Acts regulating activities that seem far removed from cops and robbers where breach of their provisions renders the offender liable to criminal prosecution. The Trade Descriptions Acts of 1968 and 1972 are examples.

It is not intended in this chapter to investigate any aspect of the law in depth. The goal is rather to review briefly some of the major areas with which the manager is likely to have contact, summarize current legislation, and indicate where more details can be found. By developing a manager's understanding of the legal factors that influence his work, it is hoped to help him make optimum use of the professional advisers at his disposal. The law can be a very dangerous field for the enthusiastic amateur.

Most managers work for companies, and their day-to-day existence takes place within a maze of rules and regulations contained in the Company Acts, generally referred to as Company Law.

6.4 Company Law

The provisions regulating the operation of companies thus represent a major part of the law of great interest to practising managers. The word 'company' has no strict legal meaning, however, and a rather general and incomprehensive definition has to suffice — 'an association of a number of people for some common object or objects usually involving business for gain'.

From a functional viewpoint there are three distinct types of companies:

1 Those formed for purposes other than the profit of their members, for example for social or charitable purposes.
2 Companies formed to enable a single trader to carry on business with limited liability for its obligations.
3 Companies formed in order to allow the investing public to share in the profits of an enterprise without taking part in its management.

English company law remains uncodified. The major piece of legislation, the Companies Act 1948, was merely a consolidation of the existing statutory rules. Subsequent legislation, notably the Companies Act of 1967 and those of 1980 and 1981, which brought the provisions of the EEC Second and Fourth Directives on Company Law into English law, added to them, but a comprehensive consolidating act is now overdue.

6.41 *Company Formation*

The most usual way to form a company is by incorporation under the Company Acts. The promoters of a company lodge certain documents with the Registrar of Companies, an official of the Department of Trade, and a certificate of registration is granted. The essential feature is public registration, and this type of company is described as a 'registered company'.

Legal personality is not restricted to individual human beings. The process of incorporation grants legal personality to a corporation, and in fact creates an artificial person. The resulting body has many of the powers of a natural person, and can for example hold property and enter into contracts even with its members in its own name.

Companies with special types of objects may be formed under such general public Acts as the Friendly Society Acts or the Trade Union Acts, being termed 'statutory companies'. It is also possible to form a company under a charter granted by the Crown. There are still a few trading companies operating under charters, but chartered companies are more usually charitable or learned bodies. The Chartered Association of Certified Accountants is an example.

6.42 *Public and Private Companies*

A company may be incorporated as either a public or a private company. The distinction between them was redefined by the 1980 Companies Act on the lines of the EEC's Second Directive on Company Law, both to remove some anomalies and also to harmonize British with European practice.

These differences, together with the forms that an enterprise can take under the Companies Acts are considered in more detail in Chapter 3.

6.43 *A Company's Constitution*

A company's basic constitution is set out in its memorandum of association. It states the company's name, its objects, domicile, share capital (if any) and whether the liability of members is limited, and determines its powers and duties. A company operating outside these powers is said to be *ultra vires* and its acts may be void or voidable.

Regulations covering all questions of internal administration are included in the articles of association. These are freely alterable by the company itself within the prescribed procedures. Together the memorandum and articles constitute a contract between the company and the member on the basis of which he subscribes his money. It is however a contract that is alterable by the other party, and it only confers rights and obligations on the member in his capacity as a member.

The form of these articles tends to follow closely the standard format given in the Acts. They contain regulations on a wide variety of matters, such as share capital, meetings, dividends and accounts. They also regulate the relationship of the board and the members.

6.44 *Exercise of a Company's Powers*

The supreme authority in a company rests with a general meeting of the members. Generally a simple majority is adequate for a decision to be valid. Sometimes however the Companies Acts specify additional formalities:

An *ordinary* resolution is one passed by simple majority of those voting and is used for all matters not specifically requiring extraordinary or special resolutions.

An *extraordinary* resolution is one passed by a three-fourth's majority without a stated period of notice. Under the Act it is only required by some matters concerned with winding-up, but often articles specify it for changes in the rights of members.

A *special* resolution is one passed by a three-fourth's majority at a meeting for which 21 days notice has been given. It is required for important constitutional changes as for example to alter the articles or to reduce capital with the consent of the court.

It would not be practical to operate in this way for day-to-day matters, and it is usual to delegate to a board of directors the right to exercise all the company's powers except those expressly reserved to the general meeting. The members cannot interfere with the management of the company whilst the directors remain within these delegated powers. They can replace the directorate and alter the articles to restrict its powers in future, but members are often relatively powerless to influence the affairs of their companies as they happen.

The question of the balance of power between the directors, shareholders and employees of a company is considered in more detail in Chapter 3. The director's current legal duty is to the members, and the interests of employees and consumers are legally irrelevant.

6.45 *Duties of Directors*

A director has a fiduciary duty to the company and must act 'bonafide' in its interests and exercise his powers only for the purposes for which they were confered. In addition to the controlling powers of members, a director is subject to a number of statutory restrictions. He has to show in the Directors' Report to shareholders details of any contracts with the company in which he has a material interest, and Articles generally include a prohibition against voting by a director in respect of any contract in which he is interested. Loans to directors are normally totally prohibited, and the amount of directors' emoluments, pensions and payments by way of compensation for loss of office has to be disclosed. Moreover the Companies Act of 1980 provides more vigorous rules of conduct for company directors. These include new provisions regulating certain transactions where the private interests of directors may conflict with those of the company; a statutory statement of the fiduciary duties and the duty of skill and care that a director owes his company; stronger powers for minority shareholders to seek remedies from the Courts; the introduction of a duty on directors to have regard to the interests of employees as well as shareholders; and provisions to outlaw insider dealing by the introduction of criminal and civil sanctions.

6.46 *Protection of Investors*

The problem here is normally that of protecting the minority, whether they be shareholders or holders of fixed interest securities from the majority. The machinery of company meetings is the means by which investors are supposed to supervize management. The Acts also provide some safeguards when securities are first issued, and it is illegal to reduce the capital of a company subsequently without application to the Courts. The *ultra vires* doctrine however is rarely effective today, and although the ordinary shareholder has an impressive list of remedies at his disposal, it is not always practical or possible for him to exercise them, especially where fraud or oppression are alleged. The famous rule in *Foss* v. *Harbottle* greatly strengthens the position of the majority, however.

It states that if a complaint is made that the directors have broken their duties of loyalty, care, or skill, the company rather than the individual shareholder is the proper plaintiff in an action against them. The rule has been extended to cover all cases where a complaint is about some internal irregularity in the operation of the company. This is because if the complaint is one that can be effectively dealt with by the general meeting it would be futile to litigate over it except with the consent of such a meeting. Generally therefore a suit by a shareholder is only allowed in four circumstances, that is where:

(a) the company is proposing to act *ultra vires*
(b) a special or extraordinary resolution is required but has not been validly passed
(c) an infringement of the plaintiff's personal rights is or may be involved
(d) a fraud is being perpetrated on the minority.

The Acts also provide a series of statutory remedies which may be available when there has been a course of oppressive conduct, even if this has not involved any particular wrongful act. Under the 1948 Act S 222(f) the court may order the company to be wound up if it believes that to be just and equitable. This is the ultimate remedy of the investor or creditor, and may incur a heavy price. The Act contains a number of provisions enabling the conduct of the directors and managers to be investigated and any unauthorized receipts recovered in these circumstances. If however it appears that a winding up would unduly prejudice the interests of the oppressed members, the court may issue an order under Section 210 of the same Act to regulate the conduct of the company's affairs in future without winding-up.

Two other forms of protection should not be overlooked.

6.47 *Department of Trade Investigations*

The Department of Trade has extensive powers to investigate companies. The Department may appoint an inspector of its own authority in certain cases specified by the Acts where fraud, misfeasance, or other misconduct towards members is suspected. It may also do so if the company by special resolution or the court by order declares that its affairs should be investigated. In less formal circumstances the Department of Trade can require a company to produce its books or papers for investigation under the provisions of the 1967 Act.

6.48 *Publicity*

Disclosure of details is perhaps the most effective protection of all. The *Companies Acts* over the years have greatly increased the amount of information that has to be disclosed about a company's operations:

> details of the company's constitution, officers, home, share capital, and financial position have to be registered at the Companies' Registry, and an annual return provided;
> registers of members, mortgages, directors and secretaries, and directors' share-holdings have to be maintained, together with separate minute books for meetings of shareholders and directors;
> its financial position has to be disclosed in the company's published accounts after a professional audit.

These are of course additional to the disclosures required when shares are being offered for sale or other specific transactions are planned. In theory at least, the investor should be able to obtain sufficient information to make an unbiassed and objective decision on the facts available to him.

6.49 *European Company Law*

Progress on the harmonization of Company Law within the European Communities has been slow. The first directive was adopted by the Council in March 1968 and subsequent delays were partly caused by the uncertainty over the entry of the United Kingdom.

There have been six directives that are briefly summarized in Table 6.1.

Table 6.1

EEC Directives for Harmonization of Company Law

Directive	Content
First	Guarantees required of joint stock companies; publication of particulars; validity of commitments undertaken; causes of nullity.
Second	Provisions relating to the function of companies; the contents of their statutes; and the maintenance and alteration of capital.
Third	Regulation of mergers of limited liability companies; publication of adequate information, shareholders rights; guarantees for creditors and employees.
Fourth	Layout of annual accounts; valuation rules; inflation accounting; contents of the notes on the accounts; contents of the annual report; publication; and auditing.
Fifth	Structure of limited liability companies; supervisory boards.
Sixth	Contents of prospectuses.

The Second Directive was adopted by the EEC Council of Ministers in December 1976, and its main provisions were embodied in the 1980 Companies Act, whilst the Fourth Directive was brought into English law by the Companies Act of 1981. The provisions of these Acts were brought into force in stages by a series of statutory instruments with transitional periods of eighteen months within which companies must comply.

Once the validly formed and constituted company has entered its market place, it will encounter another body of law that will be both a restraint and a protection. Competition in marketing is often equated with 'the enemy'. The Law however takes a broader view.

6.5 Competition Law

The legal systems of all major Western industrial powers include provisions to encourage competition as a stimulus to efficiency and to the economic allocation of resources in times of growth. Yet the case is not always clear-cut. Market power is not necessarily used against the public interest, and there may well be a conflict between competition and co-operation, particularly in industries faced by long term declining demand.

6.5.1 *Trestrictive Trade Practices*

The *Restrictive Trade Practices Acts* of 1976 and 1977 require agreements between suppliers and producers of goods and services in the United Kingdom under which the parties accept restrictions on certain aspects of their business to be registered with the Director General of Fair Trading. These matters include:

price of goods or services;
terms and conditions under which they are supplied;
quantities or descriptions of goods to be produced;
persons or areas to supply or receive products or services.

Thereafter the restrictions concerned must either be abandoned or defended before the Restrictive Practices Court. There were 321 agreements on the Register at the end of December 1978. The following examples illustrate how the procedure works:

(a)   A group of suppliers met together to allocate contracts and fix prices for ready-mixed concrete. The Court made an Order against or accepted under-takings from thirty-three companies party to the agreement, judged to be against the public interest.

(b)   A number of suppliers of Diazo copying materials and machines operated oral arrangements relating to discounts, list prices, terms, and conditions of supply over several years. The Court made an Order against the parties concerned or accepted undertakings of future compliance with the Act. These arrangements were refined by the Competition Act 1980, and new Restrictive Practices Court Rules were introduced in July 1982.

6.5.2 *Resale Prices*

Attempts to prevent suppliers fixing prices to the detriment of the public has been a central theme in competition policy. The Resale Prices Act of 1976 prohibits both the collective and individual enforcement of resale price maintenance subject to exemptions where suppliers can demonstrate to the Restrictive Practices Court that continuation of resale price maintenancce will bring benefits that outweigh any detriment occurring. Exemption may be allowed where it appears to the Court that one of the following would occur in the absence of minimum resale prices:

(a)   a substantial reduction in the quality or variety of goods available
(b)   a substantial reduction in the number of retail establishments
(c)   an increase in retail prices in general and in the long run
(d)   sale under conditions likely to cause danger to health through misuse
(e)   a substantial reduction in the necessary services provided with the goods.

The effect of this Act has been to prohibit suppliers, except in the cases of books and medicines, from seeking to compel dealers to observe minimum resale prices by discriminating against them or withholding supplies.

6.5.3 *Monopolies*

Concentration of industrial power does not necessarily lead to abuse, but sheer size may of itself stifle competition. The evidence available is ambiguous. An EEC study in 1977 among the top 292 firms domiciled in Europe found that the largest firms are hardly ever the most profitable, although it is equally apparent that certain large companies are usually among the few that excel.

The Fair Trading Act of 1973 defines a monopoly situation as one where:

(a)   at least one-quarter of all the goods or services which are supplied in the United Kingdom are supplied by or to one person or members of one group. This is known as a 'scale monopoly situation';

(b)   the parties conduct their respective affairs in any way to prevent, distort, or restrict competition. This is known as a 'complex monopoly situation'.

'Prevent, distort or restrict competition' is not defined in the Act but examples would be:

Refusal to supply goods or services to particular customers.
Refusal to supply particular types of goods or services at all.
Supply of goods or services on onerous terms — for example on condition the customer acquires other goods or services.

If a monopoly situation exists or could exist, the Director General of Fair Trading may make a reference to the Monopolies and Mergers Commission, which will determine whether it operates or may be expected to operate against the public interest. In this event an order may be made, or undertakings sought from the company concerned, that it will operate within the provisions of the Act. Thus the Commission concluded that Rank Xerox's policy of only renting and not selling its machines operated against the public interest. During the course of the enquiry Rank Xerox abandoned its rental-only policy and started to offer most of its machines for sale. On the other hand, the Commission found no monopoly conditions operating against the public interest when it investigated the supply of ceramic sanitary ware.

6.54 *Mergers*

There is no presumption that a merger is automatically against the public interest. Mergers falling within the scope of the *Fair Trading Act* are those involving the acquisition of gross assets of more than £5 million, or where a 'monopoly' (defined as 25% or more of the relevant market in the United Kingdom or in a substantial part of it) would be created or enhanced.

However, the expression 'merger' covers not only the acquisition of a controlling interest in one company by another, but also situations in which a company acquires the ability to control in practice, or materially to influence, the policy of another. It should also be noted that the application of the Act extends both to the takeover of a United Kingdom concern by an overseas concern and also to the acquisition by a United Kingdom company of an enterprise abroad.

Over the years the number of mergers coming within the legislation has ranged from about 100 to 150 a year and the number of actual references to the Commission has been about 6 a year.

All relevant public interest aspects are considered, for example the need to maintain and promote competition; the interests of consumers, purchasers, and other users; the scope for technical development and innovation; the maintenance and promotion of a balanced distribution of industry; future employment prospects; the underlying motives; the effect on efficiency; and balance of payments implications. There may also be other points in particular cases, such as possible asset stripping or tax avoidance.

A reference to the Commission is not a condemnation of a merger, only a decision that there are aspects of significant public interest which merit a fuller investigation. It is for the Commission to decide whether a merger or proposed merger falls within the scope of the Act and if so whether it is, or would be, against the public interest.

Two examples illustrate this flexibility:

(a)   Tate and Lyle's bid for Manbre and Garton was not referred to the Commission even though it would significantly reduce competition as the new group would have more than half of the white sugar market.

It was however judged that the two companies acting together would be better able to cope with the inevitable rationalization in the refining industry in maintaining employment.

(b)   Similarly Imperial Group's bid for J. B. Eastwood, the UK's largest egg and poultry concern, was not referred to the Commission since it was argued that employment would be at risk unless the merger was approved.

6.55   *Competition Legislation Abroad*

Control of anti-competition practices in UK applies only to agreements and arrangements which contain restrictions of a *form* specified in the legislation. Elsewhere agreements and arrangements which have the *purpose or effect* of restricting competition are controlled. Effects-based systems of this sort tend to differ in a number of significant respects from the form-based system operated in the United Kingdom. The EEC Law is directly applicable in the United Kingdom and all exporting companies may be profoundly affected by this type of legislation in the countries where they operate.

6.56   *United States of America*

The competition (anti-trust) rules of the United States are contained in three major pieces of legislation:

(a)   The Sherman Act of 1890 (supplemented by others) prohibits every contract, combination in the form of a trust or otherwise a conspiracy in restraint of trade or commerce. The courts apply a test of reasonableness in individual cases, but over the years some practices have come to be regarded as *per se* violations. These include price fixing, market sharing, and collective boycotts. They are criminal offences carrying a fine up to $1 million for a corporation and of $100,000 and three years imprisonment for individuals.

(b)   The Clayton Act (1914) supplemented by the Robinson Patman Act of 1936 prohibits price discrimination the purpose or effect of which is to lessen competition.

(c)   The Federal Trade Commission Act of 1914 contains a general ban supervized by the FTC on unfair methods of competition and other unfair or deceptive acts or practices in commerce.

Neither of these last two Acts carry criminal penalties, but the US authorities enforce anti-trust statutes vigorously. The number of cases brought privately, however, far outnumbers government anti-trust actions. A successful government suit provides the opportunity of claiming damages from large companies when they have been shown to have (for example) kept prices unjustifiably high or engaged in a price war to eliminate weaker competitors.

6.57 *European Economic Community*

EEC competition policy is designed to ensure that there is free and fair competition in trade between member states and that the trade barriers that have been dismantled by the Treaty of Rome are not replaced by private barriers.

The basic rules dealing with restrictions in competition are set out in Articles 85 and 86 of the Treaty. All agreements with the object or effect of 'the prevention, restriction, or distortion of competition within the common market' are prohibited. Exemptions may however be granted for agreements which contribute to improving the production or distribution of goods or promoting technical or economic progress, provided that consumers share in the resulting benefit.

The Commission has taken strong action in the European Court against illegal barriers to intra-Community trade practices that violate the Treaty. By mid-1979 it was handling over 400 complaints, and the following examples demonstrate that it is prepared to flex its muscles against the strongest entrenched interests, whether national or corporate.

Thus the Court judged that the practice of United Brands, the US banana multinational, of charging different prices in different EEC countries, was unlawful as it represented an obstacle to the free movement of trade. Similarly the loyalty discounts given by the Swiss pharmaceutical giant, Hoffmann-La Roche, were found to be an abuse of a dominant market position. These were complex cases that involved some radical new precedents. They also indicated the lengths to which the Commission would go to obtain evidence and secure convictions where apparent violations had occurred.

Governments as well as companies may indulge in restrictive practices. Thus the Court has ordered France to end its restrictions on imports of British lamb. The activities of a UK government agency, the Offshore Supplies Office, set up to aid UK suppliers of offshore equipment and services, have also been investigated following complaints that they represented a discriminatory practice that was unfair.

So far in this chapter consideration has been confined to the major systems of the law and their structure. These are of major interest to the manager or businessman because they exert a significant influence on the environment in which he operates, although seemingly remote from his own actual job. The next two sections have a much closer relationship with the marketplace. Both Contract Law and the law of Consumer Protection are concerned with the details of individual transactions, and come down to earth with a bump.

6.6 Contract Law

A contract has been defined as an agreement between two or more persons which is intended by them to have legal consequence. Contract law is thus at the root of all business since any serious transaction depends on the creation of obligations that the other party expects to be honoured. Not all contracts need to be in writing, and conversely all written contracts are not automatically enforceable.

The most important type of contract is the 'simple' contract which must possess the following essentials to have legal effect:

1 An offer and an unqualified acceptance. All offers must be communicated to the person they are made to before they can be accepted. Thus the display of an item in a shop window does not constitute an offer. If once made, a counter offer or conditional acceptance automatically rejects the original offer.
2 Valuable consideration, that is some element of exchange which is measurable in money or money's worth. It need not be money itself or tangible merchandise. A right, a forbearance, or responsibility undertaken may suffice.
3 An intention to create legal relations. It must be quite clear from the terms of the agreement that the parties intended to create a legally binding contract.
4 Genuineness of consent. Where there is no meeting of minds on a common purpose — 'consensus ad idem' — there is no legally binding contract. Mistake, duress, undue influence, or misrepresentation may in certain circumstances make a contract void or voidable.
5 Contractual capacity of the parties to the contract. An adult may enter into any contract, but there are restrictions relating to drunken persons, persons of unsound mind, aliens, and minors. A registered corporation's capacity to contract is defined by the terms of its memorandum of association.
6 Legality of objects. A contract that is contrary to either statute or common law has no legal effect.
7 Possibility of performance. Reasonable care is not an adequate defence for a breach of contract. An outside cause must make performance physically, legally, or commercially impossible to be an excuse for non-performance.

A second category of contracts does not require consideration to be enforceable. Instead 'speciality' contracts (also termed 'contracts by deed') are written on paper, signed, sealed, and delivered. A number of contracts including the transfer of interests in land for more than three years, promises of gifts, transfers of British ships, and conditional bills of sale are void (i.e. destitute of all legal effect) unless made by deed.

These elements must all be present, and if any one of them is absent, the contract will be void, voidable (i.e. where one party can terminate it at his option), or unenforceable according to the circumstances. The following examples illustrate how these principles are applied in the courts:

A farm was offered for sale at £1,000. A counter-offer of £950 was made, but the offeror agreed to pay £1,000 two days later. On being refused completion of the sale he brought an action for specific performance. Held: There was no binding contract as the counter-offer had destroyed the offer.

(*Hyde* v. *Wrench*, 1840)

A car dealer persuaded a customer to sign a partially covered-up indemnity form which he presented as a release note. Held: The customer was not liable. There was no 'consensus ad idem' as the document was of a different nature from that he intended to sign.   (*Muskham Finance Ltd* v. *Howard*, 1963)

A commercial traveller agreed that he would not seek orders from any firm in areas in which his ex-employer operated. Held: The restraint included firms that were not existing customers of the employing firm and was illegal under the Restrictive Trade Practices Acts.   (*Gledhow Autoparts* v. *Delaney*, 1965)

6.61 *Discharge of Contract*

In general only precise and complete performance of a contractual obligation will discharge a party from his duty, although if part performance is accepted by the defendant, a claim can be made for the value of the part completed.

Alternatively one party may agree to release the other from his contractual obligations. The second agreement must be under seal or supported by consideration, however. Sometimes it may be agreed that as A cannot carry out his obligations to B, C will take his place. This is referred to as 'novation' and all three parties must agree to the substitution.

If the performance of the contract is impossible at the time the agreement is made, then it is void. However the parties will be excused performance in the case of subsequent impossibility in certain specified circumstances. These include a change in law; destruction of the subject matter; personal illness; non-occurrence of a certain event on which the contract depended; a radical change in the performance of the contract; and where the commercial or practical purpose of the contract is frustrated. A party will not however be allowed to succeed in setting aside a contract if he himself is responsible for the frustrating act. Thus charterers of a ship who allowed it to enter the Suez Canal, then a known danger zone, in breach of a term of contract were not allowed to claim that the contract had been frustrated when it became trapped for two months during hostilities.

6.62 *Legal Remedies*

Where one party breaks the contract the other may have recourse to a number of legal remedies. These depend on the nature of the breach. Where a term 'that goes to the root of the contract', described as 'a condition', is broken, the other party can treat the contract as at an end or sue for damages. On the other hand if a term is not essential, it is a 'warranty', and breach does not discharge the contract but allows the injured party to sue for breach and damages.

1 *Damages* are a common law remedy for breach of contract and are compensation for actual loss. They are awarded as of right to place the injured party in the same financial position as if the contract had been performed.
2 *Quantum Meruit.* Under this remedy the plaintiff will be awarded as much as he has earned. Thus a manager appointed by a void contract could recover on a *quantum meruit* for his services.
3 *Specific Performance* is an express order by the court to a contractual party instructing him to carry out his part of the agreement. Normally specific performance will not be granted for performance of a contract for personal services.
4 *Recission* is the discharge of the contract by the order of the courts so that the parties return to their pre-contractual positions. The courts must be satisfied that this is realistically possible before recission is granted.
5 *Refusal of Further Performance* by a person suffering from a breach of contract and wishing to end his obligations under it enables him to set up the other person's breach as a defence to his own.

The Law of Contract may be regarded as the basic framework of commercial law. It establishes rules and standards for what is acceptable in business agreements between two or more parties and provides remedies and a mechanism for obtaining them when a party is injured. Agency is one important example of the application of these rules to a particular form of business activity.

6.7   The Law of Agency

In everyday speech a person who acts on behalf of another is regarded as his agent. The legal definition is however much narrower. In law:

> An agent is a person who possesses authority to act on behalf of another person (known as the principal), with a view to establishing contractual relationships between the principal and a third party.

Just because the term 'agent' is often loosely used it is vital that the businessman or manager is aware of the legal status of the agent with whom he is contracting. In particular he needs to know from what authority the agent assumes power to act on the principal's behalf, and the nature of the agent's own liability on contracts he makes; he then needs to understand the nature of the agent's relationship with his principal both in terms of duties towards his principal and conversely, the principal's duties towards him; finally he should understand when and how an agent's authority terminates.

Fortunately the law is reasonably explicit on all these points, and the position is usually made clear by the body of precedent in case law.

6.71   *The Agent's Authority*

The agent may acquire his power to act on the principal's behalf in one of two ways:

(a)   The principal may expressly authorize the agent to represent him. If the latter receives some consideration for his promise to represent the principal, there then exists a valid contractual relationship between the two.

(b)   In some cases authority may also be implied, and in those instances the law will hold one person (the agent) responsible for the contracts of another (the agent by implication) although he has given no actual authority to the person to act on his behalf.

The instances in which authority may be implied are as follows:

(i)   *Authority may be implied from certain relationships*
Where one partner enters into a contract in connection with the affairs of the partnership he is presumed to be acting as agent of all the partners, irrespective of whether he has really obtained their authority for the transaction in question.

(ii)   *Authority may be implied by necessity*
This means that if A, who is B's agent for certain purposes, has to act on B's behalf in an emergency he may enter into contracts on B's behalf which he has not been expressly authorized to make. Note, however, that A must

already be B's agent; if he were a stranger he would not, even in an emergency, be authorized to make contracts on B's behalf.

(iii) *Authority by ratification*

This is really a case of authority bestowed in arrears. It applies to a situation where a person has made a contract on behalf of another without his authority, and the principal, when discovering what has happened, decided to ratify the act of the unauthorized agent. Where an unauthorized act is properly ratified, the ratification dates back to the time when the act was done, so that the position is the same as if the agent had his principal's authority from the very outset.

(iv) *Authority arising from estoppel*

'Estoppel' is a rule of evidence according to which a person who, by words or conduct, has led others to believe that a certain state of affairs existed, will not be allowed subsequently to deny the existence of that state of affairs. Thus, if A by words or conduct lets C believe that B is his (A's) agent, he will be bound by B's acts as if he were in fact his agent.

(v) *Usual authority*

Whereas ostensible authority results from the principal's words or conduct, usual authority derives from the position which the agent holds in a particular trade or business. Thus, where a businessman instals a manager to run his business, and instructs him as to the type of contract he may make, the manager's actual authority is limited by these instructions, but his usual authority is that which a manager in his position usually possesses.

6.72 *The Agent's Liability on Contracts Made for the Principal*

Where the agent makes a contract on the principal's behalf he does not in general incur any personal liability on the contract, as the contract is one between the principal and the third party only, and does not directly affect the agent, who merely acted as intermediary between the parties. There are, however, certain exceptional situations in which the agent will be personally responsible to the third party for the performance of the contract by his principal.

Thus an agent may find himself liable personally if he contracts:

on behalf of a non-existent principal, as for example in the case of an unformed company;
on behalf of an undisclosed principal, when the third party may choose to claim performance of the contract from the agent or from the principal;
without clearly indicating that he was doing so solely as an agent. This also applies to signing a bill of exchange;
professing to act as agent, but is in fact the real principal.

6.73 *The Unauthorized Agent's Liability to the Third Party*

Where the agent acted without authority, either because he never possessed it or because the authority had expired, the third party may claim against the agent. This is based on the principle of the law of agency according to which a person who purports to act as agent warrants or guarantees to the party, with whom he is making a contract on the principal's behalf, that he possesses the authority which he claims to possess. If it is proved that he did not possess authority the third party may sue him for breach of warranty of authority.

6.74 *Duties between Agents and Principal*

The duties that an agent owes to his principal and vice versa are summarized in Table 6.2:

Table 6.2

Duties owed by:

Agent to Principal	*Principal to Agent*
The Agent must:	The Principal must:
(a) Perform the agency transaction in person unless the principal has agreed to delegation.	(a) Pay the agent the agreed commission until the termination of the agency.
(b) Perform his duties with due care, the degree of care varying with the status of paid or unpaid agent.	(b) Indemnify the agent against any liabilities incurred in connection with the performance of the transaction for the principal.
The Agent must not:	
(c) Allow his personal interest to conflict with his duties to his principal.	
(d) Make a secret profit out of the agency transaction or take bribes.	

6.75 *Categories of Agent*

A number of classes of agent will be encountered in practice, with important differences between them:

(a)   A *del credere* agent is an agent who has undertaken to guarantee to the principal that the third party with whom he has made a contract on the principal's behalf is solvent. If the principal should be unable to obtain payment from the third party because of his insolvency, he could claim from the agent. The agent will usually be rewarded for the extra risk which he is taking by receiving a slightly higher rate of commission.

(b)   A factor (or mercantile agent) is an agent who in the customary course of his business as agent has authority to sell or buy goods or to raise money on the security of goods on behalf of others. The legal position of factors is governed by the Factors Act 1889. In order to qualify as a factor an agent must be in business — i.e., he must habitually act as agent for others, and not merely occasionally.

　　　The essential point is that the owner must have voluntarily entrusted the goods to the agent in his capacity as a mercantile agent. If the agent has obtained the goods by theft, or otherwise without the consent of the true owner, the third-party buyer will not have a good title to them.

(c)   An auctioneer is an agent who has received goods from his principal for the purpose of selling them by public auction. He has authority to receive the purchase price of the goods from the buyer and to give a receipt for it. He has also ostensible authority to sell the goods at any price, so that where the owner has fixed a reserve price below which the goods are not to be sold, and the auctioneer sells them nevertheless at a lower price, the *bona-fide* buyer will be entitled to the goods.

6.76 *Termination of the Agent's Authority*

The authority of an agent bestowed on him by the principal terminates in the following ways:

1   It terminates automatically on the death of either party, on the bankruptcy of either party, and also where the principal becomes insane, or where because of outbreak of war between this country and his own country he becomes an enemy alien.
2   The principal may at any time withdraw the agent's authority. This revocation of the agent's authority must be distinguished from a termination of the contract of agency. The contract of agency, under which the agent may be entitled to some form of payment, may be terminated only in the same way as any other contract, but the agent's authority to represent the principal may be taken away from him by the principal at any time. If the agent has some contractual rights against the principal these would naturally survive.

The principal must however inform third parties who were aware of the agent's authority that it has been terminated. He is also unable to withdraw the agent's authority where it is 'coupled with an interest'.

6.8 Consumer Protection

The movement to protect the consumer from unfair business practices really began with the first Merchandise Marks Act in 1862 which amended the law relating to the fraudulent marking of merchandise. But it was the Sale of Goods Act of 1893 that made the definitive change of direction by modifying the old doctrine of *careat emptor*, i.e. 'let the buyer beware'. It stated that when a consumer buys from a trader it is automatically implied that the goods correspond to their description, are of 'merchantable quality' and are reasonably fit for the purpose for which they were sold. From the 1950s consumerism became increasingly articulate. The appointment of the Molony Committee in 1959 proved a watershed, and today there are many laws which protect the consumer. Some involve criminal penalties as well as civil liability. Their scope, combined with the activities of local authorities, particularly Trading Standards and Environmental Health Departments, Consumer Advice Centres and Citizens Advice Bureaux, and the entrenched influence of other consumer bodies, mean that no manager whose responsibilities include contact with customers should be ignorant of the main provisions of the law. The main Acts which apply are summarized in Table 6.3.

Table 6.3

Aspects of consumer law	*The main Acts which apply*
Compensation to consumers who suffer as a result of a criminal offence	Powers of Criminal Courts Act 1973
Credit and hire purchase	Consumer Credit Act 1974
Dangerous goods	Consumer Protection Act 1961: Sales of Goods Act 1893
False or misleading descriptions	Trade Descriptions Act 1968: Misrepresentation Act 1967: Theft Act 1968: Food and Drugs Act 1955: Sale of Goods Act 1893
Faulty goods	Sale of Goods Act 1893: Supply of Goods (Implied Terms) Act 1973
Faulty services	Unfair Contract Terms Act 1977
Food	Food and Drugs Act 1955: Sale of Goods Act 1893
Hygiene	Food and Drugs Act 1955
Prices: how they are stated, maximum prices	Prices Act 1974: Trade Descriptions Act 1968
Quantity for sale: how information must be given	Weights and Measures Act 1963
Short measure	Weights and Measures Act 1963: Theft Act 1968: Trade Descriptions Act 1968: Sale of Goods Act 1893
Traders' agreements and practices not in the consumer's interest	Restrictive Practices Act 1976: Resale Prices Act 1976: Fair Trading Act 1973
Unsolicited (unordered) goods and services	Unsolicited Goods and Services Act 1975

Source: *Which? Magazine*

Three pieces of legislation stand out as being of particular importance to the manager:

1 *The Trade Descriptions Act (1968)* imposed criminal penalties on any person who applies false trade descriptions, sells goods to which a false description has been applied, or gives misleading information. It gave the Department of Trade the power to require information to be marked on goods or to be included in advertisements, with particular attention to the misleading marking of prices. Thus a seller can be prosecuted if in the course of trade or business he:

gives a false indication that the price at which he is offering the goods is equal to or less than (i) the recommended retail price or (ii) a previous price at which he sold similar goods; or misleads the customer as to the price they will have to pay.

2 *The Fair Trading Act (1973)* contained other major steps towards the protection of the consumer. A Director General of Fair Trading was appointed among whose responsibilities was the identification of consumer trade practices that adversely affect the economic interests of consumers in the UK. A Consumer Protection Advisory Committee was established to consider practices referred to it by the Director and to recommend to the Secretary of State what action should be taken. The scope of the Act is very broad, covering terms, prices and conditions of supply, including the means by which they are communicated to customers; advertising, labelling and other promotion; methods of salesmanship; the way in which goods are packed; and the methods of demanding or securing payment.

The Director may make a reference to the Committee in any of these areas where a consumer trade practice appears to mislead or confuse consumers, subject them to undue pressure, or apply inequitable terms or conditions. For example, steps have been taken under this Act to prohibit a wide range of bargain offer claims, particularly 'worth and value' claims (e.g. 'Worth £10, Yours for £8.50'); 'price elsewhere' claims (e.g. 'You could pay £10 in the West End – our price £8.50'); and 'up to' claims (e.g. 'Save up to 40%').

The Act also provides for the preparation and monitoring of codes of practice, and fourteen had been launched in the period to December 1978.

3 *Consumer credit* has long been regarded as a hot-bed of abuse by unscrupulous operators, and the stigma attaching to usury is very old indeed. The Consumer Credit Act of 1974 provided for the control and licensing of anyone carrying on a credit or hire business and introduced regulations covering advertising and canvassing for credit business. The form of the credit or hiring agreement is set out and a 'cooling off' period prescribed to allow the consumer to change his mind. With hire purchase and credit sale agreements many of the conditions in the old Hire Purchase Acts are retained. Thus:

> once one-third of the total price has been paid, re-possession of the goods can only be achieved by means of a court order;
> the trader is not allowed to enter premises to take possession of goods or to charge a penalty;
> a debtor must be able to pay off the agreement ahead of time, and a rebate of credit charges must be allowed;
> the customer must be allowed the right to terminate at any time with the maximum liability of making up his payments to half the total price.

Implementation of the Act involved the largest licensing operation of its kind since the Second World War. Its scale is illustrated by the following figures:

Standard licences issued to 31 December 1980   103,379
Number of officers employed on enforcement of the Act at
30 September 1980   674

| Number of visits in year to 30 September 1980 | 26,000 |
| Number of warnings given | 716 |

6.81   *Product Liability*

One impending reform in the law may prove to be very important for consumers.

The present law makes the seller liable for the quality of the product. The injured consumer is left with only a remedy against the retailer which may leave him without compensation if the shop which sold the item closes down or goes bankrupt. Otherwise liability may be passed back along the chain of distribution with successive buyers suing successive sellers in a series of legal actions.

The aim of a draft directive of the European Commission on product liability is to make producers legally responsible for defects in the products they put into commercial circulation. A manufacturer would be directly liable for the harm that his defective product caused whether or not he could be shown to have been negligent in any way.

This apparently minor and logical change has caused a storm of emotive protest, and the Confederation of British Industries has been extremely active opposing the measure; it claims that intolerable costs for industry would be involved and that many small producers would be put out of business.

The average cost of compensation awarded after claims resulting from defective products was estimated by the Pearson Commission to be under £500, but the CBI's concern relates to the position in the US where strict product liability of the type envisaged in Europe results in claims for many millions of dollars and much wasteful litigation annually.

6.82   *Advertising*

Advertising is the perennial whipping boy of the consumer bodies and features prominently in much of the legislation discussed in this section. There are approximately seventy Acts of Parliament that affect advertising, but an extremely important part is played by voluntary control imposed within the advertising industry by the Advertising Standards Authority (ASA) and the Code of Advertising Practice Committee in securing adherence to the British Code of Advertising Practice.

All the media bodies are signatories to the Code, and various other linked organizations such as the British Direct Mail Association, the British Poster Advertising Association, and the Proprietary Association of Great Britain are associated. If an agency contravenes the Code it may find that the offending advertisement has been banned by the appropriate media until the offending piece has been removed. Thus the Code is enforced much more quickly than the law can be by the courts. Moreover an agency that offends persistently may find its recognition withdrawn by the media bodies with the result that it will no longer be entitled to commission.

During 1978 the Office of Fair Trading carried out market research to evaluate this self-regulatory system of advertising control. Its report concluded that overall it was working well, and there was no evidence to suggest that comprehensive legal controls were needed.

6.9 Conclusion

Any review of business law tends to give the impression that companies are always tumbling in and out of the courts. In practice nothing could be further from the truth. It is widely recognized that litigation can be long-drawn-out and expensive. Even where a company obtains a judgement in its favour it may be the loser financially and may incur dubious publicity.

Our guinea-pig company, Consumer & Electrical Co. Ltd, is well aware of this, and it employs a small legal department under a qualified barrister to keep itself out of the courts, in addition to retaining the services of two firms of solicitors, one City and one local.

The group will go to considerable lengths to avoid a complaint or reference to a government agency. Even if this does not result in discrimination against the group when government contracts are awarded, it will be time-wasting, may damage the group's goodwill, and may attract unwelcome investigation. The group falls over backwards to satisfy the small number of customers who complain, realizing that a case won is still business lost. Its far-sighted personnel policies have also avoided any legal cases involving staff.

In the past year its only cases have in fact been against debtors with large amounts outstanding. There were only three of these, of which two were finally settled out of court. Effective credit control means that action is usually taken long before a legal solution is necessary. In general their approach works well. They are however currently watching the progress of product liability legislation with some trepidation.

7. *Financial Management*

It was Charles Dickens' famous dictum that defined human happiness in terms of spending less than income. Conversely misery results if the individual overspends his income. Today personal savings and the existence of social welfare mean that individuals may exceed their income without incurring the draconian penalties existing in nineteenth century Britain. In the longer term it is still necessary in the final resort to balance income and expenditure or at least to ensure that enough money is available to meet ongoing needs.

7.1 The Nature of Financial Management

In business similar basic rules apply, but a company must generate enough income in addition to its ongoing current expenses to:

maintain adequate reserves to meet contingencies;
replace capital assets, such as machinery, when necessary;
cover fixed interest payments on loans and overdrafts;
permit the distribution of appropriate dividends to shareholders.

The task of the financial director is to see that adequate funds are available at the right time to satisfy those needs. Profit is one source of these funds, but there are others that are available to him at a cost, and these are considered in more detail in the next chapter.

Money differs from the other resources available to a company in a number of important ways. Its applications are infinite in variety. It can for example be invested in profit-generating equipment, given to charity, consumed in additional staff benefits, subscribed to a political party, or simply salted away against a rainy day. The choice between applications is thus an important aspect of financial management, and the range is almost infinite.

The time factor is also important. Money should never lie idle; a banker will even place his idle balances overnight to make a small percentage. The opportunity cost of idle money is the interest that it might have earned in other applications. This ability to earn interest even for very short periods means that £1,000 today is worth more than the same sum in one year's time, the difference being the interest or other return that could be earned in the meantime. Availability is another major concern of the financial director. There may be very serious consequences if he cannot get his money when it is needed.

Financial management in a company therefore has three major aspects.

7.11 *Quantity*

There must be enough money to meet the company's needs and wants regardless of other factors. This applies particularly to cash.

7.12 *Liquidity*

Funds must be in a suitable form for the use for which they are intended. It is not enough to have the money safely invested in bricks and mortar if a creditor requires payment in cash today.

Liquidity is the measure of how quickly an asset can be turned into cash. A clearing banker who must be prepared to pay outstanding balances on demand will keep his assets in a descending level of liquidity, balancing the need for fast access with the opportunity to earn interest, carefully controlled to comply with the proportions of total assets that the Government requires to be held in each category. This is illustrated by Table 7.1.

Table 7.1

Barclays Bank
Cash and Short Term Funds
(Source: Balance Sheet as at 31.12.80)

	£ m	% Total Assets
Cash in hand and with central banks	466	2.8
Money at call and short notice	1,555	9.4
Government treasury bills	100	0.6
Other bills	204	1.2
Total short term funds	2,325	14.0
Total Assets	16,492	100.0

Thus some 14% of all assets were available almost immediately to meet a run on the banks, supported of course by funds from the other banks and the Bank of England in an emergency.

It is the responsibility of the financial manager to see that creditors can be paid. The definition of an insolvent company is one that is unable to meet its financial obligations as they become due, regardless of the inaccessible wealth that it may possess. If insolvency is suspected, proceedings in bankruptcy or liquidation may follow, or a voluntary liquidation or a formal arrangement with creditors may be necessary. Thus Rolls Royce Motors, in spite of substantial net assets, went into voluntary liquidation in 1971. A more usual cause of a shortage of liquid assets is 'over-trading', the position in which a company has invested excessively in working capital and runs into difficulties in financing its operations in the interim period before sales growth restores the balance by increasing revenue.

7.13 *Performance*

The profit earned by a company will relate closely to its size and strength represented by the assets that are invested in it. The criterion for its successful performance is therefore the return that it earns on the capital employed (ROCE), defined as the whole of the assets which have a value to the business, less all liabilities except those to the owners themselves.

In management terms therefore, the task is to ensure that the best use possible is made of money in the business. In this sense the financial manager's role is analogous to that of the personnel and production manager, managing human and material resources, rather than financial ones. Financial management is a question of balance:

> too much in liquid funds may mean lost business because the firm is not using the funds available to make profits;
> it may also mean unnecessarily high interest charges if an overdraft or other fixed interest loan is retained;
> too little liquid funds can debase the financial standing of the firm, and lead to the difficulties of over-trading or even insolvency.

7.2 Financial Structure of the Company

A company's financial structure is determined in the first instance when it specifies its authorized (or nominal) capital and the shares into which it is divided in its Memorandum of Association. It will then issue a proportion of the shares, usually leaving a balance for issue at a future time when additional capital is likely to be required.

7.21 *Classes of Share*

The shareholder contributes the original capital to the company and is legally its owner. His rights and obligations are set out in its Articles of Association. The company however has a legal identity of its own, and if incorporated with limited liability, the shareholder is only liable for its debts to the extent of his shareholding.

The share capital of a company may be divided into different classes of share:

Preference Shares entitle the holders to a fixed rate of dividend before any dividend is paid on other classes of shares. They may also carry the right to prior repayment of capital in a winding up. *Participating Preference Shares* carry the right to a share of profits after a dividend of a specified rate has been paid on the ordinary shares. *Redeemable Preference Shares* may also be issued under certain conditions. These are preference shares that may be redeemed at the option of the company. They must be fully paid, and redemption is usually only possible out of profits available for dividend or out of the proceeds of a fresh issue of shares.

7.22 *Loan Capital*

A company can also issue fixed interest or loan capital, consisting of debentures and other types of loan. A lender or debenture holder is not a member of the company, but a creditor. Loan interest is therefore an expense that is accounted for before the profit out of which dividends and tax will be paid is calculated.

This fact has been a major influence on financial planners in recent years since the dividends payable on shares come out of taxed profits whilst interest on loans does not. Loan repayments and interest thus take priority over dividends and other payments to shareholders. The attractiveness of the shares of a company, and hence the ease with which further equity capital can be raised, will depend in part on the proportion that fixed interest capital bears to the total.

This relationship is known as 'gearing'; if fixed interest capital represents a sizeable share of its total capital, a company is said to be 'highly geared', and vice versa.

If gearing is high, a creditor's risk is already high and a company may have existing high fixed interest charges. An increase in gearing will increase the return to equity shareholders if the return earned on the new funds exceeds the fixed rate paid on them, but an increase in gearing will tend to make the fluctuations in the level of equity earnings proportionally greater than those in the return on capital.

In recent years there has been a tendency for companies to increase their gearing, obtaining expensive fixed interest capital as a result of failure to generate sufficient funds internally or to raise equity capital to finance their operations. Price controls, inflation, or simply the structural difficulties that small and medium-sized companies often have in raising new capital, have been responsible, associated with the generally unfavourable business conditions that have brought the return on capital employed in UK companies progressively down from 14.2% in 1960 to 4.5% in 1977.

7.3 The Company's Accounts

It is already clear that the role of financial management is broader than the traditional view of the accountant. In fact the skills and techniques employed are drawn from both categories of accountant practising in industry and commerce today.

The financial accountant (designated ACA or ACCA), is mainly concerned with the provision of the statutory annual financial accounts. A central task is to ensure that all transactions are correctly recorded in the accounts, and the preparation of payrolls is part of his work. He is also concerned with the stewardship of the company's assets.

The cost and management accountant (designated ACMA) is primarily concerned with obtaining the highest possible degree of utilization of the resources of the business. The statements he provides are aids to policy making, planning and monitoring corporate performance. They will include budget, cash flow, and product profitability reports, as well as cost and financial statistics and ratios for the board.

There is no clear distinction between these functions in many companies today, and the financial director will choose his weapons from both armouries.

The annual financial accounts of a company comprise a statement of assets and liabilities in the form of a Balance Sheet, and a Profit and Loss Account that discloses in terms of profit or loss earned the aggregate financial result of carrying

on business in the period under review. The Companies Acts specify in some detail
the information that should be disclosed in each case and companies tend not to
exceed the minimum required. Many companies now produce simplified versions
for their employees to meet the criticism that their accounts were deliberately
obscure. The cartoon, Figure 7.1, taken from GEC's statement for 1978 makes
the point with robust good humour.

Figure 7.1 'How about letting the shareholders have the same **Annual Report**
as the workers???'

7.4 The Balance Sheet

The balance sheet has been described as a 'financial snapshot' of the company at
the end of its financial year, and a good idea of its financial health may be drawn
from it. It shows how the liabilities of a company, that is value that it owes to
other people and organizations, is represented by the assets that it holds in the
form of property, machinery, investments, stocks, debtors, cash or other
resources.

Today balance sheets will be encountered in two forms, the traditional double-
sided sheet and the newer vertical presentation. These include basically the same
information, but many companies have gone over to the vertical form because it
highlights financing and liquidity positions and generally makes analysis easier.
Thus Net Current Assets is shown on the face of the balance sheet itself. Table

7.2 is based on the balance sheet of the Associated Newspapers company as at 31 March 1978.

Table 7.2

Net Assets Employed	*£000's*	
Fixed Assets	8,698	
Subsidiary/Associated Companies	28,473	
Investments	1,099	
Current Assets		
Stock and Work in Progress	2,782	
Debtors	11,800	
Short-term Deposits	14,139	
Cash	813	Note the shorthand of the Balance Sheet that at first sight is confus-
Total Current Assets	29,534←	ing. From *Total Current Assets*
Total		
Current Liabilities		
Creditors	13,923	
Taxation	922	
Bank Overdrafts	—	
Dividends	1,203	
Total Current Liabilities	16,048←	the *Total Current Liabilities* are subtracted to show the
Net Current Assets	13,486←	*Net Current Assets*. This is then added to the other assets
	51,756←	to give the *Balance Sheet Total*. But the intervening totals are
Financed as Follows:		not shown.
Share Capital	7,600	
Reserves	41,780	
Total Share Capital and Reserves	49,380	
Loan Capital	464	
Deferred Taxation	1,912	
	51,756	

Total Share Capital and Reserves represent the shareholder's stake in the company, since revenue reserves represent retained earnings that have not been distributed as dividend. There are however other forms of reserves that may appear in a balance sheet that are outside the scope of this book. It is important to recognize that the reserves are invested in the assets of the company. There is no idle balance of £40,000 + that can be withdrawn on demand. Share capital is made up of

Ordinary Shares of 25p each and Authorized capital at £8.1 million exceeds Issued
and Fully Paid capital by £0.5 million. Loan capital consists of 6½% and 8¾%
Unsecured Loan Stock repayable at par at the Company's option on or after 31
March 1989.

7.5   The Profit and Loss Account

The Profit and Loss Account is really two or three accounts in one.

In a manufacturing company it is correctly termed the Manufacturing, Trading
and Profit & Loss Account. The first section is debited with the costs of materials,
labour, stocks and overheads to present the total cost of production. This figure is
debited to the Trading Account and adjusted for changes in stock levels. Sales
revenue is credited, and the balance, gross profit, is carried down to the Profit and
Loss Account proper. Interest, dividends, and other income are credited, and
establishment, administration, and finance costs are debited. The balance is the
net profit for the period and, in the case of most concerns, is carried down to an
Appropriation Account.

A company like a retailer or wholesaler that does not manufacture but confines
its activities to buying and selling at a profit will debit the cost of purchases and
related expenses, like delivery charges, to a General Trading Account, adjust for
changes in stock levels, and credit the account with sales revenue. The balance will
be gross profit, an important indicator of trading effectiveness. This figure will be
carried down to a Profit and Loss Account similar to that described above.

It would not be in the interest of companies to disclose such a wealth of
information, and the law does not require them to do so. The full accounts as
described above are provided for the directors whilst the published versions appear
as in Table 7.3.

Table 7.3

Examples of Published Profit and Loss Accounts

Manufacturing Company: The Dreamland Group
for the year ended 31 December 1978

	1978 £
Group Turnover	8,317,325
Group Trading Profit	1,163,294
Non-Trading Items	(11,751)
Group Profit before Taxation	1,151,543

Notes to the Accounts state that Turnover excludes VAT and that Trading Profit is
stated after charging depreciation, auditors remuneration, hire of equipment and

remuneration of directors. Non-Trading Items include interest and other receivable and interest charges. Figures are given in each case.

Non-manufacturing Company: TESCO Stores Holdings Ltd
52 weeks ended 25 February 1978

	£000s
Sales to customers at net selling prices	979,333
Deduct Value added tax	26,339
Sales excluding value added tax	952,994
Trading profits of the group	35,105
Add Interest and dividends	1,378
	36,483
Deduct	
Emoluments of directors of parent company	
Amortization, amounts written off and depreciation of fixed assets	7,921
Net profit subject to taxation	28,562

Notes to be read as part of the accounts give figures for auditors remuneration, debenture interest, and a surplus on redemption of debentures that have been charged to trading profit. Details are also provided for interest and dividends, depreciation, and directors' emoluments.

7.6 Financial Health and Strength

The financial accounts supplemented by reports and statements produced by management provide the means for appraising and monitoring the financial health and strength of the organization. There are six sets of questions that need to be asked to arrive at a valid conclusion. They are:

(a) *Profitability.* Are profits adequate in relation to the capital employed or can they be improved?
(b) *Trend.* What are the trends in the level of profit earned; and is the company financially able to take advantage of opportunities as they arise?
(c) *Borrowing Powers.* How good is its standing with lenders; and will it be able to obtain the resources it needs?
(d) *Solvency.* Can it meet the demands of creditors as they fall due; is working capital adequate; and is there a safe proportion of liquid funds?
(e) *Ownership.* Who owns the business; how far is it financed by its creditors; are its assets mortgaged beyond a safe limit; is it vulnerable to the threat of takeover?

(f)   *Gearing and Cover.* Is the amount of loan capital excessive; is the dividend satisfactorily covered?

The order of priority will differ from company to company and from situation to situation. The financial manager will tend to ask questions that vary in detail from those that interest the bank manager, the shareholder, the creditor, or the tax inspector. The six headings above however cover the most important aspects that will be of interest to all of them.

Analysis of the Profit and Loss Account and Balance Sheet provide the answers to these questions or at least point to further questions that need to be asked. Accounting ratios are a technique that can be very helpful in identifying trends and appraising progress. They may be used to compare salient figures in the balance sheet, to appraise changes between two periods, and for inter-firm comparison. It is obviously important to ensure that figures are produced on similar bases. Even so they should be used mainly to support other figures and as planning guides rather than as definitive statements in their own right.

The analyst needs to use all the information at his disposal and should not confine himself to one technique or approach. Often he will interpret the non-statistical parts of the report in reaching his conclusions on the company's financial health and strength. The following comments which refer to the Associated Newspapers' balance sheet on page 107 cover the main areas to be considered.

7.61 *Authorized and Issued Capital*

The difference of £0.5 million represents a potential source of liquid resources with which to meet current liabilities or the cost of an expansion programme. Calls in arrear or forfeited shares if shown in this section may indicate possible difficulties.

7.62 *Loan Capital*

It should be noted whether this capital is secured by a fixed, floating or other charge on the company's assets. The importance of gearing has been discussed earlier, but is very low in this case. A gearing ratio calculated by the formula

$$\frac{\text{(Fixed dividend capital + long-term loans)}}{\text{Equity funds}}$$

of more than 50% is usually regarded as high, whilst a ratio above 100% should be very seriously regarded in almost every case and efforts made urgently to increase equity investment. Often this may mean accepting a holding from an institution with a corresponding dilution of the directors' freedom of action.

7.63 *Fixed Assets*

The terms of tenure of land and buildings need to be examined, and the imminence of the renewal of any leases may be significant. Arrangements for replacing plant, machinery, and vehicles should also be considered.

If intangible assets such as goodwill appear, they should be regarded with caution. Often assets like patent rights for example do have real value. Sometimes however fictitious or nominal assets result from expenditure that is not represented by current value but has not been written off. In general it is safer to confine analysis to tangible assets, and it should be regarded as a sign of potential weakness if nominal assets represent a major proportion of the total.

7.64 Solvency Ratios

7.641 *Liquidity.* This ratio relates short-term obligations to the funds likely to be available to meet them. A ratio significantly below 1:1 may indicate inadequate credit control or underutilized cash. In this case (Debtors + Short Term Deposits + Cash) relate to Current Liabilities in the ratio (£26,752 : £16,048), i.e. 1.7 : 1.

7.642 *Current ratio.* The current ratio is the ratio of current assets : current liabilities. Sometimes termed the working capital ratio, it shows whether there is an adequate amount of working capital to meet running expenses and service fixed assets. A rule of thumb should be about 2 : 1, although industry averages tend to be lower. In the case of Associated Newspapers the ratio is (£29,534 : £16,048), i.e. 1.8 : 1.

7.65 Debtors, Creditors and Stock

An early sign of financial stress is often indicated by the ratio of debtors to creditors and stocks to sales. If debtors increase disproportionately, it may suggest weaknesses in credit control. An increase in creditors may either mean that the company is having difficulty paying its debts or it is successfully making the trade finance a larger share of its business, depending on circumstances. Similarly large increases in stocks should be investigated with care. They may represent seasonal trends or a build up before a big campaign. Alternatively they may herald a slow-down in business that could leave the company over-stocked.

These ratios are expressed either as a percentage of annual sales or in terms of week's or month's sales. Thus debtors representing 20% of sales value might be referred to as 10 weeks sales. In the interests of consistency, debtors are compared with sales at selling prices while creditors and stocks should be compared with purchases or sales at cost or buying prices.

7.66 Sales Ratios

The ratio of gross profit to sales is an overall guide to the efficiency of production in a manufacturing business and an indication of trading profitability in a non-manufacturing organization, where it should coincide with the trade mark-up.

The ratio of net profit to sales takes all expenditure into account and provides a measure of overall performance. It is however necessary to eliminate expenditure and income that are not related to sales.

The ratio of sales to capital employed demonstrates the rate at which assets are being turned over, and is an important indicator of how successfully the company is taking its opportunities. In general a high ratio is a healthy sign unless the company is seen to be overtrading. A low ratio suggests that assets are underutilized.

7.67 *Profitability*

The main profitability ratio is the profit earned on assets employed. Earlier in this chapter we equated profitability with performance and considered the most widely used form of this ratio, return on capital employed, (ROCE).

Ratios are not definitive data in their own right. They are indicators, guides, and tools to aid in planning. They are most useful to the manager when comparing a company's performance between years or for inter-firm comparison. They can also be a useful diagnostic technique, explaining as well as identifying changes.

For these purposes a ratio may be split into component parts, and each examined separately. Thus ROCE can be regarded as a combination of Pre-Tax Profit: Sales and Sales: Net Assets. The former indicates profitability as a percentage of Sales whilst the latter indicates efficiency in the use of funds expressed as the rate of turnover of Net Assets in relation to Sales. Each has its own group of subsidiary ratios which in turn reveal strengths or weaknesses and point up the need for appropriate action. This is shown in Figure 7.2.

The other ratios specific to the business could include Production, Marketing, Distribution, or any function that had significant impact on overall profitability.

7.68 *Sources and Applications of Funds*

A further technique for analysing the Balance Sheet is the Movement of Funds Statement that is now a standard item in most annual reports. It illustrates the changes that have taken place in the structure of assets and liabilities during the accounting year by the simple technique of subtracting the opening figure for each item from the closing one with certain adjustments. Table 7.4 is taken from the 1978 accounts of Unigate, the milk, meat, and food group.

Table 7.4

Source and Application of Funds

	1978 £000	Notes
Source of funds		This part of the statement shows
Profit before taxation	31,459	the value of fresh funds generated
Extraordinary items	(199)	during the year and retained in the
Depreciation	12,783 ←	business. Depreciation and other
Other movements in reserves		items not involving the movement
including exchange adjustments	(338)	of funds are added back because
	———	although committed they are still
Funds generated from operations	43,705	available for use in the company.
Funds from other sources:		This section shows funds obtained
Fixed assets and goodwill sold		⁄ from external sources.
(book value)	3,206	
Loan capital	918	
	———	
	47,829 ←	This is the total available for use.

Table 7.4 (continued)

	1978 £000	Notes
Application of funds		
Fixed assets	28,468	These items represent the long term
Acquisitions and goodwill	651 ←	changes in the company's financial
Investments	45	structure
Decrease in interest of outside		
shareholders in subsidiaries	271	

Increase in working capital:		Here are shown changes in working
Increase in stock	5,787	capital with creditors deducted as a
Increase in debtors	19,040	liability from the other current
(Increase) in creditors and		assets. An increase in creditors is a
provisions	(22,380)	source of funds because the busi-
		ness is being financed to a greater
	2,447	degree by outsiders.
	31,882	
Loan capital repaid	2,226	The total application of funds is
Dividends paid	6,185	less than the total of funds obtain-
Taxation paid	4,403	ed. There is therefore an increase
		in net liquid funds which the
	44,696	Balance Sheet shows is made up of
		an increase in Bank, cash and short
		term investments (a source) and a
Movement		reduction in Bank Loans and over-
Increase in net liquid funds	3,133	drafts (an application).

7.7 Financial Planning and Control

Financial planning follows the principles set out in Chapter 6. A corporate strategy will be designed to achieve the objectives of the organisation in both the short and long term. This will have financial implications that determine in turn the objectives and strategy of the financial plan. A growth plan may well include new factories, outlets, or even the acquisition of other companies, that will require the raising of new finance. It is clearly important that all aspects of the plan should be closely co-ordinated with that of the enterprise as a whole. At the same time targets for profit, percentage return on sales and return on capital employed require careful planning and control over the assets to be utilized.

7.71 *Budgetary Control*

Budgetary control is the major technique used. It is both a planning and control mechanism. It provides a detailed plan of action for a business over a definite

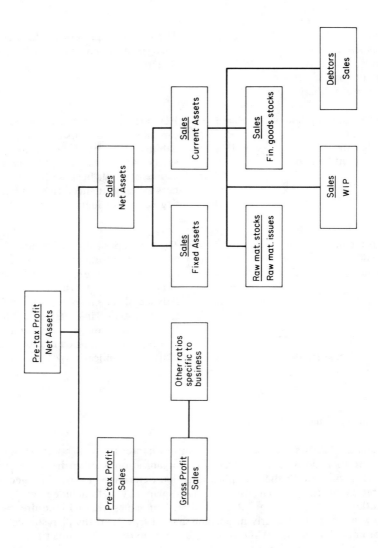

Figure 7.2

period of time and helps to co-ordinate the activities of the organization in achieving it. Two budgets are of particular value in this context.

7.711 *The Capital Expenditure Budget.* Preliminary proposals to invest in new buildings, vehicles, or equipment will have been embodied in the corporate long term strategy. They will be planned in detail in this budget, evaluated in money terms, and the timing of their acquisition specified. The budget for the current year will be calculated more precisely so that the funds needed can be made available to plan. Strict control is essential, firstly to ensure that all expenditure is consistent with long-term corporate objectives, secondly to ensure that liquidity problems are avoided, and thirdly to confirm the viability of the investment. This control takes two major forms:

(a)   *Investment Appraisal*
The expected costs and revenues associated with each major investment should be carefully assessed in one of the following ways:
the pay-back method estimates the period in which the expected operating profits from the project will add up to the amount spent on it. The shorter the period, the higher is the rating of the project;
the annual rate of return on the investment may be calculated in a number of ways. The higher the return, the higher is the rating of the investment;
the discounted cash flow (DCF) technique estimates the net cash flow from the investment and discounts it with the use of tables to calculate today's value of the flow over the life of the investment.
These very brief thumbnail descriptions do no more than identify the techniques available. Further detail is outside the scope of this chapter.

(b)   *Variance Analysis*
Analysis of the variance between budgeted and actual expenditure provides the second form of control. This helps to identify unauthorized expenditure and will indicate where additional funds may be needed, or existing funds re-allocated.

7.712 *Cash Flow Budget.* The inadequacy of cash resources to meet current needs can be both embarrassing and expensive. Similarly excessive idle bank balances are also expensive and wasteful of potential earning power. The Cash Flow Budget provides a means of maintaining an adequate level of liquidity.

Forecasts are made of sales revenues, other receipts, payments for goods and services, wages and salaries, and other payments such as rent, rates, dividends etc. Particular care is taken to determine the timing of the actual receipt or disbursement of cash. Sales receipts for instance will be subject to the length of the collection period and credit control policy. Similarly allowance is made for the amount of credit taken on purchases.

Table 7.5 illustrates a typical annual cash budget.

The annual budget is then broken down into twelve monthly or thirteen financial period budgets, each of which is revised at regular intervals since opening and closing balances are unlikely to correspond exactly with planned totals, and there will also be other changes necessary. Analysis of the variances between budgeted and actual results will again indicate where fresh action is needed.

Table 7.5

	£000	£000
Opening Bank balance at 1 April 19.........		110
Inflow:		
Sales Revenue	4,680	
Dividends from investments	10	4,690
		4,800
Outflow:		
Materials and Services	2,000	
Wages and Salaries	1,700	
Rent and Rates	200	
Capital expenditure	500	
Corporation tax	100	
Loan interest	20	
Dividend to shareholders	150	4,670
Closing Bank balance at 31 March 19		130

7.72 *Control over Other Assets*

Profitable operations imply that effective control will be maintained over all assets, with particular emphasis on fast moving items of working capital. Control over stocks is discussed in Chapter 11, and the important technique of Standard Costing is covered in Chapter 12. The control of debtors has a central place in financial management however, both to control the company's credit risk by not allowing slow payers to develop into bad debts, and also to ensure that working capital locked up in debtors is kept to a minimum. It is helpful to have a target for the number of days' sales outstanding in debtors at the close of each month. Table 7.6 is a reasonably good indicator of the trend, but needs to be associated with a Debtors Analysis that concentrates on the older items and lists them separately.

Table 7.6

Target days' sales in debtors: say, 75 days. Debtors at 31 March 19xx: £100,000
Actual days' sales in debtors:

Month	Sales	Debtors	Days	
	£	£	in month	in debtors
March	40,000	40,000	31	31 (All)
February	35,000	35,000	28	28 (All)
January	35,000	25,000	31	22 (*)
		£100,000		

* $31 \times (25,000/35,000) = 22$ approx.

Table 7.6 (continued)

Actual days' sales in debtors	81
Target days' sales in debtors	75
Excess debtors	6 days

Barclays Bank offers the following practical advice on debtor control to the clients of its Business Advisory Service:

1 Check a new customer's credit rating before despatching any goods. Ask him for credit references, and refer to other sources where possible, e.g. credit agencies, other known suppliers, Companies House, trade press, representatives, personal experience.
2 Establish a credit limit for the customer and when each order is received, check that the outstanding debtor balance plus the amount of the new order does not exceed the limit.
3 Debts cannot be collected promptly if they are not billed promptly. Make sure you have a system which enables the invoices to go out the same day as despatch, or the next day at the latest.
4 When an item becomes overdue, don't delay. The following is often a sensible procedure:

   (a) Send a 'first letter' seven days from the due date for payment.
   (b) Send a 'second letter' fourteen days later.
   (c) Thereafter, telephone, telex, cable, or for large sums consider paying a personal visit. Don't be put off by plausible-sounding excuses.
   (d) When six weeks overdue, stop supplies and send a 'third letter'.
   (e) When eight weeks overdue, place the matter in the hands of solicitors or a debt-collection agency.

5 If you have a reason to think there is a genuine but temporary problem, you will have to decide whether to risk losing the money or the customer.
6 Don't offer settlement discounts unless it is absolutely essential because it is very expensive. Take for example the commonly quoted '2½% monthly' cash discount. This must be viewed in terms of the difference it makes to outstanding debtors when compared with its cost. If average debtors are outstanding for, say 2½ months (75 days) then payment within 30 days would save 45 days. For this you pay 2½%, equivalent to an annual interest rate of

$$2\tfrac{1}{2}\% \times \frac{365}{45} = 20\% \text{ approx.}$$

Is it worth it? It may be, but only in exceptional circumstances.
7 The biggest risk in a debtor balance is that it will become a bad debt. Example:

Sale of	£500
Gross profit, say,	£200

   To recover the total loss if this debt were to go bad would require additional sales of £1,250 (£500 lost × (500/200)).

8 The work involved in exercising proper debtor control may be time-consuming
   for the accounts section. But the risk of not doing so is one which the average
   business cannot afford to take.

7.73 *Computer Models*

Financial modelling has been described as 'merely a sophisticated version of the
backs of envelopes which have been used for years'. However the use of computers
does enable highly complex calculations to be done very quickly and accurately and
allows the planner to ask many more 'what if . . . ?' questions about possible results
of his decisions than would be practical using purely manual methods.

A model is simply a set of relationships establishing the links between the
various financial aspects of the business. With a computer, all the elements of a
budget with all their interlocking relationships can be included in the model. A
model is a simulation of the firm's business. Managers are therefore not confined to
making a single set of decisions or forecasts about what is likely to happen but can
explore a number of possibilities and use the conclusions as a valid base for planning, forecasting, and control. Of course the accuracy of the model depends on the
quality of the data base introduced, much of which may well involve managerial
judgement as well as objective fact. The main applications are for corporate planning, budgeting, and investment appraisal.

The value of a model depends on the number of important variables in a firm's
business and their volatility. A large firm with a very stable environment will get
less out of modelling than a smaller firm in a very dynamic market. It is not
necessary to own a computer to operate a model as there are many computer
bureaux available. Circumstances will determine whether it is necessary to design
a completely new programme or satisfactory to rely on one of the many existing
packages available. The Tootal Group of textile companies for example built their
own modelling system to execute the basic profit planning calculations for sales
forecasts, in volume and value, together with standard costs and resulting margins,
stock movements and margin analysis. Previously managers provided their
estimates at the start of the planning process and were only able to make limited
changes thereafter.

Models in most companies are designed to produce answers to the sort of
management questions discussed so far. However there is a trend towards corporate financial planning models that are integrated with the standard accounting
computer programs. In these systems periodic data for forecasts is extracted from
the day-to-day transactional systems, such as general ledger and stock control, and
from the corporate data base. Automatic interface routines are interposed between
the transactional systems and the corporate model so that revision and updating of
the plan occurs as an integral part of the process.

7.74 *Profit Planning*

The objective of most businesses is to earn profit, and an acceptable level of profit
is a central consideration in financial management. Conceptually profit improvement is very simple; there are only three ways of increasing profits:

(a)   *Volume.* More volume can be obtained at the same price and cost by increasing the level of sales and/or increasing production.
(b)   *Price.* Prices can be increased without affecting volume or cost by increasing list prices, reducing discounts or introducing new charges. As an adjunct to this, sales of more profitable items can be increased at the expense of the less profitable.
(c)   *Cost.* Expense may be reduced for the same volume at the same price by reducing the cost of materials, labour and overheads and using such techniques as Value Analysis described in Chapter 11.

In practice this is the formula for running a profitable business and is very far from simple. The factors affecting profit do not interact in a simple way.

Because of the fixed nature of some expense, total costs do not change in proportion to volume and the profits of some businesses are more sensitive to volume than others.

Increases in price tend to deflate volume and may increase costs per unit. The highest selling price may not therefore maximize sales revenue.

Some products make a greater contribution to profits than others, so a change in the sales mix may disproportionately affect total profit.

Relative product profitability is often incorrectly measured by calculating profit as a percentage of sales. Where there are limiting factors in production, linear programming may be necessary to determine the optimum mix.

The complex relationships between these factors emphasize the need for a company to have cost information in a form that will help decision-making through evaluation of the probable outcome of planned activity.

7.75   *Fixed and Variable Costs*

The analysis of costs into fixed and variable elements is a method used by the majority of companies.

Fixed costs are those which tend to be unaffected by variations in the volume of output.

Variable costs are those which tend to vary directly with variations in volume.

Semi-variable costs are partly fixed and partly variable.

If variable product costs are deducted from the sales revenue received, the balance is available to meet fixed costs and to provide profit. This amount is termed Contribution. Whilst fixed costs remain fixed within defined levels of operation, variable cost will alter. Thus although contribution is not the same thing as Net Profit, it is clear that it will move in the same way as net profit in total and trend terms. Profit planning can therefore be carried out with contribution estimates in place of net profit figures with the following advantages:

the exact relationship between cost, price and volume is brought out clearly;
the relative contribution to profit of each of a number of products may be shown, guiding business planning and the allocation of sales effort;
information is provided on which products should be made in the company and which bought out;
the separation of fixed from variable costs provides an effective means of

controlling selling and production costs and the volume and mix of sales; it discloses how the greatest overall profit can be made.

There is a danger with all forms of marginal costing that attention will be diverted from fixed overhead cost control. If however the need for contribution to cover these costs before any profit is earned is kept in mind, the approach offers significant advantages, enabling techniques like Break-even Analysis and Flexible Budgeting to be used.

7.76 *Break-even Charts*

A break-even chart is a convenient method of indicating the relative profitability of an organization at different levels of activity. Sales are plotted against cost, as is shown in Figure 7.3.

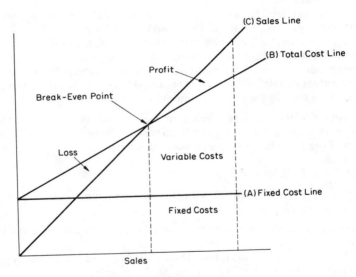

Figure 7.3

The fixed cost curve (A) shows those costs that will be incurred at all levels of sales, and this line therefore runs parallel to the horizontal axis.

The total cost curve (B) represents the sum of the fixed costs that do not change with output and the variable costs that do. Thus before any sales are obtained, total cost will equal fixed cost, but from then on variable as well as fixed cost will be incurred.

The sales line (C) will rise proportionately to volume, and will cut the total cost line at the break-even point, the point at which neither profit nor loss are made as cost equals revenue there.

Clearly for any given volume of sales, the higher the break-even, the lower the profit. A company with a high break-even is described as 'cost sensitive' because a small change in the level of costs will make a disproportionate impact on profit.

Similarly a company with a low break-even may be regarded as being particularly sales sensitive since a given increase in sales will yield a proportionately larger increase in profit.

One measure of the financial strength of a business is its 'margin of safety'. This is simply its sales in excess of the break-even point. Where the break-even is high in relation to sales, there will be little margin to meet reductions in price or sales volume before losses are incurred.

The ratio of profit to volume, or P/V ratio, is most significant as it reveals at once how much additional profit will be made for any given increase in volume. It may be used to calculate the net profit appropriate to any volume as follows:

$$\text{Net Profit} = (\text{Sales} \times \text{P/V Ratio}) - \text{Fixed Costs}$$

The P/V ratio and the Margin of Safety are linked by the following formula:

$$\text{P/V Ratio} \times \text{Margin of Safety} = \text{Net Profit}$$

In practice it may be said that:

a lower margin of safety coinciding with a high P/V ratio is usually a sign that fixed costs are too high in relation to normal sales;
a low margin of safety coupled with a low P/V ratio generally indicates that the unit variable costs are excessive in relation to the selling price.

7.77 *Profit and Loss Forecasting*

A more formal method of profit planning is the Profit and Loss Forecast. Each component of the P & L Account is projected to the end of the financial period and a complete account representing the position at the end of the year is constructed. Plans are made to ensure that the resulting net profit is acceptable. Similarly monthly P & L forecasts are produced and actual results are monitored against forecast, with appropriate action to ensure that each month's achievement does in fact build up to the year's planned profit.

7.8 Conclusion

There are very few things prized as highly as sound financial management at our guinea-pig company, Consumer & Electrical. The Chairman is an accountant but understands that, taken to excess, the virtues of accountancy can discourage enterprise and stifle management initiative. He noted with interest the experience of a major competing electrical wholesaler who seriously damaged the morale and effectiveness its staff by making sudden demands for ratios and statistics which were not understood.

At C & E every department manager is expected to take an interest in the financial health of the group. Thus Marketing reports the contribution earned each month, as well as the sales revenue and volume. Margins are carefully watched, and the critical ratios and variances are extracted and carefully studied. This department is also vitally interested in the costs of its products, working mainly with variable product costs within the framework of the group's standard costing system.

The group does not indulge in financial modelling, which the Chairman privately believes is 'new fangled'. On the sly however, the Finance Director has been experimenting with forecasting models like PASTAN and PASFOR of PA Management Consultants. In the meantime much reliance is placed on cash forecasting and cash flow planning to keep C & E on a stable keel. The gearing ratio is held at a steady 10–15%, and a vigilant watch is kept for share holdings that may be building dangerously high stakes in the group. On the basis that 'a stitch in time saves nine', debtor control is regarded as vitally important, and a serious investigation takes place if the total shown in the monthly accounts exceeds eight weeks sales. Particularly in C & E (Distribution) it is recognized that a long overdue account may entail the loss of a good customer as well as the sum involved.

The details of inflation accounting are outside the scope of this book, but C & E are only too well aware how the progressive fall in the value of money has falsified the picture presented in the traditional accounts. Accordingly a Current Cost Statement is produced in accordance with the interim recommendations on inflation accounting by the Accounting Standards Committee. Cost of Sales is adjusted to allow for the difference between the actual cost of goods sold and their replacement cost; similarly Depreciation is adjusted on the basis that fixed assets are valued at replacement cost; whilst a gearing adjustment reflects the extent to which operations are financed by net monetary liabilities, usually representing an offsetting inflationary gain.

Almost all C & E's expenditure is financed from funds available within the Group. That however takes us on to the subject of the next chapter.

8. Sources of Funds

The function of finance may be defined as the provision of the required amount of money at the time it is wanted at an acceptable cost. If expenditure matches income in a regular and even way this is not difficult to arrange. In practice of course it does not. Sales revenues may fluctuate quite dramatically for seasonal and other reasons, and whilst some expenditures, like wages, flow uniformly month by month, major purchases, like new capital machinery will provide peaks that demand special provisions. The finance available to a company has to provide cash for all its needs. These will include working capital for its operating expenses like rent, labour, work in progress and stocks. These are short term investments in the sense that they should be recouped with profit when the sale of the product takes place. A turnover rate of five times a year is not unusual in a wide range of industries and in this case the average life of the investment is only ten weeks.

However, the company will also need to make fixed investment in plant and machinery from time to time, may acquire financial assets or subsidiaries, and perhaps make capital expenditures abroad. All these will tie up money for considerably longer. The factor of time is thus central to financial planning, and it could obviously be serious if the maturity of an investment and the period of finance were not closely linked. The legal solvency of a company is expressed in terms of its ability to pay its debts as they become due, and this, of course, includes capital repayment of loans.

In the case of a small company it may be necessary to relate particular sources of finance to specific projects. Thus bank overdrafts may be used for working capital and equity finance for longer periods. In these cases it may be necessary for individual investments to be justified individually. However, in general large companies raise money to provide a pool of finance that is then available when any funds are required for the whole range of its activities. The best time for a company to raise money may not coincide with the best time to invest it. It therefore tries to raise money when it can do so on the most favourable terms, funding short term debt, or adding to cash balances in the interim period.

The availability and cost of finance from external sources depends on a number of factors. The company should be seen as one link in a chain. It will assess its own investment prospects in terms of the likely return and the risk involved, using techniques like Discounted Cash Flow to compare one with another. A financier providing it with funds will tend to look at its operation in much the same way, relating his return to the risk involved. A 'blue chip' organization will pay a smaller margin over base rate for its overdraft than most private individuals for example. The risks involved in finance fall under the following headings:

Management risks relate to the management's ability to implement the planned course of action profitably.

Physical risks are risks that some accident may destroy or spoil some physical asset of the operation financed. Fire, flood, and theft are examples.

Technical risks cover the possibility that either the technical expertise available is inadequate for the purpose, or perhaps that technical obsolescence may reduce the profit of the scheme.

Economic and *Political* risks include the possibility of a downturn in economic activity, new measures of taxation, changes in government policies and in some countries civil disturbance and revolution.

Almost every company can obtain finance if it is prepared to accept very high rates of interest. In practice, successful companies of some size with good profit records and sound prospects do not, in the normal way, have difficulty in raising capital on acceptable terms. Smaller organizations, particularly if unlisted by the Stock Exchange may encounter problems, and much attention has been given to their difficulties by both the Bolton Committee (1971) and the Government itself. A small firm undeniably suffers from a number of disabilities that do not affect larger firms. Some facilities are, in fact, only available to larger firms, and it generally costs more proportionately to raise small sums for reasons of risk and administrative expense. Some small firms do not use all the facilities available either through lack of information or from an unwillingness to relinquish partial control to outsiders. In addition firms of all sizes have experienced particular financial difficulties over the last few years as a result of inflation and reduced profitability.

8.1 Internally Generated Funds

So far it has been assumed that 'finance' means money from an external source. However, retained funds within a company are the prime sources of finance for investment in the UK. These funds have accounted for about three-quarters, on average, of manufacturing industry's total sources of funds over the years. They derive from retained earnings and provisions for depreciation and taxation. If a company is to maintain the substance of its business it must be able to finance the replacement of its existing assets from its own internal source. Internal funds also have advantages over external borrowed funds as a source of finance for new investment because, like new equity capital, they are risk capital and do not create a further prior charge against profits. Nevertheless they are not without cost. The company should take into account the 'opportunity' cost represented by the notional interest that the funds would have earned if placed in other external investments, when evaluating the return from a project. Moreover sufficient has to be earned on this capital to maintain its stock market valuation relative to other companies, both to avoid the threat of unrealistically low take-over bids and to retain its ability to raise further capital in the market.

8.2 Finance from Trade Credit

Maximization of the use of working capital through the use of trade credit is of considerable importance to the individual firm. By delaying payment for as long as reasonably possible and persuading customers to pay for goods sold as soon as possible a company can release a flow of funds for other uses which in practice is an important source of working capital for all firms.

Credit management covers all aspects of the company's use of working capital. Effective stock control and planning of work in progress can minimize the amount of money tied up in these uses. The strategic use of discounts for prompt payment and adequate credit control procedures can significantly accelerate payment by customers, although the costs involved have to be carefully considered. Credit factoring, the sale at a discount of a company's debts, can also improve cash flow. A factor may pass on to his client up to 80% of the value of a debt as soon as the invoice is despatched to the customer. The rest of the debt is passed on when the factor has received it. Other services provided by factors may include a straight-forward accounting service and some protection against bad debts. In some cases it may be more economic in the long run to use outside factoring services than maintain an internal organization for sales ledger accounting and credit control.

Small and newly established firms find themselves at the bottom of the trade credit pyramid, pressed on one side by larger suppliers who can exert pressure for immediate payment and on the other by customers who can delay payment unreasonably. Tight credit control is, however, an essential part of efficient funds management and the following example from the General Electric Company's 1977 Accounts illustrates the principle.

Table 8.1

	1977 £m	% change	1976 £m
Sales	2,054.6	+17.3	1,752.4
Debtors (at selling prices)	480.0	+15.1	417.1
Creditors (at cost)	407.5	+19.3	341.7

Some caution has to be exercized in interpreting these figures. Debtors and Creditors shown in the table are as at 31 March, and may not be representative of the whole year. However, on the face of it a 17% increase in sales has been financed with only 15% increase in debtors, implying a smaller total tied up in trade debts. Creditors have, however, increased more than proportionately to sales, so the trade is giving marginally longer to the company to pay and is shouldering a correspondingly greater financial load. Both indicators are moving in GEC's favour and, without detailed evidence to the contrary it would appear that some additional funds have been released for other purposes.

8.3 External Sources of Finance

The main sources of external funds are bank borrowing, ordering shares issued for cash, and preference shares, debentures and other long-term loans and mortages.

8.31 *Finance from Banks*

By far the largest source of short-term finance for industry in the UK is the traditional overdraft provided by the Clearing, Scottish and Irish Banks. These overdraft facilities are essentially to provide funds for working capital, to cover the cost of stock, work in progress and other short-term needs as already mentioned. Traditionally UK banks have avoided providing long-term investment capital to industry, shunning the involvement in management that German banks, for example, habitually practise.

The banks, through their local branches, maintain close contact with their customers and offer overdraft finance at fluctuating rates of interest on a revolving principle — receipts by the company being used to reduce an overdraft and payments to increase it. The banks often, but not always, take some security — perhaps in the form of a floating charge over the company's fixed assets. The overdraft system is relatively cheap, very flexible, and available without much legal formality. In practice the distinction between short-term and long-term finance is blurred because overdrafts tend to continue from year to year and, since the banks seldom terminate a facility entirely unless the recipient's credit rating has deteriorated severely, represent lines of credit that may be open for ten to fifteen years or longer.

More recently, the banks have been extending the length of time for which they are prepared to provide finance, and now offer medium-term loans from two to seven years, and in some cases for up to ten years. This form of finance is slightly more expensive than overdraft, but is available for a fixed term (with an agreed repayment plan) and is not recallable at short notice except in certain agreed circumstances; the interest rate is not so variable. Rather more security may be required, however. The merchant banks and overseas banks also provide short and medium-term finance.

Many other sources of finance are available through the banking system. Acceptance credits provide a convenient method of financing goods against bills of exchange. These bills are drawn by the manufacturer on the customer, or his bank, and may be either held to maturity (commonly ninety-one days), or sold through the Discount Market at a discount reflecting current interest rates to provide immediate cash. The customer, to whom the goods have been sold, will provide cash to the accepting house at the end of the agreed period from the final sale of the goods involved.

Some large companies have borrowed money from abroad, with the help of the banks. In recent years such loans have generally borne rates of interest well below market rates for sterling loans and have thus had attractions for companies. The difference in interest rates, however, reflects the exchange risk and such borrowing has often only been attractive to companies with sizeable overseas operations or sources of revenue from overseas.

A company may also need to raise money to maintain or expand its overseas operations. Exchange control severely restricts the extent to which companies may use money raised in the UK for investment overseas, so that a company with substantial requirement for funds overseas is generally limited in its choice of finance to retained overseas profits or foreign currency loans raised abroad.

The development of the Euromarkets in recent years has provided a new mechanism for these operations. There is no physical market place, the market consisting of a number of registered 'market makers' who deal largely on the telephone. In 1981 the total of foreign and international bond issues and publicized Euro-currency credits reached $US137 billion and growth has continued since then. Originally issued only in $US these bonds are now expressed in Euro-versions of many currencies, and attract funds widely from outside the country of the nominated currency. A limited number of Euro-sterling issues have appeared, but at the time of writing their status in relation to UK exchange control is ambiguous. Normally only the largest institutions can participate in the Euro-markets and banks usually form international syndicates for this purpose. Thus the issue of $US30 million 9% Bonds due in 1989 by United Biscuits was managed by Morgan Grenfell, Kredietbank SA Luxembourgeoise, and the Swiss Bank Corporation and the securities were sold through 116 merchant and clearing banks in most European countries, Japan, Hong Kong, and the Middle East.

Other means of raising finance through the banks and other financial institutions include:

block discounting (the sale at a discount of a block of rental contracts, for example for televisions or cars);
contract hire, for example on a fleet of company vehicles as an alternative to using scarce funds on outright purchase;
the hire-purchase of plant and other assets for similar reasons;
leasing, again enabling the lessee to obtain access to equipment without capital expense.

Leasing is probably the fastest growing category of industrial finance today. It is a means of converting short-term money into medium-term financing. Lessors rank equally with industrialists in being able to take advantage of full first year depreciation allowances on new assets purchased for industrial use. These allowances are passed back to the lessee by way of reduced rentals. However, the assets can never become the property of the lessee to preserve the legality of the allowances. Instead he enjoys a second lease term at virtually peppercorn rentals or a rebate in rentals to reflect the secondhand sale price of the asset.

The asset concerned may be large or small. The largest lease to date in the UK for a single industrial asset was signed early in 1977 for the £70 million catalytic cracking unit for the Lindsey Oil Refinery on Humberside.

To summarize this section it may be said that these facilities are generally more expensive than the traditional overdraft, but may provide a company with additional sources of finance or enable it to acquire, or have the use of, particular assets without tying up its own money.

8.32 *Market Finance*

The sources of finance from the banking system are essentially designed to meet short- and medium-term needs. Companies which are unable to meet all their needs for finance from retained profits or from the banks can raise long-term money on the stock market by issuing equity or loan capital.

The choice between raising equity or loan capital depends partly upon the capital structure of the company — the extent to which it has relied upon one form of finance rather than another in the past — and what is regarded as an acceptable ratio between the various sources of funds. This acceptable ratio is not unique and varies between countries and between industries, as well as between individual companies. Much depends upon the nature of the business, in particular upon the extent to which the assets can be marketed and the degree of variability of the cash flow. Essentially, it is a matter of the assessment by the market of the risk involved. 'Gearing', the relationship between loan capital and shareholders' company's funds, is traditionally regarded as one indicator of financial risk.

There are several ways of issuing equity capital.

(a)   A public company may issue shares that have been authorized but have not been issued so far. 'Authorized' or 'nominal' capital is the capital mentioned in the company's Memorandum of Association and represents the maximum amount that it can issue without passing a resolution to increase it and paying duty on the increase.

Alternatively it may introduce a new class of shares. These generally take one of the following forms:

A Private Placing is when a company arranges for an institution to buy a block of its shares without making them more generally available through a stock exchange.

A Stock Exchange Placing is when a broker, frequently with the assistance of an issuing house, arranges for a large number of investors to purchase the securities to be issued.

A Public Issue by Prospectus is when an issue is offered to the public, usually through the Press, with the help of an issuing house expert in dealing with a large number of applications.

An Offer for Sale is when securities are offered to the public, not on behalf of the company itself but of one or more holders to whom they have already been issued. Normally the holder is the issuing house itself and it will attempt to sell at a price that includes a margin of profit for itself.

Issues by Tender are made when it is difficult to predict either the price or demand for the issue. The method generally used is to fix a price and to invite tenders either at or above it. Shares are allotted at the highest price that will take up the issue.

(b)   Public companies may make a rights issue, offering new shares to existing shareholders. Each is given the opportunity to subscribe for the new shares up to a given proportion of those he holds already. Alternatively he can assign part or all of his rights to somebody else, and since offers are invariably made on favourable terms, he will be able to sell his rights on the Stock Exchange.

Since the price to be paid for the new shares is below the current market price of the existing ones, the price per share of the enlarged issue will usually fall, and the individual who neither takes up his allocation nor assigns it will suffer an uncompensated loss on the shares he holds already.

A bonus or scrip issue is quite different from a rights issue. It is usually made free to the shareholder in proportion to his existing holding. No funds are raised, and the price per share tends to fall in proportion to the relative size of the issue. It is a device for translating reserves that are really part of the shareholder's equity formally into paid-up shares.

(c)   Private companies may go public by making a public offer of shares for sale.

All these methods entail the publication of an offer of shares together with a description of the company's plans and prospects, which have to meet the stringent requirements of the Stock Exchange. The share issue needs to be underwritten by financial institutions who agree to take up any unsold shares in return for a fee or a favourable discount. The effect of this is that a company is sure of raising the full amount of the shares on offer, but, as a corollary, companies are unable to make such issues unless institutions can be found which will underwrite the issue at an acceptable price. Attitudes of underwriters to proposed offers depend upon the general state of the market for shares, as well as on the characteristics of the company wishing to raise money.

The function of the Stock Exchange as a source of new capital for industry should not be confused with its operation as a secondary market in existing shares. The sale or purchase of an existing share merely transfers its title from one shareholder to another. It does not generate new finance and it does not affect the company concerned except for registration procedures unless a change in control is involved.

8.33 *The Institutions*

The role of the long-term savings institutions has become increasingly predominant in the provision of finance through the Stock Exchange in recent years. Pension funds, insurance companies, investment trusts, unit trusts, and charities were estimated to account for 65% of all equity purchases in 1975, which represented £5.2 billion of new money to invest in the following year.

The ways in which these funds have been directed has been at the centre of political controversy, culminating in the detailed investigation by the Wilson Committee. It has been suggested that their emphasis on high security, their preference for large companies, and their tendency to act together when reacting to short-term changes has distorted the flow of finance to British industry. On the other hand companies that have wanted to raise equity at the going market price through rights issues or stock market placings have usually found the institutions to be an almost inexhaustible source of funds. Moreover they have participated in some projects involving high risk and long-deferred returns where there was the prospect of a commensurate return. The North Sea oil fields are a prime example.

In general the institutions avoid taking a direct part in the management of the companies in which they invest. The appointment of a director to the board is however not unusual, and it is easy to see why 'the institutions' figure so frequently in the boardroom conversations of many companies.

The pie charts in Figure 8.1 illustrate the destinations of the investment funds of the two largest groups of institutional investors, the insurance companies and the pension funds. In spite of the concentration of equity investment in their hands, almost half their total goes into gilt-edged stock.

The prime function of both these institutions is, however, the safeguarding of their depositors' funds. Investment is subject to very stringent security precautions and this explains the high proportion of British Government Securities, or 'gilts' in the total.

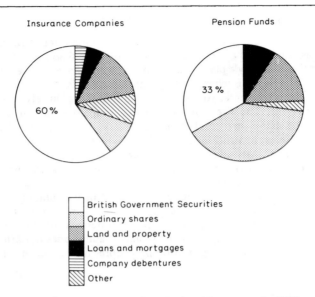

Insurance Companies   Pension Funds

British Government Securities
Ordinary shares
Land and property
Loans and mortgages
Company debentures
Other

Figure 8.1   Breakdown of Institutional Investment in 1975
(Source: *The Economist*)

Insurance companies are among the limited number of financial institutions
that provide mortgages on industrial property. A related source of finance is
'Sale and Lease-back' whereby a company can raise finance by selling some of its
real capital assets to a financial institution, normally an insurance company or a
pension fund, and then lease them back for use. This is principally of help for
factory and office buildings, but may also be extended to major items of capital
equipment.

The major institutions are often dealing with funds that individuals have saved
to provide for their future, and their tolerance of risk is correspondingly low. As a
result a number of specialist institutions exist to fill particular needs which may be
difficult to meet from traditional sources.

(a)   *Finance for Industry Limited* (FFI) is owned by the English and Scottish
Clearing Banks and the Bank of England, and was formed in 1973 by a merger
of Finance Corporation for Industry (FCI) and the Industrial and Commercial
Finance Corporation (ICFC). FCI provides long-term fixed interest capital for
medium and larger-sized companies which cannot find the necessary finance
elsewhere. ICFC provides equity and loan capital to small and medium-sized
companies, and also provides a wide range of financial and specialist services with
a number of regional offices and through specialist subsidiaries: financing new
technical developments (Technical Development Capital); assisting with company
mergers; assisting with Stock Exchange floatations; providing credit instalment
facilities; financing shipbuilding; and assisting family businesses with provision for
capital transfer tax on the death of one of the proprietors through the Estate Duties
Investment Trust (EDITH).

(b)   *Equity Capital for Industry Limited* (ECI) was established in 1976 with an issued capital of approximately £40 million, subscribed substantially by insurance companies, pension funds, investment trust companies, unit trusts and FFI. It is intended specifically to help companies to raise equity capital where they cannot for one reason or another raise such capital on the market.

(c)   *National Enterprise Board* (NEB) was established in 1975 under the Industry Act 1975 to provide finance for industry, to promote efficiency and profitability by re-organization or development of industry, and to be a holding company for Government shareholdings.

(d)   *Other Institutions.* Other specialist institutions exist to provide advice and finance particularly to smaller firms, and also to individual industries, including the Agricultural Mortgage Corporation, the National Research Development Corporation and the National Film Finance Corporation. Funds are also available through the European Investment Bank and other institutions of the European Economic Community, particularly for projects in the assisted areas.

There are also a number of institutions who specialize in the provision of venture capital. By definition this business carries a high risk element, providing start-up capital for new businesses and rescue capital where needed. The range of funds injected is usually between £15,000 and £1 million and an equity stake with a seat on the board are generally required. The term of funding is between five and ten years. Other conditions vary greatly between institutions. Table 8.2 illustrates the variety available, but is not comprehensive. There are about thirteen specialist venture capital institutions in the UK at the moment.

8.34 *Government Activities*

The increasing involvement of Government in the affairs of commerce and industry has been a characteristic of the post-war period. High interest rates combined with high levels of inflation have provided disincentives to industrial investment, and the Government has introduced a number of policies designed to release funds for investment.

8.341 *Deferred Taxation.*

Since October 1970, when the Investment Grant Scheme was ended, the basic national incentive offered by the Government to encourage investment has taken the form of accelerated depreciation allowances against taxation. Under the current system, tax allowances are given on a national basis without any regional differential.

(a)   *Plant and machinery.* The most important single incentive is the first year allowance for expenditure on plant and machinery. Since March 1972, up to 100% of such expenditure can be set against profits for the year in which the expenditure is incurred.

(b)   *Industrial buildings.* Complementary to the allowances for plant and machinery expenditure are the allowances given for expenditure on the construction of industrial buildings (including additions to existing industrial buildings).

(c)   *Stock relief.* The stock relief introduced by the Chancellor in 1974 enables some element of inflationary price increases to be disregarded in the

Table 8.2

Some Venture Capital Institutions in the United Kingdom

Vehicle for capital	Backers	Capital earmarked	Type of client or situation	Min/max funds injected	Start-up capital	Rescue capital	Equity stake	Seat on Board	Term of funding	Exit criteria	Special features	Portfolio
ICFC	Clearing and other banks	Unlimited	Good management in fresh operation; existing operation with new management	£5,000 up to £1m – when Finance Corporation for Industry (FCI) can take over	Yes; but only currently running at 1 in 40 projects	No; but Estate Duties Investment Trust Ltd will take minority stake in appropriate situations	In 10% of customers & not more than 25% of funds advanced	No	7–20 years	Aim to have loans repaid in regular instalments. Equity policy not to promote sale but accommodate position to suit major shareholders	Network of branches. Branch managers provide local link and advice when required	2,200 companies £165m committed
Charterhouse Development	Charterhouse Group	Not disclosed	1. Mature companies 2. Swiftly growing companies	£50,000 to £1m	Not normally	Only within portfolio	Yes	Yes	5–7 years	Looking for dividends as well as appreciation	Financial skills and experience	60 companies at cost of £6m
Hambros Bank	Hambros and syndicate	Open	Avoid high technology and service industries	£25,000 upwards	Only when considerable management potential	No	Yes	Yes	5–7 years	Looking for dividends	Panel of outside businessmen to take director-ships	Cannot be differentiated from total bank holdings
Small Business Capital Fund	Cooperative Insurance Society	Open	Avoid property & retailing. Go for rapid growth and proven management. Aim at pre-tax profits of £200,000 in 5 years	£50,000 upwards	Yes	Yes	Yes 25–49%	Yes	5–8 years	No dividends taken. Sale when convenient for majority shareholders. Loans in package	Team with line management experience	18 companies at cost of £4m
Hill Samuel Development Finance	Hill Samuel	Open	Industrial or commercial with proven track record	£15,000 to £500,000	No	No	Yes	Yes	Open	Looking for dividends	Involvement with management	10 companies £1m

Table 8.2 (continued)

Vehicle capital	Backers	Capital earmarked	Type of client or situation	Min/max funds injected	Start-up capital	Rescue capital	Equity stake	Seat on Board	Term of funding	Exit criteria	Special features	Portfolio
National & Commercial Development Capital	Royal Bank of Scotland. Williams & Glyn's Bank	£2½m equity £6m loan	Good track record £100,000 pre-tax profits	£100,000 to £500,000	No	No	Yes. Ultimately 10–30%	Yes	5–7 years	Sale or merger by agreement with majority shareholders. No dividend	Lend at roughly same rate of borrowings from parent banks. Highly selective	6 companies £1½m committed
Citicorp International Capital	Citicorp, parent company of First National City Bank	World-wide £70m	(a) Mature company, sales over £1m and opportunities to create capital growth by better management. (b) Growth sectors	£100,000 to £500,000	No	Only considered if rescuing shareholders from a stagnant situation	Yes. Prefer convertible stock – structure must satisfy US banking regulations	The right to a seat	6–8 years	Corporate sale. Look for dividends or coupon yield	International presence. Willingness to join in syndicated situations	1 in UK £100,000
European Business Development	Funds based in Luxembourg	Open	Client must not be restricted to a single national market! Looking for fast growth in international markets	Open	Unlikely at present	Yes, if appropriate techniques can be utilized	Yes	Yes	5–7 years	Capital appreciation, not dividends	Can refer clients to shareholder banks	40 throughout Europe

(Source: *Investors Chronicle*)

calculation of taxable profit.

The effect of these reliefs is that, at present, substantially the whole of the profits which a manufacturing company continues to re-invest in its business, whether by way of stock or plant, are effectively relieved from corporation tax, although the allowances are strictly a deferment of tax liability rather than outright exemption. Nevertheless it must be noted that at least over the last two or three years, a number of companies (and groups) have not had sufficient taxable profits to enable them to utilize immediately all of the allowances due to them. The phenomenon, known as 'tax exhaustion', reduces the effectiveness of tax incentives for investment.

(d)   *Selective Investment Scheme.* An initial allocation of £100 million to the new Selective Investment Scheme was announced in December 1976, designed to promote investment projects which will, through improved performance, yield significant benefits to the economy. The scheme operates on a selective basis; applications are examined individually in their industrial context and against the aims of the Government's Industrial Strategy. The scheme is directed towards manufacturing industry with particular attention to the engineering sector, but desirable projects from other sectors are eligible for consideration.

(e)   *Industry schemes.* Over £240 million has been allocated under Section 8 of the Industry Act 1972 to be spent on schemes to assist individual industries. These schemes have been drawn up to meet the needs of particular industrial sectors in discussion with both sides of industry and where practical through the industrial sector working parties that are the main vehicle of the Government's industrial strategy. Major schemes have been implemented in Clothing and Textiles, Machine Tools, Paper, Print Machinery, Meat Slaughtering, Foundries and Electronic Components.

(f)   *Regional schemes.* In addition there is a variety of grants and allowances available to assist investment in selected areas that have suffered in the past from high unemployment and structural depression.

No plans for raising capital should be finalized before a careful analysis of the help that Government can provide in the particular circumstances has been made. Grants and loans from the European Community may also be a useful source of funds, although in most cases this money is available only with the agreement of, and usually with some contribution from, the appropriate national authorities. The most staunchly independent organization should not reject these facilities out of hand; most do not require the board to relinquish the smallest degree of control over the operations concerned. Their availability may be regarded as the more positive side of the coin of high corporate taxation.

8.4 Summary

At this stage it is worth summarizing the availability of the sources of finance discussed so far.

In general banks lend only for the short- or medium-term and avoid long-term capital investment. The Government has taken pains to ensure that priority is given to finance for productive industry from these sources within the overall constraints placed on the banks by official economic policy.

Internally generated funds are the main source of finance overall and the equity market is the other main private sector source of risk capital for industrial firms. Like retained earnings it avoids an increase in loan charges, but unlike retained earnings it involves diluting the existing equity, and may imply some diminution of control over a company.

Table 8.3 sets out the salient differences between these various sources.

Table 8.3

Institutions	Over-drafts	Term lending and loan capital	Other financial services*	Equity finance†	Size of company	Sums available
Banks	√	√	√	–	All	All
Merchant Banks (including Clearing Bank subsidiaries)	–	√	√	√	Most	Probably minimum £50,000
Finance Houses	–	–	√	–	All	All
Specialist Bodies‡	–	√		√	Small	Probably minimum £50,000
ICFC	–	√	√	√	Small to medium	£5,000 to £1m
FCI	–	√	–	–	Medium to large	£1m to £25m
ECI	–	–	–	√	Turnover £10m to £100m	£½m to around £4m
NEB	–	√	–	√	Most	Around £50,000
Insurance companies and pension funds	–	√§	√	√§	Most	
Stock Exchange	–	–	–	√	Minimum market value about £½–¾m	Minimum probably

*Including leasing, hire purchase and sale and lease-back (not necessarily available from all institutions)
†Includes development capital, venture capital, long-term equity capital and assistance with flotations (not necessarily available from all institutions)
‡Includes, for example, SBCF, Charterhouse, Moracrest NRDC
§Usually via Stock Exchange
Source: Wilson Committee Working Papers

At the beginning of the chapter the function of finance was defined as the provision of the required amount of money at the time it is wanted at an acceptable cost. Means and sources will differ with the circumstances, size, and creditworthiness of the company concerned.

Table 8.4

Sources and Uses of Funds
Sources and uses of funds of large listed companies in
manufacturing industries

(Per Cent Total Sources/Uses)

Sources of funds	Estimate 1975
Net trading income	86.2
Other income	11.1
Depreciation	36.4
Gross Income	133.7
Other capital receipts	4.0
Taxation payments	−26.5
Dividend payments (net of tax)	−15.8
Interest on long-term loans	−10.6
Other expenditure on capital account	−3.7
Total internal funds	81.1
Bank borrowing	1.0
Ordinary shares issued for cash	12.2
Preference and long-term loans	5.7
Total external funds	18.9
Total sources of funds	100.0
Uses of funds	
Tangible fixed assets	60.4
Acquisition of subsidiaries	7.9
Less shares and loans issued in exchange	−1.6
Cash cost of acquisitions	6.3
Working capital	
Stocks	31.0
Liquid assets	15.9
Debtors	20.2
Creditors	−37.8
Debtors less creditors	−17.7
Total working capital	29.2
Other expenditure	
Investments	4.8
Intangible assets	0.4
Consolidation adjustment	−1.0
Total uses of funds	100.0

Sources: National Income and Expenditure Tables and Financial Statistics 1976

Table 8.4 shows how large manufacturing companies financed their operations in 1975. It is seldom a simple process involving a single source. More often it will be a question of balancing a number of sources and of re-structuring the company's debt to meet changing circumstances in the most favourable way.

8.5 Conclusion

In this chapter the romantic image of high finance has been deliberately dented. For the average company debtor control is at least as important as the excitement of an operation on the Stock Exchange. Sound finance is closely related to sound funds management, the day-to-day task of making sure that the company has the money that it requires to implement its corporate plan from the most appropriate source, on acceptable terms, at the lowest possible cost.

Our guinea-pig company, Consumer & Electrical, only has reason to raise funds in the market very rarely, but the Chairman appreciates fully the value of professional advice, and retains the services of a London merchant bank in addition to C & E's clearing bank. The City of London is a mine of all sorts of business information, and he values his regular meetings with his merchant bankers as much for their wide perspective of commercial intelligence as for the services they actually provide.

Table 8.5 is a summary of the services provided by Morgan Grenfell, one of the leading London merchant banks.

Table 8.5

Banking
Acceptance Credits in both sterling and other currencies
Short and Medium Term Loans in both sterling and other
    currencies
Negotiations and management of ECGD-backed sterling and
    currency export credits
Financing of large international capital projects
Financial advice and support for international tenders
Guarantees, performance and other bonds
Foreign Exchange
Exchange Control advice
Deposits in sterling, dollars and other currencies
Equipment leasing
Tax relief schemes
Ship finance

Investment Management
Pension Funds
Private and Charitable Funds
International Funds
Property
Asset Management

Table 8.5 (continued)

Corporate Finance
Mergers, acquisitions and disposals
Issues of debt and equity both in sterling and other currencies
Stock exchange quotations for share and loan capital
Public flotations
Advice on Channel Islands operations
Advice on general financial matters including requirements
    of the Stock Exchange and of the Takeover Panel
Advice on compensation and incentive arrangements
    (through an associated company MWP Incentives
    Limited).

There are few areas of finance where it is not qualified to advise. Most clearing banks also have a merchant banking subsidiary, for example Barclay's Merchant Bank, offering a similar range of services.

The sources of finance are constantly changing. New services become available, tax changes alter the relative attractiveness of available methods, exchange and interest rates change every day, and inflation prospects condition the atmosphere of investment. No one source is permanently 'right'. C & E's policy is to monitor its arrangements monthly, with a full scale review once a year at the time of the AGM. It is also of course the Finance Director's responsibility to keep in touch with the situation, and to make interim proposals as required.

9. *Sources and Materials Management*

A recent Census of Production showed that across the broad spectrum of British industry the purchase of materials and services generally accounts for over half of total costs, almost double the figure for wages, salaries and their related costs.

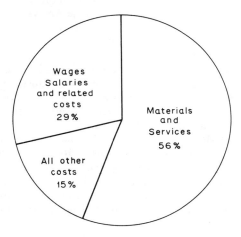

Figure 9.1

Similarly stock, including raw materials, work in progress, and finished goods usually represents a major share of the assets of a manufacturing company. The table below shows that stocks often account for between a quarter and one-third or more of the total assets of companies of a wide range of sizes and industries.

Table 9.1

Levels of Stock

Company	Sector	Turnover (£m)	Stocks (£m)	% Total Assets
GEC	Electrical	2,343	589	27.6
Unigate	Food	974	96	23.4
Turner & Newall	Industrial materials	414	132	29.4
Chubb & Sons	Security	199	55	38.2
Sidlaw Industries	Textiles	40	8	28.4

Source: Annual Accounts for 1977/78

Traditionally however companies have paid more attention to their resources of money, manpower and machinery than to control and exploitation of that other major commitment, their stocks of materials. Often the procurement function is the 'Cinderella' among the departments, with a general ignorance of what the process actually entails on the part of top management.

Yet significant progress has been made in recent years as rapid rises in the price of raw materials have awakened a greater awareness of the need to ensure value for money in their procurement and utilization. The old style buyer or purchasing officer, whose main responsibilities were to keep within budget and maintain cordial relations with suppliers and his 'client' departments within the company, is gradually giving way to the integrated approach of Materials Management. This includes the conventional activities of stores operation and stock control, as well as purchasing. The emphasis is on making the most economic use of the materials available to the company, and techniques like Value Analysis consisting of detailed investigation and analysis of a product and its various components may generate new ideas, resulting in simplification, the use of new materials, improved design, and cost reduction.

The buyer's expertise in obtaining the best terms and his knowledge of suppliers and markets are a central aspect of materials management, but this wider concept involves the control of materials through the processes of production and responsibility for the way they are utilized, as well as their procurement. It is a function that cannot be carried out in isolation, and the manager concerned, who may be termed supplies manager, purchasing manager, or buyer, as well as the newer title, materials manager, will be concerned with a wide range of other departments. He will work closely with marketing because the materials budget will be closely related to the sales forecast, either directly or through the production budget. Marketing may also be responsible for the design and specification of some materials, chiefly the promotional aspects of packaging, and also be influential in the development of new products.

New product development with its emphasis on new and improved materials will associate him closely with R & D, and the need to monitor the performance of materials in day-to-day production will involve a close relationship with production department. Then in addition, almost every department will have material needs that have to be supplied in ways that are often a compromise between the specification of the order and the economic reality of the market place.

The stores itself is an important part of materials management, and handling frequently accounts for 15% and occasionally as much as 85% of total cost. Maximum use of space and minimum waste of time is the objective in planning the stores. Over-the-counter service may be suitable for items with low and medium turnovers, but fast handling becomes more critical as turnover increases. Conveyors operating mechanically and by gravity, cranes, fork-lift and pallet trucks, pipelines, and systems of palletization are among the mechanical handling equipment available. At the extreme, goods are loaded straight into conveyors, the stores being represented by loops or sidings, with materials being fed direct into the productive process. Thus storage tends to become integrated with production, and the warehousing of parts and supplies is an integral part of the process by which a constant flow of items available outside the organization finds its way to the sections inside that require them.

For the non-specialist manager it is convenient to begin with a consideration of stock control, because it is here that answers to some of the questions that concern him most are derived.

9.1 Stock Control

The purpose of a stock control system is to maintain a bank of materials that is adequate to meet operating requirements but is not excessive. Materials have been regarded so far as a resource, and like any other resource it is necessary to ensure that the company obtains the best value for money from it that it can. The financial manager regards the return on capital employed as a valid criterion of the organization's overall performance. Since stock represents a major part of the average company's assets it has a major part to play in this calculation. Clearly the lower the stocks held for a given level of production the more efficient will be the usage of this resource. Stock control is the means of monitoring stock levels and avoiding stock imbalance. It is also closely related to profitability because over-zealous stock reduction can cause shortages that may hinder the whole operation of the company. British Leyland for example is so dependent on the supply of some components that if deliveries are delayed even for a matter of days, large sections of the whole organization can be brought to a halt. At the retail end of the distribution chain, stock shortages can force customers into the arms of competitors and undermine the whole future of a product in a competitive market.

Thus the objectives of stock control are the avoidance of excessive stocks on one hand and of stock shortages on the other. The costs of ordering supplies and of carrying stocks may also be significant, and a good stock control system should be designed to ensure that these are kept to optimum levels.

The costs involved in stock investment are not always apparent. They include:

(a) The notional financial cost of the funds employed in this way that could be used in other applications. A stock of £100 million represents an annual opportunity cost of £12 million if the cost of marginal funds to the company is 12%. This is likely to be a minimum if instead of financing stocks the money were used to reduce the overdraft. If there are real opportunities to employ capital profitably, the opportunity cost might well be 25% or more.

(b) The expense of providing storage space, employing storemen, and arranging security or other specialized facilities. This may be substantial, but may usually be regarded as a fixed expense independent of the volumes involved. They will however tend to increase in steps as a new warehouse or additional staff are needed, and these points need to be recognized and provided for.

(c) The costs of procuring and replenishing stock. These include the cost of the time of buyers, clerks, typists and expediters, as well as the costs of unloading and checking goods, processing invoices and paying bills. The stationery element alone can be quite substantial when postage, internal requisitions, requests for quotations, placing and chasing orders, goods received notes, statements, cheques, envelopes, carbons and copy paper are taken into account.

Large orders reduce costs because the purchase price tends to be lower, reflecting the supplier's savings from limiting the number of transactions. Similarly the purchaser will also make savings because fewer purchases are made. On the other hand large orders increase the total stock at any one time and consequently the overall investment. The correct answer is a balance between the two which can often be misleading. The decision on when to accept a quantity discount, whether in the form of a seasonal offer or promotional 'loader', illustrates this point.

A manufacturer uses £2,000 worth of a particular industrial consumable every year. There are some minor fluctuations, but he maintains an average stock of £400 by ordering monthly. His supplier offers him a 5% discount if he is prepared to order a six monthly supply (£1,000) for delivery in June. On the face of it he will make a saving of £100 per year and will also save by placing two orders per year instead of the current six. However he will incur increased finance and stock-holding costs because his average stock holding could well double to £800. As Table 9.2 shows, the £100 saving is really a difference of only £32, and it will be a management decision whether this is worthwhile or not. If shortages or price increases are expected it may well be an acceptable proposition.

Table 9.2

	Standard Price (£)	5% Discount (£)
Purchase Price	2,000	1,900
Notional stock finance (@ 12% x average stock)	48	96
Stockholding cost (say 15% x average stock)	60	120
Ordering Costs (say £10 per order)	60	20
Annual Cost	2,168	2,136

(Difference £32)

In real life, of course, costs will not behave in this totally variable way and each organization will have a different structure of costs relating to the nature of its own product and operation. It is also customary for a supplier to offer a range of quantity discounts relating to different sizes of order, and the task is more often to select the optimum from a range of price: volume relationships.

9.11 *Economic Ordering Quantity (EOQ)*

The EOQ is calculated by balancing the two opposing sets of unit costs. Financial and stockholding costs increase as the order quantity increases, whilst ordering and purchasing costs should decrease. When the two sets of the equation are equal, total costs are at a minimum. This is shown in Figure 9.2.

The EOQ is clearly a valuable parameter of cost control, providing a criterion of cost effectiveness for materials management. For most stock purchases the size of the order is important because it determines the size of the average stock. For most

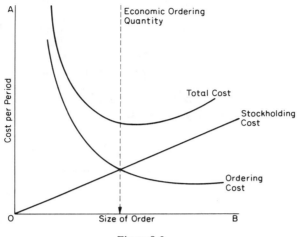

Figure 9.2

high volume manufacturing processes however, the idea of separate orders is not really appropriate because regular requirements are met by regular deliveries from suppliers, and stock is carried mainly to meet emergencies. The main consideration is to control the flow of material.

The second basic question of stock control is how to establish the level of stock of any item at which fresh supplies need to be initiated.

9.12 *Re-order Level*

The level of stock at which it is necessary to place an order to replenish stock is termed the re-order level. In some systems the buyer is automatically advised when this level is reached. This total has three components:

(a) the amount of stock expected to be consumed in the period under review
(b) the amount of stock required during the lead time needed to obtain supplies
(c) a 'buffer' or 'safety' stock to allow for fluctuations in the amount of materials used or for delays in delivery.

The safety stock is also sometimes called a minimum stock because the total stock will never fall below this level if lead time and consumption perform as expected. It is a permanent reserve.

9.13 *Stock Forecasting*

The value of the stock control system will depend on how accurate the estimates for these levels turn out in fact to be. In many companies it is general practice to use a rule of thumb based on experience, for example to make safety stock cover for one month's supply. However the key to minimizing the size of the safety margin is to improve the accuracy of forecasting usage in the delivery and production periods.

If all stock items are classified by the value of annual usage and plotted on a graph, as in Figure 9.3, it will be seen in the vast majority of cases that a very small proportion of all items account for a high proportion of the total value. Known as 'Pareto's Law' or the '80:20 Principle', this provides the basis for differential treatment of stock. In the example below 10% of items stocked account for 70% of the total annual usage. These Class A items represent the main focus for the controller. Class B are goods that are intermediate in value or volume, whilst Class C contains the slow movers and/or low value items, making up 70% of the stores contents, but accounting for only 10% of value.

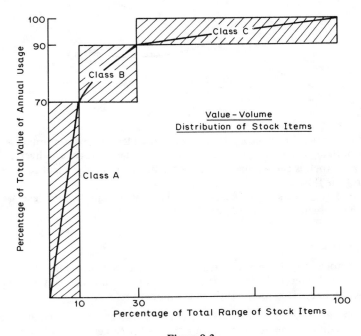

Figure 9.3

One of the commonest methods is to use a moving average covering the last six or twelve months. Alternatively exponential smoothing can be used to derive a trend from historical data. Probability theory can also be helpful in stock forecasting. Thus if we know that average consumption during lead time is 100 and actual consumption would not exceed 110 in 95% of such periods, then we would know that a buffer stock of 10 and an ordering level of 110 would give us a 95% protection against stockouts, which would occur in the 5% of cases when actual consumption exceeds 110. It is clearly uneconomic to develop probability distributions to determine every item's safety stock. However it has been found that a particular probability distribution known as the Poisson can be applied to the fixing of order levels when most stock items are separate identities issued in fairly small quantities. The statistical methods required are however beyond the scope of this book. The forecast for materials used in regular production is generally an exploded version of the production programme, which in turn should be based on the customer demand forecast produced by Marketing.

9.14 *Differential Treatment of Stock*

Stock is seldom an homogeneous category, and the basis of an effective control system is to classify items into groups and provide them with an appropriate degree of control. Thus merchandise with limited shelf-life will require careful rotation to ensure that its quality is not impaired by long storage. Control will need to identify each batch to ensure that this is done. High value stocks may require special security arrangements or frequent counting. Thus in a Cash and Carry grocery warehouse it is customary to lock spirits and tobacco in a separate compound. The supply of some items may be attended by special risks or particularly long delivery dates. Foreign sources or exclusively made custom-built goods or components may be examples.

9.15 *Value: Volume Analysis*

The most important differences from a stock control viewpoint between items are:

volume of usage;
speed of turnover;
cumulative value.

Class A items should be ordered frequently, tightly controlled and requirements may be computed exactly from the explosion of the production programme. Shortages are prevented by frequent checks and energetic chasing. Class B items are still important but should receive a lower level of attention. Order periods will tend to be longer and safety stocks will tend to require some expediting. Class C items on the other hand are ordered in large lots, perhaps a year at a time, with ample safety stocks.

9.16 *Stock Control Methods*

Methods of stock control fall into two categories, those whose data source is a physical check and those that depend on a separately maintained record. A second characteristic is between those that are continuous and those that are periodic in their working.

The Imprest System is probably the most widely used system in factory sub-stores. A pre-printed sheet for every item notes the normal stock level and has blank spaces for the insertion of quantity in stock and quantity required, calculated during a weekly stock check. The document is dated and signed and may be used as a requisition on the central stores.
The Two-Bin System consists of two bins, a working bin and a reserve. When the working bin is empty, the storemen switch to the reserve bin and advise the buyer. In a variation of this there are three bins, coded green for free stock, yellow for order level, and red for danger level. When the yellow bin is broken into, action is taken to replenish stock. There are no paper stock records, and

reliance is placed on simple visual control.

Order Level Cards represent a straightforward application of continuous stock control. The appropriate order quantity and order level are calculated for each item and entered on a stock card. The stock clerk posts issues and receipts, advising the buyer by purchase requisition when the stock balance reaches order level.

Max—min is probably the most common record based control system. In its simplest form, maximum and minimum stock levels are fixed for each item, and the stock clerk is held responsible for keeping stock between the defined limits. There is a tendency for Max—min to lead to hidden overstocking as stocks may be permanently higher than intended because of numerous small topping-up orders. Moreover changes in demand may outdate the figures used for max and min, and the system can sometimes be inflexible.

Cyclic Ordering is designed for tight control of costly items and is also good where it is important for the supplier to know the customer's requirements at regular intervals. In this system stock is reviewed at regular intervals so that the order size varies with consumption, rather than allowing the interval between orders to vary with consumption. Thus orders are normally for the actual amount used in the previous month once an initial order has covered the regular lead time and buffer stock.

9.17 *Stocktaking*

However efficient the day-to-day process of stock control, the need for stock checking remains. Both errors and pilferage are always possible, and internal audit procedures often include spot store checks for these reasons. Moreover the production of the year end stock record for the balance sheet inevitably requires an audited stock-take. There are two approaches:

(a) In *Annual Stocktaking* the stores are closed if possible and every item is counted and valued, very often under the supervision of the firm's internal auditors. The process involves a great deal of concentrated effort and causes much inconvenience both to staff and to other departments.

(b) *Perpetual Inventory* however is a continuous process of checking and counting throughout the period. It minimizes disruption, encourages checkers to become familiar with the job, and enables slow-moving stocks as well as discrepancies to be identified early.

The interface between stock control and purchasing requires a high level of co-ordination and co-operation. Through its reports, records and controls, stock control has the function of ensuring that stock items are replenished in accordance with the pre-determined re-order level and economic order quantity established in conjunction with purchasing and confirmed by management, as agreed operating policy. Purchasing in a strict sense starts from the point at which stock control answers the questions:

What merchanise should I buy?
How much do you need?
When do you need it?

9.2 Purchasing

The objectives of the Purchasing Department follow logically as part of the same series. They are to procure goods as required:

from the right supplier;
at the right qualities;
at the right price;
at the right time.

This is not to discount the contribution of the buyer whose creativity and flair are influential factors in determining his company's degree of cost effectiveness. Rather it emphasizes his close co-ordination with stock control and his integration with production. In most cases he will himself have established minimum, maximum, and re-order stock levels in accordance with lead time and other safety factors in conjunction with the stock controller, and will be responsible for reviewing them as conditions change. In most manufacturing companies purchasing reports to the Production Director, and it seldom makes sense to consider purchasing out of this context. Figure 9.4 is a typical organization chart demonstrating this relationship.

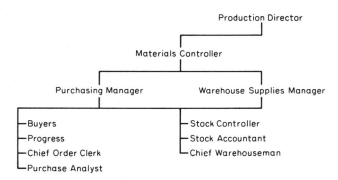

Figure 9.4

The standing of the buyer within his organization differs from company to company. The nature of the product is an important element in determining the scale of management participation and the status of the buying function. This will determine the need for skilled and economic purchasing. Much industrial buying is not the preserve of a single manager. Many sections take part, and it makes better sense to think in terms of a decision-making unit made up of a number of managers from different disciplines. A purchase of plant and equipment may well involve Design Engineering, Production, R & D, Sales and Marketing, and Finance, as well as Purchasing.

Table 9.3 illustrates the participation of management in the selection of a supplier. Naturally the Managing Director is involved about twice as often in the selection of a supplier for major investment items like Plant and Equipment as he is for Component Parts that are likely to be routine purchases, controlled tightly to specification, and bought relatively frequently. The part played by Purchasing Department will be more extensive for all three categories once the order placing stage has been reached.

Table 9.3

Participation of Management in Selection of Suppliers

Product Categories	Part played by Managing Director	Part played by Purchasing Department		
		Director	Manager	Other
	(% times involved)			
Plant and Equipment	26	6	20	—
Materials	19	11	51	8
Component Parts	12	8	46	8

Source: *How British Industry Buys* (IMR/FT)

Component parts are likely to be a routine purchase controlled tightly to specification and demand significantly less attention than plant and machinery which will be relatively infrequent, high cost purchases.

9.21 *Organization of Purchasing*

In a small to medium-size company, purchasing may be very small, perhaps consisting of one or two buyers only. In general a degree of specialization is desirable, and it is usual to allocate a commodity or group of commodities to a particular buyer so that he can develop knowledge of particular products, foster relations with suppliers, and become experienced in the working of the markets concerned.

In a larger group the degree of centralization desirable has to be considered. In general centralization enables larger orders to be placed and market power to be exerted in a number of ways with consequent cost savings. Conversely some flexibility of supply is lost and relationships with suppliers become less close.

A central purchasing department is more likely to be responsible for procuring raw materials, machinery and other capital goods than for components, sub-assemblies and supplies. The former are obtained from a recognized market or from a small group of candidate suppliers. The number of orders placed per unit of time is relatively small and therefore administratively feasible for a central department. The latter products however may involve a large number of orders and decisions, a large number of suppliers, and local conditions may vary so that decentralized selection may provide the best results. In these circumstances it makes sense to supplement a centralized department with local buying offices. The organization of the supplier may also be a factor. For certain products a company may have no alternative but to purchase from local sources. Both IBM and Xerox for example force buyers to deal with their regional organizations rather than.worldwide. In other cases a national agreement with a company like ICI can provide spin-off benefits in terms of economic deliveries or even R & D.

9.22 *The Buying Function*

The functions of the Purchasing Department differ in emphasis between category of product and size of company, but generally fall under the following heads:

(a) *Market Intelligence*

The buyer needs to keep constantly up to date with developments that concern products, markets and suppliers in whom he has or may conceivably have a future interest. In each area he will be aware of alternatives available and will monitor trends in price and development that could provide an advantage over his current purchase. The buyer for a carpet mill for example will trace relative prices between jute and synthetic carpet backing, keeping an eye on research that could produce a product advantage for the synthetic product. He will also watch for take-overs, amalgamations, or other changes in relationships between suppliers that could change the competitive balance.

(b) *Vendor Appraisal and Selection*

A company may put every order out to open market tender, but where a continuing flow of goods is required or where there are many small orders, time can be saved and closer working relations developed by selecting a panel of approved suppliers often following a rigorous appraisal. Accredited suppliers may be awarded a certificate to this effect and either be invited to quote when new business is available or be allocated a share of available business by rotation. The buyer is then able to place an order as he judges best at the time. A growing practice is to identify second sources once a major contract has been awarded and to guarantee this supplier enough business to ensure that he can fill the gap if the first choice fails for some reason. Thus in November 1978 Ferodo, the French motor components group was seeking an agreement with Lucas of the UK for 'second sourcing' some of the products it supplies to the French motor industry. French motor manufacturers were insisting on having alternative and competing supplies of essential components.

(c) *Procurement*

The actual procurement process begin with the receipt of a requisition from a 'client' department authorizing the purchase of goods. Depending on the nature of the requirement the buyer either selects an approved supplier, or requests quotations from a number (usually three) of suppliers. Negotiation of prices, contract conditions, and delivery terms follows: official orders are prepared, signed, and despatched; and as time goes by orders are progressed or expedited to obtain delivery on time. While the buyer himself may not do all these things, they remain the function of the department. Co-ordination should be maintained throughout with the department issuing the requisition to keep the staff concerned informed of probable delivery dates.

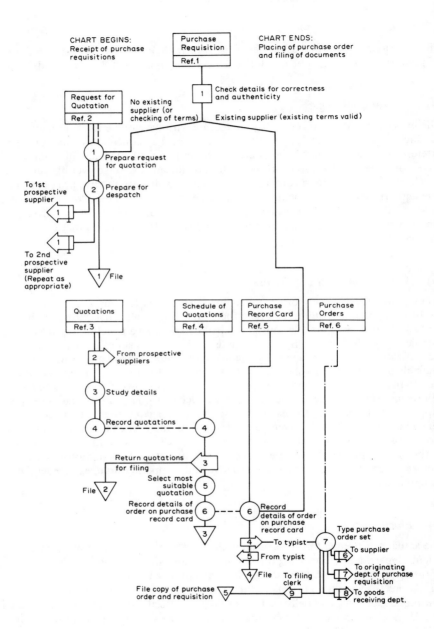

CHART BEGINS:
Receipt of purchase
requisitions

Purchase
Requisition
Ref.1

CHART ENDS:
Placing of purchase order
and filing of documents

1 Check details for correctness
and authenticity

Request for
Quotation
Ref. 2

No existing
supplier (or
checking of terms)

Existing supplier (existing terms valid)

1 Prepare request
for quotation

2 Prepare for
despatch

To 1st
prospective
supplier

1

To 2nd
prospective
supplier
(Repeat as
appropriate)

1 File

Quotations
Ref. 3

Schedule of
Quotations
Ref. 4

Purchase
Record Card
Ref. 5

Purchase
Orders
Ref. 6

2 From prospective
suppliers

3 Study details

4 Record quotations 4

3 Return quotations
for filing

File 2

5 Select most
suitable
quotation

6 Record details of
order on purchase
record card

3

6 Record
details of order
on purchase
record card

Type purchase
order set

7

4 To typist

5 From typist

4 File

To filing
clerk

File copy of purchase
order and requisition

5

9

6 To supplier

7 To originating
dept. of purchase
requisition

8 To goods
receiving dept.

Figure 9.5

(d) *Receipt of Goods*

Incoming goods are recorded on Goods Inwards sheets by the receiving department, and Purchasing will record the details of goods received against each order, showing undelivered balances. Alternatively a copy of the purchase order set may be sent to the Goods Inwards department who will record receipts, returning the order to Purchasing when it is complete.

(e) *Payment*

Finally it is usually a function of Purchasing to verify the purchase invoice and approve it for payment, having checked all details for compatibility and confirmed that the delivery is acceptable in every way.

9.23 *Value for Money*

The functions described so far are very largely routine. The concept of value for money however is inherent in all supply work. The effective buyer should always be looking for ways in which he can obtain better value for the money he spends. Since the items he purchases are required for usage in the company, as part of the production process, or for re-sale, this objective inevitably involves him in close co-operation or even integration in his 'client' departments.

Things never stand still, and even the completely non-technical buyer will receive from his suppliers suggestions for improving the specification, making the item easier to produce, or reducing its cost. Suppliers often recognize that involvement in this type of activity with a customer strengthens their hold on the account by providing an advantage over competition. The supplier has a real interest in the cost effectiveness and hence competitiveness of his customer. An increase in production levels invariably means more orders for him.

A buyer may also identify opportunities for standardization that result in major cost savings through bulk buying. Price however is only one aspect of value. A recent survey among American industrial buyers revealed that quality control, punctual delivery, engineering capability, and new product innovation all ranked ahead of low prices in their minds. Value encompasses the whole of the product package, and the buyer must take into account the whole pattern of utilities associated with his purchase. Distribution arrangements, packaging, credit, spares, servicing, and supply availability are all factors that may decide the buyer against the lowest priced quotation.

9.24 *Value Analysis*

Value Analysis has been defined as an organized, creative approach with the purpose of identifying unnecessary cost which can be eliminated without reducing the quality, reliability, durability or performance of the end-product. It is a team effort in which design, manufacturing, and purchasing executives apply a planned procedure of investigation into the possibilities of cost reduction without reducing value. The most dramatic results have been achieved where the product is multi-component assemblies which give each member of the team a chance to apply his own specialist skills to the item under review. It has been estimated that at least three-quarters of the value analysis currently undertaken is applied to bought-out parts and components, a statistic that underlines the central contribution of the buyer. Typically value analysis will include such questions as:

Can we cut the item out altogether?
Can it be simplified?
Will any thing else serve the same purpose better?
Can it be replaced with a standard part?
Would a cheaper material do as well?
Would a dearer material do proportionately better?
Would a cheaper production process be satisfactory?
Can a cheaper supplier be found who will be satisfactory?
Is anyone buying it for less?

These will indicate such improvements as:

Simplification of design and adoption of alternative methods
Material cost savings and use of substitute materials
Re-definition of manufacturing tolerances
Rationalization of production processes
Increased standardization
Labour savings from modified assembly
Discounts from bulk buying
Savings in transportation, packing, and handling costs
Changes in make or buy policies.

9.3 Computers in Materials Management

The subject of electronic data processing is outside the scope of this book. However it would be unrealistic to totally ignore the part that computers now play in materials management. A well designed system can sort, process, and analyse many thousands of items very rapidly and reliably. Use is not however confined to routine 'number crunching'. A modern computer can be programmed to carry out work that could not be done at all, or at least not in an acceptable amount of time, by staff. The flow of mini-computers into the market in recent years means that most companies can afford at least a basic model today.

Stock control is a classic computer application. Stock may be recorded on magnetic tape or other appropriate media and updated with receipts and issues as convenient. No perpetual inventory record is needed, and the machine will print out balance slips at pre-determined intervals. While updating, a computer can test for exceptional canditions to determine when expediting or ordering is needed. Department (retail) stores with perhaps 150,000 to 200,000 items in stock are now taking advantage of computer techniques to maintain current stock balances updated directly from the point of sale. In the system used at Argos, the assistant obtains an immediate statement of the availability of each item by passing a 'wand' connected to the terminal over a stock list printed in magnetic coded characters.

Buying routines involve a smaller volume of clerical work than stock control, but the use of computers is also widely spread in purchasing. Name, address, terms applicable and other detail for each supplier can be recorded in an electronic supplier directory. Costing, lead-time, end-product, ordering history, quantity, price, and supplier may be filed for extremely large ranges of items. Conventional explosion of production programmes and stock recording transactions can be carried out, and the machine may print reports on request, purchase orders, and cheques to pay for the goods. Larger systems may also incorporate appraisal of the performance of suppliers and buyers in terms of prices, quality, delivery, and other factors.

The rapid update capability of computers, coupled with the logic that is now available in software packages and appropriate data, enables managers to cope sensibly with the thousands of day-to-day changes in the materials planning process. One result is that the individual functions are moving closer together and sometimes integrating. Figure 9.6 shows a computer based materials requirements planning (MRP) system that illustrates this trend.

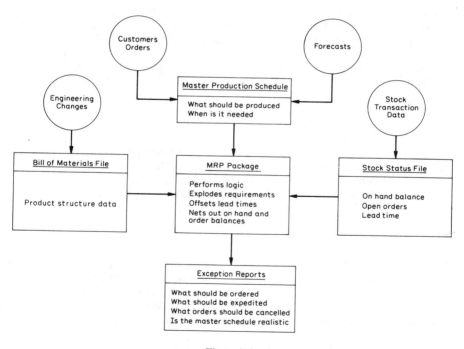

Figure 9.6

9.4 Marketing Opportunities in Materials Management

The marketing executive with one eye on the satisfaction of his customer and the other on the activities of his competitor can find many opportunities in the area of materials management, and in most companies the brand or product manager will work closely with his purchasing counterpart.

9.41 *Product Enhancement*

Through his contacts with suppliers, the buyer will often be able to pass on details of new developments that can be incorporated as product improvements. New materials can often replace traditional ones and provide a cost saving at the same time. Thus

> a cheap, light petrol cap may replace a costly heavier metal one
> aluminium foil cans may supersede expensive, tin-plate ones
> polypropylene bagging may replace traditional jute sacking.

In each case a product improvement is combined with a cost saving, and often there will be incidental benefits derived from distributing lighter products as well.

Packaging is a traditional means by which an old product is updated and given new sparkle. Many cardboard manufacturers maintain teams of designers who are able to produce solutions to complex packaging problems as part of customer service. A typical example is the cosmetic or toiletry manufacturer who produces Christmas packings to make his product appeal to the gift market. A packaging facelift may also be an effective response to a competitor's new product launch.

9.42 *Cost Reduction*

The value analysis exercise can often indicate ways in which the company can improve its market position. A materials-based cost reduction may enable price levels to be trimmed to gain an advantage over competitors. But a saving can often be used in more creative ways. It frees funds that can be used to improve the product, raise the level of promotion, or simply increase its profit contribution.

9.43 *Product Range Development*

Also, analysis can often point the way to range extensions. A value analysis exercise indicated to a domestic appliance manufacturer how he could up-grade his top volume refrigerator within existing costs and introduce a new economy model with very little addition to on-going fixed cost. Five years later the economy 'X' model retained third place in the UK market whilst the original product had been withdrawn.

Diversification can take a number of different forms. Thus a company engaged in aluminium wire drawing can manufacture aluminium roofing nails for the building industry, decorative chain for the costume jewellery trade, or wire for specialist welding purposes. The possibilities of such a conversion operation may be virtually endless, and systematic analysis of the functions and characteristics of an existing range can often indicate new product prospects.

A company need not necessarily manufacture all the items it sells. The practice of selling factored products is very common. Wherever a volume is expected to be too small, where there are production problems that require significant investment, or simply where outside specialist manufacturers have a cost advantage, the possibility of filling a perceived gap in the range with a bought-in product should be considered. Thus GEC Osram carry a very wide range of General Lighting Service lamps, many with relatively low volumes. It would not be economic to set up a line to manufacture Christmas Sets, but these lamps complement the domestic range at a particular time and make a worthwhile contribution. They are therefore bought in from an outside supplier. A good buyer will make suggestions on his own initiative, but 'make or buy' decisions should be reviewed at regular intervals as a matter of course. New processes, components and materials are becoming available constantly and can upset the economics of the *status quo* literally overnight.

9.5 Quality Control

Decisions on product quality may be central to product range planning. A market may segment on quality lines, and a manufacturer may be able to develop a profitable corner where substitutes may be virtually absent. Rolls/Royce is the obvious example, whilst at one time Wilkinson razor blades held a similar position. Consumers were prepared to go to great lengths to obtain these blades, although the difference from Gillette's 'Super Silver' competitor was marginal in terms of purely physical characteristics.

A marketer may move his product up and down the quality scale, projecting the change through advertising and other promotion. In this way he may:

relaunch an ailing product
justify a price increase
move away from a troublesome competitor
introduce a premium or economy range member.

Branding however implies consistent quality since brand loyalty is based on a familiar and acceptable standard. Quality control therefore has an important role to play.

Rates of consumption are very closely associated with quality and durability. Through 'planned obsolescence' a marketer can deliberately reduce the life of his product to stimulate re-purchase. This practice may well prove counter-productive. A customer will not be satisfied if his purchase proves less durable than expected, and he may re-purchase elsewhere. A more generally acceptable means of hastening re-purchase is the introduction of new features or styles that render an item that continues to be serviceable obsolete or obsolescent. This marketing strategy is familiar in fields as far apart as computers and women's haute couture, office copiers and motor cars, as well as wallpapers and washing machines.

9.6 Stockholding

As with Quality Control, the marketing manager can vary the extent of his service when it comes to stockholding. Initially he will need to ensure that sufficient finished goods are in stock to meet regular or expected demand, but his decisions on safety margins and the depth and width of the range stocked can affect the availability offered to the customer. Immediate availability of all items may be too costly to be viable, and a marketing decision has to be taken on the level of acceptable stock-outs.

It may also be possible to offer special facilities to selected customers, perhaps stocking a wider range than normal at selected depots. Indeed the employment of regional depots in addition to the central store may add a valuable element of customer satisfaction and a major competitive advantage.

Stockholding may also add value to the product itself:

holding stock in an inflationary situation to take advantage of expected price increases may contribute worthwhile stock profits;
some products improve with age. Thus Glenfiddich malt whisky makes a product advantage of its eight years stock life;
stockholding to meet a seasonal trend, perhaps providing special facilities to keep consumables fresh, is another example.

At this stage it is healthy to remember that the disciplines of the market still apply. No new product, modification or development should be considered simply because we know how we can make it. That is production-orientation at its most extreme. There is often a real temptation to launch something because it is new and revolutionary. To succeed there must be a perceived customer need for it and the prospect of creating a valid customer satisfaction, i.e. there must exist a gap in the market to be exploited. It does not matter whether the basic idea derives from a market study, a value analysis, a purchasing discovery, or the existence of spare capacity on a machine. It must be validated in terms of market demand before investment is begun if unnecessary risks are to be avoided.

9.7 Conclusion

Sourcing and Materials Management are seen as key functions at our typical company, Consumer and Electrical. You do not have to be an accountant to see that stocks of one sort or another may represent a very high proportion of Current Assets. As a mixed manufacturing and trading group, C & E usually hold about 45–50% in Stock, and, conscious of the cost of neglect or mismanagement, the Managing Director has arranged for the appointment of a Purchasing Director to the Board.

C & E experience many of the problems of materials management. C & E (Manufacturing) have to control raw material and work-in-progress stock levels, as well as those of finished goods. Their calculations are based on sales forecasts from the Marketing Department, but as their smaller appliance range has strong gift appeal, demand tends to be seasonal to meet the Christmas rush, and they smooth out the peaks and troughs by manufacturing for stock in the quieter periods. This obviously demands careful control, and the early sales trends are anxiously watched as the trade starts to buy in September.

C & E (Distribution) have related problems, but concentrated on finished goods stock. Procurement from C & E (Manufacturing) is at national arms' length prices, but is controlled as carefully as purchases from outside the group.

Although each division has its own Purchasing Section, their activities are carefully co-ordinated at group level. The decision on whether to make, buy, or sub-contract is particularly important for C & E with its mixed interests, and purchasing staff spend as much time on Value Analysis, standardization, and cost improvement programmes as actually visiting and negotiating with suppliers. The group tries to foster good relations with its suppliers, and operates an effective vendor rating system, with certificates for approved suppliers, within, of course, its established policy of putting significant requirements out to competitive tender.

10. *Production Management*

In most companies the great bulk of assets are employed in the production or operations function. The factories, machinery, and vehicles associated with manufacturing usually represent the largest proportion of fixed assets; the largest group of employees (except in the least labour intensive concerns) work in production; and correspondingly a major share of management, particularly in the lower and middle echelons, is employed there. Moreover the assets utilized in production tend to be larger, more closely linked with one another, and longer-lived than marketing and most financial assets. Production processes often represent the core of the company; it may be difficult to redirect them and 'fine tuning' may be almost impossible.

Nevertheless the production department has no separate or independent existence from the rest of the company, even where it may be organized as a semi-autonomous division or cost centre. Its activities are an integral part of the overall corporate plan and in some production-oriented companies may well represent virtually all of it. However plans change from year to year and it is a major responsibility of management to see that the technology, organization, and output capacity of the manufacturing facility remain closely geared to the demands of marketing strategy. Four aspects are of particular relevance to production management:

10.1 Growth

The demands on production management will differ between a company satisfied with a low rate of growth and one that requires a higher rate, particularly where this entails major increases in volume and aggressive new product policies.

10.2 Orientation

Mention has been made earlier of the concepts of market or product-orientation. Within these overall postures a company may see certain aspects as being of particular relevance to its planning and operating. A materials — or technology — oriented company will tend to develop its specialization in these directions, and the production facilities it requires will differ accordingly.

10.3 Diversification

A company's approach to diversification has obvious production implications.

Product diversification, if achieved by purchasing new production units may have relatively little impact on a particular unit, except in as far as its management may undertake a new work load. Diversification based on the current range however often entails a complete re-organization of factory facilities.

10.4 Competition

Competitive strategies almost always affect manufacturing. Price competition involves the choice between seeking high profit margins or high sales volumes, determining the scale of production output. Decisions to compete on quality, durability, after-sales service, availability, fashion, or delivery all affect production planning, or the closely related functions of stock control and distribution.

Production is therefore something of a challenge to the marketing man. He may need changes in the level of output, pack modifications, minor adjustments to product details, quality changes, or fundamentally new products, and he may need them fast. The production manager knows that the efficiency of his own performance and the productivity of his plant relates closely to the length of uninterrupted run he can organize. The two positions are frankly irreconcilable. Both parties need to make conscious and continuing efforts to recognize the problems of the other and to work out sensible methods of co-operation and compromise. Nowhere is the interface between two departments as critical to the final success of the organization as that between marketing and production.

Because of these differences in approach any manager who desires to influence the production process needs at least a basic knowledge of the principles and methods involved.

10.5 The Production Process

Production is a conversion process in which certain items are introduced as inputs and products emerge as output. If the process is to be planned and controlled in an effective way, four steps are necessary. These are to:

(a) set standards for inputs and outputs
(b) compare actual performance to standard
(c) take corrective action where performance is unsatisfactory
(d) measure productivity by comparing output to input.

This of course bears a very close relationship to the principles of planning and control outlined in Chapter 6. The use of ratios is also not unlike that made in financial management. Thus the efficiency of converting inputs into outputs may be expressed by the productivity ratio: output/input x 100.

10.6 Methods of Manufacture

The manufacturing methods used in the conversion process are mainly determined by the nature of the product and the volumes that are to be made. There are four basic manufacturing methods and these are outlined in Table 10.1.

Table 10.1

Method	*Description of Method*	*Examples of products*
Jobbing, unit or specification production	Unit or very small quantity production of articles generally to individual customer requirements. Items produced by this method will tend to wait between the various operations.	Ships, bridges, special machine tools, castings and forgings.
Batch production	Involves the multiple production of articles in batches of five up to many hundreds. Items made by this method of manufacture could be to customer requirement or in anticipation of orders. Like jobbing production, batches of work will tend to queue between operations	Furniture, clothes, machine tools, screws, steel, books, fisheries and mining products
Mass, flow or line production	Involves the continuous manufacture of very large quantities of products. The products made by this method are nearly always some kind of consumer goods, and are made in anticipation of sales, often using many manufactured components	Motor cars, TV sets, radios, soap, cigarettes, electric light bulbs and refrigerators
Continuous or process production	Certain products, because of their nature and the large demand for them, lend themselves to the process method of production. In this method the whole factory is like one huge machine where the raw material enters at one end and emerges at the other end as a finished product.	Chemicals, petrol, domestic gas, plastic and brewery products

There are similarities between jobbing and batch production on one hand and between mass and process manufacture on the other. It is therefore possible to consider them in two major groups, each offering distinct marketing advantages and disadvantages.

(a)   *Jobbing–Batch Production* is suited to small to medium quantities. General purpose machinery is often used that can be modified to suit particular products. It is thus possible to produce a wide range of small volume products with a relatively high number of variations. Often the needs of individual customers can be reflected in product modifications and at one end of the scale products may be made to specification. This means however that production will be of an intermittent nature, and the time to make one product may be extended. Similarly the large number of different products makes sales forecasting difficult and complicates the balancing of demand and production capacity. Future planning tends to be on the basis of analysis of customers' past orders.

(b)   *Mass, Flow, Line, or Process Production* is appropriate for large-scale quantities. The number of products will be smaller and more standardized than for small quantity production, and this makes it possible to gear demand to capacity, so permitting continuous flow. This however requires a greater sophistication in sales forecasting and may involve sampling and other techniques of market research. It is relatively difficult to make minor modifications to the product and it will seldom be viable to make to a customer's specification unless very big volumes, like those of 'private label' products, are concerned. Unless market demand is totally stable and uncyclical, it will regularly be necessary to build for stock. This provides marketing with the opportunity to offer guaranteed availability to meet customers needs, but it also places an additional burden on demand forecasting and stock control. Mass production generates a large volume of relatively low cost products that puts continuing pressure on distribution. The nature of this process will determine both the size and organization of the sales department and the characteristics of advertising and promotional plans.

There are thus special marketing problems associated with each method of production and the scope of the functions of the marketing department will vary accordingly. Particular difficulties are experienced when a company grows to a stage when a change in its methods of manufacturing is appropriate. A company moving from batch to mass production, either through product diversification or volume growth in its current range, needs to recognize the need for a revised manufacturing organization structure, and similar adjustments to procedures and systems throughout its operation.

10.7 Factory Layout

Factory layout is one of the principal factors contributing to manufacturing efficiency. If production is to flow smoothly the location of departments and the siting of equipment need to be carefully planned, not only with regard to current products but also with an eye on possible future changes in demand. The general nature of the layout will be largely influenced by the method of production employed, and there are correspondingly two basic types of layout:

(a)   *Product layout:* when a company manufactures large quantities of a standardized range of products the equipment is arranged in operation sequence. This is called a product or line layout. Examples of articles produced by this method include motor cars, television sets and washing machines.
(b)   *Process layout:* in most factories engaged in jobbing/batch production the equipment is arranged in a process or functional type layout. In this type of layout similar kinds of equipment are placed in groups. Products include castings, furniture, machine tools, and forgings.

A product layout for a small part engineering operation is shown in Figure 10.1. Control tends to be easier because routes are less complicated and the time for a product to pass through the factory is decreased. On the other hand, unless volume can be geared accurately to capacity, machine utilization will be bad, and the

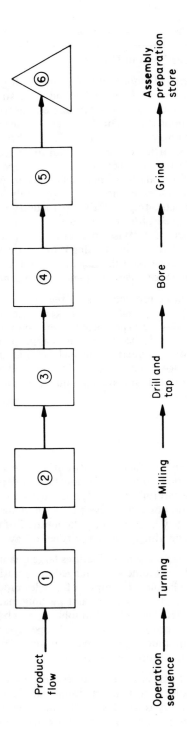

Figure 10.1 Product Layout

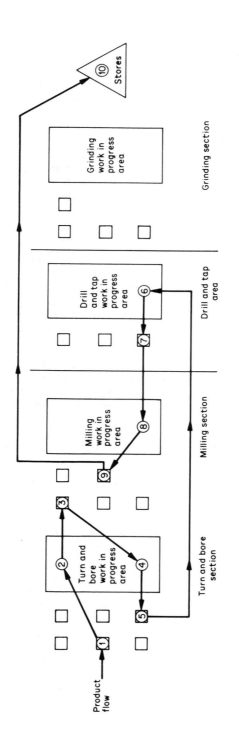

Figure 10.2 Process Layout

system is inflexible, not being able to accept change easily.

A process layout for the same operation is illustrated in Figure 10.2. It is extremely flexible and can accommodate many different products, and machine utilization will be correspondingly high. However control will be difficult because of the complicated product flow, and it may be necessary to hold stocks of work-in-progress as a buffer between operations.

The design of a satisfactory layout takes into account details of likely demand over the next five years; production methods; details of buildings, departments, equipment, and the area available for work-in-progress; the capacity and location of such services as electricity, gas, water, lighting, and pneumatics; and of course statutory and local government aspects, such as building restrictions. A good layout however may become inefficient if conditions change. Very often these changes derive from the marketing area, as in the following cases:

1 Order size: if the size of orders has increased or decreased a different form of layout may be more suitable.
2 Product type: a change in product type may alter materials handling, plant requirements, and processing times.
3 Competitiveness: an increase in price competitiveness may necessitate an improvement in methods, reduction in work-in-progress or a different kind of layout if it involves cost economies or increases in volume.

Inevitably this brief summary of the nature of the production process has touched only on salient points of major interest. In most instances the complete and equipped factory already exists and the marketing manager has to accept that in his day-to-day operation it can only be adapted to his interpretation of the market's needs in a marginal way. He does however play a major role in how production capacity is programmed through his responsibility for the demand forecast on which production planning is based. This aspect is discussed in more detail in Chapter 14.

10.8 Production Planning and Control

A factory's methods of manufacture may be specified, its layout designed, and its machinery installed, but manufacturing cannot begin until a production plan has been produced and finalized.

Production planning and control is practised by industrial enterprises in order to ensure that delivery dates are met, that materials and components are available when and where they are needed and that workers and machines are neither overloaded nor left idle. It consists broadly of relating what is wanted (sales requirements) to what is available (production capacity) on a time basis. It may be defined as the group of activities employed in planning and controlling the flow of materials into, through, and out of the plant in such a manner that the planned product quality and volume is produced on schedule by the least costly methods.

Production planning and control may be regarded as the nervous system of the factory. Its activities cover all the stages of the course of production operations from the procurement of materials to the shipping of finished goods. Materials and facilities must be available according to plan, work must flow from one operation to the next according to a set schedule without unnecessary delays and stoppages, and a means of controlling the progress of work according to the production programme must be provided.

Production planning and control is a series of related and co-ordinated activities performed in an orderly sequence, consisting of planning production programmes, releasing orders for production, and following them through to completion. The major functions of production planning and control can be grouped into two categories, as follows:

10.9 Planning

Planning embraces three functions that must be specified before production can start, they are:

1 Preparation of Production Programme
2 Routing
3 Scheduling.

Each of these planning functions provides the answer to one or more of the six questions basic to production planning:

(a) What is to be done?
(b) Who is to do it?
(c) Where is it to be done?
(d) How is it to be done?
(e) When is it to be done?
(f) Why is it to be done in this particular way?

10.91 *Preparation of Production Programme*

Preparation of the production programme provides the answer to the basic 'what' question.

It is produced on the basis of the sales demand forecast from Marketing, and it reconciles the potential demand for products or groups of products with the available production capacity for a stated time period. In a situation of high machine utilization it may well require a compromise between market development and customer service needs and production considerations. Depending on the facts of the situation agreement will be reached somewhere on the spectrum between 'You'll just have to wait' and 'We will instal new plant immediately to meet your requirements'. It is important that this dialogue between Marketing and Production actually takes place at this stage because it enables both sides to maintain realistic attitudes about, respectively, supply conditions and the market place, and they are able to adjust their subsequent actions accordingly.

A detailed short-term production programme is then drafted, providing for all product variations. Detailed stock projections are made at each stage as it should always be kept in mind that demand can be met from finished goods stock on hand as well as current production. An astute marketing manager will be as interested in current and projected levels of stock as in the production plan itself.

10.92 *Routing*

Routing provides the answers to the basic who, where, and how questions of the production planning problem.

It comprises the selection and determination of the most efficient and least costly path which the raw materials and parts of the product will follow, from one machine to another and from department to department, while being transformed into finished products.

Beside mapping out the path, routing handles the detailed specifications included in the plan.

Product specifications are the basis for routing. They come in various forms, as written specifications, engineering drawings, or formulas, for example. Naturally, they must not conflict with practical production possibilities. Ordinarily these specifications are obtained either from the customer, or from the staff responsible for product engineering and design, or from both sources. The detail included will vary greatly with the products and processes involved.

Procedure specifications are commonly developed within staff units responsible for methods study and time and motion study, the information being often prepared in the form of 'Standard Procedure Instructions' and/or 'Route Sheets'. When such aids are available, and this is usually the case in mass production, routing entails a comparatively simple routine, and the routing staff has merely to make references to these instructions and sheets. Still, to specify routing the routing staff must have information about all the available production facilities, and they must be able to determine how best to accomplish the desired result cost-effectively.

The routing function in production planning breaks down the production programme into detailed work orders for individual processes or machines. It entails the job of specifying for the production departments, the operation sequence, the location, the equipment, and the procedure required for the work indicated by the product specifications.

The detail in which this is done depends on the nature and type of manufacturing, on the volume and complexity of production, on the repetitive nature of the order, and on the assistance provided by other staff units of the enterprise.

In continuous production industries, the problem of routing is relatively simple, since the sequence of operations and the path of production is normally fixed by production lines. Nevertheless standardized route sheets must be used as basic documents when preparing work orders and when giving specifications. Production times should be included in the route sheets in order to allow balanced work loads for the various processes to be planned.

10.93 *Scheduling*

Scheduling answers the basic question 'when', and, as the term implies, the scheduling function involves the time element in production. The simplest schedule for a production-order specifies either the date when the order is to start production, or the date when it is to be completed. In most cases the elapsed time for the work and the limits for individual operations should also be specified. In addition, the time required for procurement of materials for tooling, and for other essential preliminaries should be carefully scheduled.

Effective Scheduling depends on complete and up to date information on the following factors:

(a)   Delivery requirements for finished products, quantities and dates.
(b)   Production capacity, available plant facilities and manpower.
(c)   Existing work loads and future commitments.
(d)   Standard processing times.
(e)   The quantity of materials and parts, including supplies, on hand and available for new work.
(f)   Determination of the Lead Time, which is the time required for procurement of materials, parts, tools and supplies.

A plan, however carefully drafted, has little value until it is put into effect. Control is needed to ensure that subsequent action is indeed in accordance with plan.

10.10   Control

Control means more than planning; it is one thing to work out a plan for a production programme and quite another to see that the plan is carried out. That is the essence of control.

Control involves the use of various techniques and methods for ensuring that the production programme is carried out. Hence various functions of execution and appraisal are involved. They include the release of orders authorizing the production programme, they entail a follow-up on progress, and they involve action to correct irregularities where progress falls out of line with the plan.

Control functions begin with the start of production and accompany it through to completion. These major functions are:

Dispatching
Follow-up
Corrective action

10.101   *Dispatching*

Dispatching is the 'go-ahead' for work to begin when essential orders and instructions are given. Dispatching gives the necessary authority to production departments to start a particular job which has already been planned under Routing and Scheduling.

Major tasks of dispatching are to:

release production orders to production centres authorizing the start of work as per schedule;
distribute machine loading schedules, route sheets, schedule charts, and other necessary instructions and forms including drawings, specifications, and procedure instructions to production centres;
check-up on the completion of pre-requisites to production, i.e. delivery of parts, materials, and tools to work centres;
issue subordinate orders such as work orders, requisitions, inspection orders, and

other orders authorizing the desired work to be done.

Dispatching is usually conducted at a centre called the 'Dispatching Station' where records of all orders pending, orders in process, and work load data are maintained.

The dispatching station may also hold copies of drawings specifications, and processing instructions that apply to repeated orders, since releasing those papers is one of the dispatching functions.

The dispatching function is not to be confused with the despatch of goods for shipment or delivery. Dispatching, as part of Production Planning, takes place before manufacturing begins; despatch is the final job of sending products out of the factory to their next destination.

10.102 *Follow-up and Corrective Action*

A separate follow-up section is sometimes formed, but usually the same group handles dispatching and follow-up action as they are closely related. Its responsibility is to:

see that materials and parts reach production centres at required times so that production can be started to schedule;
check on production progress including starting and finishing times, quantities, inspection results, and movement of work from one centre to the next;
maintain up-to-date progress records including revision of schedules and the work load situation;
check on delays, investigate their causes, and try to remove them;
report to factory management all significant deviations from schedules and delays so that appropriate corrective action can be taken.

10.11 Importance of Effective Production Planning and Control

The effectiveness of production planning and control is of vital interest to the marketing manager. Few other functions have such a direct impact on his customer, whether through the availability of the product range or through the cost implications of inefficient utilization of production capacity. The following list of symptoms indicating weak control and planning illustrate the point:

failure to get customers' orders delivered on time;
frequent need to 'rob' one order to fill another;
numerous rush production orders;
short production runs due to uneconomic lot sizes;
frequent product changes, resulting in excessive set-up costs;
frequent operation delays due to materials and parts shortages;
operations delayed by unbalanced flow of materials and parts;
excessive overtime;
high production costs.

Production Planning and Control seeks to organize the various elements of production so that productivity is maximized for a given level of output. This requires a detailed knowledge of all aspects of each process, and in particular how each section relates to the others and how sensitive each is to changes in its environment. The most volatile of these elements is of course the human one, and the planner needs to be continually alert to ways in which its contribution can be improved. The most important source of this information is Work Study.

10.12 Work Study

Productivity was earlier defined in terms of the ratio of output to input. The object of work study is to improve this ratio by investigating and analysing the operations in the production process to identify opportunities for improvement. It is a scientific approach providing management with the objective facts needed to reach correct decisions. Thus it is a service to management rather than a line function.

Although work study projects can be very complex and invariably involve a great deal of detail, there are two simple themes that underlie a large proportion of study work. They are:

(a)   *Simplification*
In general the simpler an operation the more cost-effective it will be, assuming of course that it achieves the same end result. Simpler systems, methods and production layouts may enable higher speeds to be achieved, lower wastage rates incurred, and other economies, such as a lower supervision ratio, to be made.

(b)   *Standardization*
The use of standard components and methods is an important aspect in the economies of large scale production. Diversity may mean the need for more checks and controls, and all the costs associated with small production runs. Standardization and Simplification are closely related as they both tend to seek common features between separate parts of the production process.

The subjects for study differ from situation to situation, focussing on factors that can adversely affect productivity. These may be classed in two categories:

Factors that add to the work content of the job, such as bad design, lack of standardization, inappropriate quality standards, unsuitable machines, processes, conditions, tools or materials, bad layout and weak methods.
Factors that add time and thus cost to the job, such as excess product variety, non-standard methods, frequent design changes, bad planning, maintenance or working conditions, and such operator problems as absence, lateness, careless work, idleness or accident.

Work study has three basic techniques for tackling these questions, each of which is subdivided into a number of procedures applicable to the nature of the work being studied. They are:

1 Method study is concerned with analysing how work should be done considering the current state of technology and the nature of the production facilities available.

2 Work measurement involves determining how long and how hard operatives have
   to work to do a job whose methods and working conditions have been specified.
3 Job evaluation assesses the relative value of work done in different jobs in terms
   of skill, responsibility, effort, and conditions.

10.13 Method Study

Like all work study, Method Study should be characterized by a strict and rigorous
attitude to the ascertainment and analysis of facts. The Glossary of Terms in Works
Study published by the British Standards Institution defines it as 'the systematic,
recording, and critical examination of existing and proposed ways of doing work
as a means of developing and applying easier and more effective methods and
reducing costs'. It is applied in six distinct and separate steps.

Step 1 is to select and identify the problem. This is not simply a platitude; it is
a very serious difficulty knowing where to start, particularly as it may not be
apparent which job will yield the greatest economies. It is therefore vital to define
as closely as possible the objectives of the study. Cost reduction for example may
require a different study approach from productivity improvement.

Step 2 involves ascertaining and recording the facts about the problem and
analysing them into appropriate detail. The questions to be asked are simply:
What is done?; Where is it done?; When is it done?; Who does it?; and How is it
done?. Questioning however must be comprehensive and may be complex. For
example the 'when' question includes the sequence or order in which work is
done as well as the simple frequency and time of day aspects.

Step 3 is criticism of the facts collected. In some cases valid conclusions may
be reached by very superficial consideration of the facts collected. More often
valid criticism requires the use of such techniques as the process chart. Every
operation is recorded either in terms of the flow of materials or the actions of
the operator, during the process. The function of the chart is to visualize the
process and provide information such as the duration of each event, the distance
travelled, the class of labour, and the methods employed in a form that makes it
easy to see where time or cost can be reduced and methods improved. String
diagrams, flow diagrams and outline charts may also be used. Two handed or gang
charts may be used to record the simultaneous activities of two or more workers
and to compare the old method with prospective new ones.

Figure 10.3 is an example of a typical process chart designed to record two
aspects of an operation and present them in a form to ease comparison. This form
shows the activities of the right and left hands or compares the present with the
proposed methods.

A brief description of each movement is entered in the spaces numbered 1 to
20, and a brief analysis of quantity, time, or distance travelled as relevant to the
study in hand is included in the appropriate vertical column. It is then classified
into one of five categories: Operation, Inspection, Transport, Delay and Storage/
Hold. By drawing a line through the symbol for each activity, a visual picture of
the operation is produced that can help to identify wasted time or other
opportunities for improvement (Figure 10.4).

Step 4 is the development of a better method. This should spring logically from

TWO HANDED OPERATION CHART
PROCESS CHART
MATERIAL FLOW/OPERATIVE FLOW

Part or Ref. No.

Sheet No.   of

DEPARTMENT   Charted by   Date

Job Description	SUMMARY						

		Present		Proposed		Difference	
Chart begins		L.H.	R.H.	L.H.	R.H.	L.H.	R.H
		No.	Time	No.	Time	No.	Time
Chart ends	○						
	□						
Dwg. No. M/c No.	◇						
Jigs and Tools	D						
	▽						
	Totals						
Suggestions Incorporated	Time or Distance						

Present Method Left Hand	Quantity or Time	Distance	Operation	Inspection	Transport	Delay	Storage/Hold	Operation	Inspection	Transport	Delay	Storage/Hold	Distance	Quantity or Time	Proposed Method Right Hand
1			○ □ ◇ D ▽					○ □ ◇ D ▽							
2			○ □ ◇ D ▽					○ □ ◇ D ▽							
3			○ □ ◇ D ▽					○ □ ◇ D ▽							
19			○ □ ◇ D ▽					○ □ ◇ D ▽							
20			○ □ ◇ D ▽					○ □ ◇ D ▽							

P.A. MANAGEMENT CONSULTANTS LIMITED   P.S.25/1

Figure 10.3

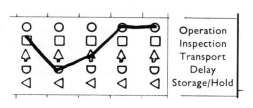

Operation
Inspection
Transport
Delay
Storage/Hold

Figure 10.4

the analysis of Step 3. Charting existing methods enables weaknesses to be noted and eliminated. The actual movements of the operator need to be planned so that energy is preserved and both hands work together with a natural balance and rhythm. Unnecessary movement can also be eliminated at this stage, and some-times whole jobs can be deleted or pre-planned in radically different ways.

Steps 5 and 6 consist of installing and maintaining the new method. This may require new tools and equipment but will certainly involve operator and supervisor training. Instructions sheets need to be prepared, and the timing of introduction should be carefully planned, particularly if other processes are affected. The maintenance of good industrial relations is at least as important as maintenance of the new method, and in many plants the process of consultation with employees' representatives will have proceeded in gear with the study from the beginning.

10.14 Work Measurement

Time study is the best known technique of work measurement and is traditionally subject to much opposition from trade unions. It is a tiring and tedious job calling for long periods of high concentration and attention and it depends absolutely on the co-operation of the subject who can frustrate the objects of the study by simply deviating from his usual work practices. Where rigorous standards of accuracy are not required the surreptitious use of a wrist watch can often provide enough data for informal performance comparison. The activities of a territory salesman can be monitored in this way to provide a basis for sales forecasting and territory coverage. However in its full application time study is a scientific, analytical and systematic procedure, and the highest standards of accuracy and objectivity are essential. The steps in making a study have much in common with other work study techniques. Thus Steps 1 and 2 are to select the job to be studied and to record and analyse the operations to be studied into elements, checking that conditions assumed to be standard do in fact apply.

In Step 3 each element of the job is timed as an indication of how long it should take. Pace will vary between operators and even from time to time with the same operator, according to how he feels. Assessment of the amount of effort being expended is an important aspect at this stage. In Steps 4 and 5 each actual observed element time is multiplied by its rating figure calculated in Step 3 and divided by the specified level of performance figure, resulting in the time for performing the element on that occasion at the specified rate. A basic or standard time is then selected for the element.

Step 6 consists of determining the frequency of each element and in Step 7 the incidence of fatigue is assessed and allowed for. This is done on the basis of fatigue allowance factors that typically include strenuousness and dexterity, concentration, posture, noise, eyestrain, conditions and personal needs.

Finally in Step 8 the time value of each job and operation will be worked out and issued for use in production planning and remuneration systems.

The process described so far has required the actual measurement of each element of every job in order to produce time values for planning. It is however possible to compile standard times from existing data with the advantages of reduced cost and less of the disruption of work sometimes caused by stopwatch studies. There are many proprietary systems of pre-determined motion times. A major advantage of such a system is that it is possible to determine the time value of the whole of an operation with consistent subsidiary values as all are calculated from the same basic data.

10.15 Job Evaluation in Production

The application of job evaluation is now much broader than the production department and in recent years has been developed to cover clerical workers and higher management as well as manual workers. It offers a means of establishing pay differentials between jobs scientifically and (hopefully) in a socially acceptable way that may reduce disputes in future.

The process begins with the assessment of all the work factors in the jobs that are to be evaluated. Jobs that can be differentiated in a valid way and all aspects of duties and responsibilities are included in a Job Description. The core of the exercise is then to assess the relative importance of the jobs in the scheme in terms of skill, responsibility, effort, and conditions. This step is potentially controversial and is usually taken by a panel on the basis of the work of the study officer, including of course representatives of the staff concerned. It may also be necessary to offer staff the facility of personal appeal against particular evaluations. There are four main methods of evaluation in current use (*see* also page 181):

Ranking is a direct system of comparing jobs so that they are ranked in order of importance, starting with the least important in the first rank and moving to the most important in the last. Jobs are not divided up into constituent factors but are considered as complete and a scale of values, that is more or less arbitrary, is applied.

Grading is the system most commonly used currently. A job description is written for each job and a specification is also drafted for a set of grades. These cover status in the organizations, duties, responsibilities, and work functions. Jobs are then put into appropriate grades.

Points assessment is an attempt to differentiate between jobs by awarding a number of points to each of the factors of the job according to its merit. Such factors as skill, responsibility, effort, experience, and working conditions are weighted according to their importance in the job and marked out of a theoretical maximum.

Factor comparison is the analysis of jobs into factors representing their most critical elements. A number of key jobs serve as bench marks, and the pay of other jobs is determined by grading them according to their factor content in comparison with these jobs.

Work Study is concerned with time, output, the allocation of resources, and productivity. One other factor has to be considered before the production process can really be regarded as being under effective control. That is the quality of the end product.

10.16 Quality Control

Quality is an extremely important element in the marketing mix. The marketing manager needs to be aware of the relationship between quality, price, and demand in each of the market segments within which he operates and keep alert to possible changes in the balance between these factors since they may offer a valuable opportunity to re-position his product in relation to its competitors. By increasing quality and price he may be able to go up-market and meet the specific needs of one section of his customers more closely. Alternatively he may seek volume by reducing price and quality. Very often he can extend his product range by adding a 'de luxe' or an 'economy' model. Quality costs money and it is part of the marketing function to specify as clearly as possible the optimum level of quality demanded by the market: too much represents unnecessary additional cost whilst too little may reduce the attractiveness of the product. Branding of consumer goods implies a level of quality that the customer can recognize and rely on when he makes a purchase. Quality consistency is therefore also a major interest of the marketing manager. He has the responsibility of ensuring that the factory does not despatch inferior goods that may result in loss of customer goodwill. For this purpose he will liaise closely with production management, and may:

sit on a regular liaison committee;
receive quality control reports on current production;
participate in Value Analysis or Value Engineering exercises;
use market research to confirm the acceptability of current standards.

'Quality' to the consumer or user is a subjective element meaning that the product conforms to an expected standard and provides an acceptable degree of service. The factory manager must be much more precise, requiring specific standards of manufacture if he is to maintain an effective control over quality. Different articles require different standards, but the following groups are typical of a wide range of manufacturing.

1 *Dimensions:* most goods are made to dimensional standards such as diameter, length, and thickness, with defined tolerances.
2 *Volume:* weight, cubic and fluid content are important particularly where exceeding the stated tolerance involves increased cost.
3 *Specifications:* in engineering goods especially the chemical or material composition of the product may be critical, and performance standards are always important.
4 *Surface Finish:* smoothness, colour, type of chemical finish, and durability make a major contribution to the attractiveness of the product.
5 *Surface Defects:* similarly cracks, blemishes, discoloration, rust spots and bad joints detract from the quality image of the product.

Quality standards should always be related to the requirements of the product. It would obviously be ridiculous to make a doorknob to the same exacting specifications as a micro-processor for example.

Product quality is affected by a number of factors in the production process. First is product design which can influence both the efficiency of manufacture and the performance of the final function. Manufacturing methods may be influential. If these are not suitable there will be difficulty and additional cost in meeting design standards. Similarly plant must be capable of meeting these standards and the level of maintenance will affect this capability. Adequate tooling is essential if consistent sizes are to be produced. Production and inspection personnel need to be trained to recognize faults and to rectify them when necessary. Finally an effective inspection team is needed to maintain quality standards.

It is clear therefore that quality assurance is an integral part of the production process, and constant vigilance is needed to prevent standards being eroded. Quality control requires the checking of production at pre-determined times and at selected operation stages.

Two methods, or a combination of the two are in general use:

1 *Inspection:* a team of inspectors make regular physical tests to ensure that

standards are being maintained. They will examine:
    raw materials and bought out parts used in production;
    work in progress at each production stage;
    the output of such processes as heat treatment, electro-plating, paint spraying and metal melting;
    the final product prior to packing and despatch.

2 *Statistical Quality Control:* often mathematical techniques related to probability are used which may involve the use of a computer. A pre-determined sample of products is taken at each production stage and at regular intervals. The sample is subjected to 100% inspection, but the sample itself may represent only a small proportion of total production. In this way it is possible to control a process economically and within very small boundaries of error. It is particularly appropriate when the examination process involves testing to the point of destruction.

The need for Production Control, Work Study, and Quality Control emphasizes that, however carefully production is planned, it is seldom a totally stable process. Quality standards tend to slip, work study values loosen, and incentive schemes lose their bite. Constant attention to detail is an essential of good factory management, and planning without effective control systems may be no better than a waste of time. At the same time however it is necessary to look ahead to ensure that use is made of the best methods and equipment available. Manufacturing is constantly changing, and it is the role of the R & D and Design departments to keep the company at least abreast of competition where innovation is concerned.

10.17 Research, Development and Design

The R & D and Design departments are normally organized within the Production department because they usually are most closely related to the production process. Every company is faced by the need to keep pace with continuing change. Technologies, processes, and products become obsolete at an alarming rate, and an extensive R & D programme may be necessary for survival. These three functions represent the innovative side of the department. Their scope includes innovation in plant, processes, methods, and control engineering, as well as new products themselves.

Most companies need at least some research, development, or design, depending on the nature of their products and markets. But it may not be necessary to maintain a large staff for the purpose. In general there are four main approaches:

1 *Company Research*
A company may well regard R & D as of sufficient importance to justify its own department, especially where there is a high premium on technological advance.

The research centre of the ICI fibres operation at Harrogate for example employs about 1,200 staff at a campus site just outside the town. Its main function lies in machine development designed to ensure that ICI remains one of the most efficient producers of fibre, although it also does some basic fibre research.

2   *Co-operative Research*
The smaller company may organize its development work through the use of a
co-operative research association. There are about 50 of these associations supported both by member subscription and grants from the Ministry of Technology.

3   *Contract Research*
There are also a number of commercial research organizations that will undertake
projects of research and development on a fee or contract basis. PA Management
Consultants' PATS Centre at Melbourne near Cambridge has advanced laboratory
facilities which are capable of carrying out basic research in electronics for example
on one hand or product development like the design of a new record player on the
other.

4   *Government Research*
The Government through the Ministry of Technology co-ordinates a comprehensive range of research activities, including the National Physical Laboratory developing basic standards of measurement on which industrial quality control is based for
example. The National Research Development Corporation (NRDC) provides
finance for research projects in certain circumstances.

   The Department of Industry employs some 1,500 qualified scientists and
engineers in its five industry orientated research centres, backed up by another
1,000 skilled technicians and craftsmen. One project has been to encourage
industry to make greater use of micro-processors, the micro-miniaturized computer
around which new control systems for almost every type of process are expected
to develop in the next decade.

10.18   The Design Department

The role of the design department is to provide a bridge between R & D and
production. The design engineer has the task of converting ideas into sufficient
detail for them to be made into products by developing detailed drawings and
specifications. These will include the amount and quality of tooling, depending
on the volume of production and the quality control standards applied. A company's product must be competitively priced, function effectively, give reasonable
service, and have an acceptable appearance if it is to succeed, and these factors are
the basis of good product design. They may be summarized under three headings:

1   *Technical Design* includes the details of the product's performance, the avoid-
    ance of breakdowns, and the achievement of its basic function.
2   *Industrial Design* deals with ergonomic aspects, that is the suitability of the
    product for human use, and its shape and appearance.
3   *Manufacturing Design* covers equipment, layout, labour, and tooling involved
    in manufacture; specification and reduction of wastage of materials; operating
    standards and the rationalization and simplification of methods; specification of
    the appearance, durability and cost of finishes.

10.19 Conclusion

Production Management, as has been seen in this chapter, has much in common with the other forms of management discussed so far. The techniques employed are similar to those used in the other sectors of the business where the object is to optimize the output of a limited supply of resources. Non-manufacturing organizations like airlines, hotels, banks and other service companies are similarly interested in the efficiency with which their service is provided, control over its quality and ensuring that it is available where needed. These themes are important wherever managers work, not only in Production.

This chapter has dealt with the theory and practice of Production Control with deliberately few references to computer aided systems. Manually prepared controls are certainly not obsolete, but there is now available a range of standard programme packages that all but the smallest manufacturing companies should be at least aware of, particularly as the existence of computer bureaux means that it is not necessary to possess a mainframe to be able to process control data electronically.

11. *Management of Human Resources*

However technologically advanced, the success of any business depends on the behaviour, attitudes, and motivation of the people who work in it, and effective inter-personal relationships may be seen as the sinew that binds an efficient organization together. People differ in their motives, mental and physical abilities, emotional needs, and other personality characteristics. They are individuals who cannot be regarded as an homogeneous resource, and there are particular problems in motivating people to give of their best at work that do not apply to the other factors of production.

Nevertheless, people are a major operating expense to almost every business enterprise, and it is common for aggregate staff remuneration to represent between a quarter and a third of total turnover. The human resource therefore has to be managed as productively and as cost effectively as other resources. Recognizing this, most major firms employ a specialist Personnel Department to deal with staff matters.

11.1 The Personnel Department

Since the Second World War there has been a revolution in the relations between employees and management. Rising standards of living, broader educational opportunities, the breakdown of traditional social barriers, and the advance of organized labour have virtually eliminated the old subservient attitudes of workers to employers. There has been a major change in the balance of power, together with a wider acceptance that the employee should participate, at least to some extent, in the decisions that affect the organization for which he works. In line with these developments the Personnel function has grown out of its original preoccupation with welfare. It may well have a director on the board and be involved with management, generally in such areas as Corporate Planning, Organization, Staff Development, Manpower Planning, and Industrial Relations.

Getting things done through people is central to every manager's job, and cannot be hived off to a specialist, however expert, without seriously diluting his responsibility for the results of the unit under his control. The Personnel Manager therefore has a functional or specialist relationship with both line and staff managers to whom he relates in a purely advisory capacity. A staff relationship exists between him and the Chief Executive to whom he is an assistant with specialist responsibilities; at the same time he has a line relationship with his own departmental staff.

His responsibilities and duties may be briefly listed as follows:

178

(a) Recruitment of personnel as circumstances and the manpower plan dictate
(b) Training and Education, including management development programmes
(c) Wages and Salaries structures, including regular reviews and any necessary negotiating machinery
(d) Disputes Procedures and their operation
(e) Channels of Communication to provide quick and effective flows of information both upward and downward
(f) Promotions and Transfers, with systems to allow for consultations and appeals
(g) Staff Appraisal schemes, and their relation to promotion and remuneration
(h) Redundancies, with provision for proper consultation with staff representatives
(i) Health, Safety and Welfare
(j) Implementation of all corporate staff policies.

11.2 Recruitment

Recruitment is invariably high on the list of priorities, and the sheer scale of many companies' efforts to obtain the staff they need is often not appreciated. Of Tesco Stores 38,000 staff in 1978, almost half had less than one year's service whilst 15% had five years or more. It is easy to see the numbers that had to be recruited over the years to obtain this basic cadre.

The process begins with a Job Description setting out the duties and responsibilities of the job to be filled, with a Person Profile describing the qualities and experience needed to fill it. The head of the department in which the vacancy occurs completes a staff requisition form as formal authority for Personnel Department to begin. After discussion with the trade union or staff association concerned, the vacancy will usually be advertised both in outside media and within the company. Depending on the nature of the vacancy it is not unusual to receive more than a hundred applications, and an initial screening may be necessary before application forms are sent to the most promising applicants, asking for details of education, qualifications, experience, and personal background. Those with real potential are then called for interview.

11.3 Interviewing

Interviewing is itself a specialist skill, and care has to be taken to ensure that personal preferences do not lead to ill-considered selections. One effective discipline is to work from a check-list of job requirements that have to be met. If each applicant is awarded a rating of marks out of ten for each, the interviewer has a rough and ready means of comparing a number of applicants who may be interviewed over a number of days. Interviewing is an imprecise art and it is notoriously difficult to be objective about other human beings. It is therefore common practice today to combine interviews with one or more selection tests. The first category will be designed to evaluate skills and abilities. They range from the specific trade test to the more general tests of word power, physical ability, and mathematical aptitude. Psychological tests provide a second category, providing some indication of intelligence, special aptitudes, and personality factors. Few of these methods are adequate alone, but taken together they give the selector considerably more information about the candidate than an interview alone.

11.4 Induction Training

The cost of recruitment is high, and the company already has an investment in the employee before he actually joins. Turnover in the early months of engagement of new employees is very high, and a well-planned induction programme may make all the difference to their attitudes in the critical early days.

First of all there is clearly a need for information about the organization as a whole. Entrants may be told a little of the firm's background, its objectives, its history, and its attitudes to its employees, its customers, and the public at large. A member of corporate management could explain the organizational structure of the company, its product range, profitability and other related factors. A tour of offices, factories, and leisure facilities could also be included.

Information focussed on the job itself is clearly necessary. A tour of the department, with explanations of how each job fits into the production flow or the overall pattern of activity, with introductions to the supervisor or other staff with whom they will be concerned, is the normal practice. Departmental rules about timekeeping, refreshment breaks, safety rules, and other routine matters also need to be explained. If the organization recognizes trade unions, the new employee should be introduced to the shop representatives of the union.

Some matters should be discussed with the individual by a member of the Personnel Department. These include the development of his career; the firm's policies and practices in helping with personal, domestic or financial difficulties; details of the pension scheme; and information about how and when salaries and wages are paid. At this stage information is given verbally, followed at a later stage by the written details required by law.

Induction training is merely the first step in a process of training and development that may continue throughout the individual's career. For the employee, training programmes demonstrate that the company is still interested in him and provide an outlet to promotion; to the company they represent investment in its most valuable resource. A more detailed discussion of training topics is included in Chapter 2, but the activities of the Commercial Union Assurance Company illustrate the importance placed on training in a labour intensive industry. The average number of CU staff in 1978 was 7,908, and its Douce Manor training centre carried out some 6,500 training days during the year.

11.5 Job Evaluation

Training is unlikely to produce material results unless it is geared to a sound promotion policy and jobs are related to each other in a systematic, logical and progressive way. Job Evaluation is the technique by which the value of a job is assessed so that remuneration levels can be set fairly between jobs, career paths can be planned more realistically, training courses can be designed to meet training need more closely, and recruitment of new staff can be made more precise in the light of the information about a job that an evaluation scheme provides.

The introduction of equal pay for women in Great Britain entailed the need to establish what represents equal work. Job Evaluation however is applicable wherever it is desired to compare one job with another, and it often provides a solution to pay disputes where questions of differentials are involved. A typical scheme evaluates a job in terms of experience, initiative, and skill or knowledge required, the degree of responsibility involved, and the amount of supervision or direction needed. There are four basic methods:

1 *Ranking*

Each job is placed or ranked in the order of its relative importance to other jobs in the organization. This system is simple to understand and to administer, but, except in the smallest companies, does not indicate sufficient differences between jobs for most purposes.

2 *Classification*

Both Ranking and Classification schemes deal with the job as a whole. Here a number of bench mark jobs are identified and other jobs are classified in comparison with them.

3 *Points Rating*

This is the system most commonly used in British industry. After an exhaustive examination, each job is given a points value based on the mental and physical effort, experience, training and other requirements of the job. The points value for the job may then be translated into money, using a suitable formula. Figure 11.1 shows the distribution of the Commercial Union's staff by the rating in

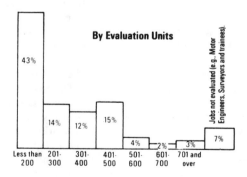

Figure 11.1 Distribution of C.U. staff

Evaluation Units of their jobs. Thus 57% of employees had less than 300 units, whilst only 5% had more than 600, a pattern that is common to many organizations.

4 *Factor Comparison*
Each job is analysed into factors, and a number of key jobs of reference for grading the others. Analysis reveals the pay award for each factor within these jobs. The extent to which each of these factors is required in each of the other jobs is determined, and a financial award is made based on its relationship to the degree of the factor included in the key jobs.

11.6 Staff Appraisal

Performance appraisal is a vital part of optimizing the output of employees, whatever the nature of their job, their experience, or their age. Appraisal schemes usually attempt the following or some of the following tasks.

Improvement of current performance
Provision of data for promotion and succession planning
Communication between staff and management.

For appraisal to be effective there needs to be a high degree of agreement between the employee and his manager on what he is trying to do. Most Management by Objectives (MBO) schemes include definition of the Key Result Areas in each job with a Personal Performance Plan for the achievement of agreed objectives in each area. These provide a sound base for performance appraisal at the end of the review period. In this way appraisal is closely linked with day-to-day work and is really an extension of the normal, informal management review of results achieved.

Appraisal tends to be highly charged emotionally, with neither appraiser nor employee totally at ease. It is therefore important that the system is seen to be fair and as objective as possible. To this end it should be divorced from the salary review, and the outcome should be an agreed plan for future action which the employee sees as being in his interest and to which he feels himself committed. It is now widely accepted that criticism has a negative effect on the achievement of goals and that praise has little effect one way or the other. Counselling should avoid both as far as possible and should be a day-to-day, rather than a once-a-year activity.

Appraisal schemes generally have two aspects; the performance of the employee in his current job, and his personal characteristics. The first concentrates on what has been achieved in the review period, whilst the second indicates his state of development and readiness for promotion. Assessment is an extremely subjective exercise, particularly when assessor and assessed are working closely day to day, and detailed guidelines should be provided to induce a degree of standardization into the ratings given by different assessors. The use of numerical scales and pre-printed grids can also reduce the scope for personal bias.

The detail of each assessment scheme will depend on the nature of the job under review. In the case of a consumer goods salesman the following could be appropriate:

1 *Performance Achievement*
Volume and value sales against target; display and distribution levels obtained;

new business developed; trade co-operative promotions run; success in selling the planned product mix; quality of relations with the trade and public.

2 *Personal Qualities*
Personal acceptability to customers; determination and industry; sales ability; territory organization; product knowledge; personal impact; ability to answer objections and to close the order; recognition of business opportunities; potential for leadership; and progress towards promotion.

The documentation of the appraisal is of particular importance. It represents a permanent record of the employee's performance that may be extremely valuable to the company, not least if a dispute arises under employment protection legislation. One leading clearing bank uses a five-part form that corresponds to each stage of the appraisal, and provides a useful example:

Stage 1 is a statement of achievement against pre-agreed job objectives. The bank uses either MBO or CWIP (Clerical Work Improvement Plan) standards for this purpose, and the form is completed by the employee himself.
Stage 2 is the assessor's evaluation of the performance, with comments explaining his decisions.
Stage 3 is the development appraisal, summarizing personal strengths and difficulties, recommending ways to make the employee more effective in his current role, and rating his potential for longer term development on a five-point scale.
Stage 4, the assessment meeting, is attended by supervisors, managers, and directors who have been involved with the work of the employee in the review period. They discuss the appraisals made and agree a whole job rating. They then confirm the objectives that have been set for the next period.
Stage 5 is the feedback meeting at which the employee discusses his appraisal with his manager. Activity plans are agreed, the whole job assessment is finalized following the employee's comments, and the manager enters his confidential comments on the form following the meeting.

11.7 The Role of Management Consultants

Consultants can help Personnel in a number of valuable ways, contributing an objective, outside view, specialist skills, and up-to-date knowledge of conditions in other comparable firms. This is particularly true of recruitment, where knowledge of the advertising media and permanent staff to handle the preliminary sifting of applications and interviewing can save time and cost. The client need only interview half a dozen serious applicants from an initial list of a couple of hundred. At a more senior level, an Executive Search Consultant may be able to identify and approach a prospect who might not have applied of his own initiative.

Consultants may also design appraisal and other staff systems, carry out job evaluation schemes, and advise on wage and salary scales. Thus in 1977 the Hong Kong and Shanghai Bank hired PA Management Consultants to carry out a survey of its personnel policies worldwide, comparing them with those of similar international companies. Proposals covered remuneration, fringe benefits, pension

schemes, and job contracts. Staff appraisal, job evaluation, training, career planning and promotion policies were also reviewed, whilst manpower planning was
given increased importance. A series of action plans for implementing the changes,
with specific dates and the names of people responsible for carrying them out, were
drafted. A forward-looking company recognizes that its personnel policies may
become outdated, just as those in other parts of its business can.

A major part of the Personnel Manager's work is ensuring that the requirements
of the law relating to people at work are met. Since 1971 there has been a flood
of legislation that has been described as 'breathtaking and bewildering'.

11.8 Employment Legislation

Many managers are not aware of the extent to which legislation has affected their
relationships with their employees. The Employment Protection (Consolidation)
Act that came into operation on 1st November 1978 brought together in one
enactment the provisions on individual employment rights previously contained
in the following Acts:

Redundancy Payments Act 1965
Contracts of Employment Act 1972
Trade Union and Labour Relations Act 1974
The Employment Protection Act 1975 — the Employment Acts of 1980 and
1982 supplement this legislation.

11.81 *Prior to the Commencement of Employment*

The basic legal principle has been in the past that the employer has the right to
select any employee he requires for a particular job.

There are now several statutory exceptions to this principle, the Sex Discrimination Act 1975 and the Race Relations Act 1976 being the most important. The
employer must take great care in the way he advertises vacancies, selects or refuses
an applicant, and in the terms of employment he offers to ensure that there is no
discrimination on the grounds of sex, colour, race, nationality or ethnic or national
origins.

11.82 *The Contract of Employment*

The relationship of employer and employee is a contractual one in which the
employee undertakes to do work and the employer in return agrees to pay wages.
This is so whether the contract is in writing or not and there is no statutory
requirement in most cases for an employee to have a written contract of
employment.

However the 1972 Act requires that an employer must give to an employee not
later than thirteen weeks after the commencement of the employment a written
statement dealing with three types of information:

1 The names of the parties, the date when the employment began and whether
   employment with a previous employer counts as part of the employee's continuous employment and if so the date on which such period began;

2 Any terms or conditions affecting:
 (a)   the scale or rate of remuneration
 (b)   hours of work
 (c)   holiday entitlement and holiday pay
 (d)   incapacity for work due to sickness or injury, and any provisions for sick pay
 (e)   the length of notice which the employee is obliged to give and entitled to receive
 (f)   the title of the job which the employee is employed to do.
   To avoid possibilities of misunderstanding later it is prudent to regard this as a minimum to be developed rather than as a complete agreement.
   The Code of Practice, first included in the Industrial Relations Act of 1971, notes the following commonsense suggestions for other matters to be included:
   'Apart from the statutory requirements, management should ensure that each employee is given information about:
 (i)   the requirements of his job and to whom he is directly responsible
 (ii)   disciplinary rules and procedures and the type of circumstances which can lead to suspension or dismissal
 (iii) trade union arrangements
 (iv)   opportunities for promotion and any training necessary to achieve it
 (v)   social or welfare facilities
 (vi)   fire prevention and safety and health rules
 (vii) any suggestion schemes.
   The contract of employment is not therefore simply a legal and technical matter. It is at the very heart of the relationship of the employer and employee.

3 A 'note' about disciplinary rules and grievance procedures.

11.83 *Rights of Employees during Employment*

An employee has a number of other statutory rights that may not be included in his contract of employment. The most important of these are as follows:

(a)   *Guarantee Pay*
      Employees are entitled to receive guarantee payments for a day on which they would normally be expected to work under their contracts but on which the employer has not provided them with any work.

(b)   *Suspension from work on medical grounds*
      If an employee is suspended from his normal work on the medical grounds that his health would be endangered if he continued to be exposed to the process in question, then he is entitled to receive from his employer his normal pay during the suspension up to a stated maximum.

(c)   *Trade union membership and activities*
      Employers may not take any action against employees as individuals for being members of, or for taking part at an appropriate time in the activities of, an independent trade union.

(d)   *Time Off Work*
      An employee who is an official of an independent trade union, which is

recognized by the employer, must be allowed reasonable time off with pay during working hours to carry out trade union duties or receive training in trade union duties.

Employers are also required to permit employees who hold certain public offices reasonable time off to perform their duties. This provision covers such offices as Justices of the Peace and members of a local authority.

An employee who is being made redundant after at least two years service is entitled to reasonable time off with pay within working hours to look for another job.

(e)   *The Expectant Mother*
A woman who is expecting a baby after a period of continuous service has the right not to be dismissed because of pregnancy, is entitled to time off with maternity pay to have a baby, and to return to her job afterwards. (The details of these rights were modified by the Employment Act 1980.)

(f)   *Redundancy Pay*
Employers are required to make a lump sum compensation payment, called a 'redundancy payment', to employees dismissed because of redundancy. The amount of the payment is related to the employee's age, length of continuous service with the employer and weekly pay.

(g)   *Sex and Race Discrimination*
Under the Sex Discrimination Act 1975, it is unlawful for employers to discriminate on grounds of sex or against married persons. The Race Relations Act 1976 outlaws discrimination by employers on the grounds of race, colour, nationality (including citizenship) or ethnic or national origins. The Acts cover training and promotion as well as recruitment.

(h)   *Equal Pay*
Employers are required to afford equal treatment in terms and conditions of employment to men and women who are employed on 'like work' or work rated as equivalent under a job evaluation study.

The measures concerning employment that have been discussed in this section are supported by the body of factory, workshop, shops, and offices acts that regulate safety and other conditions of work at the workplace.

Thus current legislation represents a significant extension of the rights of the employee at work and his claims to social security; the statutory sick pay arrangements that came into effect in April 1983 have been described as 'a company-based social security scheme', for example.

The law seldom seems to help the manager in his basic task of getting the best out of his work force. Motivation takes on a new significance in these circumstances.

11.9   Motivation

Manpower differs from other resources because it has a mind and will of its own. Thus a man may spend a whole day on a task and so be fully utilized, but his output may be influenced by a number of subjective factors that are difficult to identify and control. The reasons why people behave in the ways they do range from purely instinctive urges to rational decisions to achieve desired ends.

The pioneers of scientific management at the end of the nineteenth century, led by F.W. Taylor and F.B. Gilbreth saw the need for standardizing methods of work and the conditions under which it was done. Time standards were introduced both to aid management and as the basis of a differential piece-rate system that was felt to be necessary to motivate workers. This approach developed into modern work study and methods engineering. Incentive payment systems were introduced to encourage the worker to higher levels of productivity through payment by results schemes which attempt to relate payment to assumed effort.

Yet money as a motivator has severe limitations. Herzberg regarded it as an 'hygienic' factor. It had to be got right as part of the working environment, but it was not a 'motivator' that would induce permanent increases in effort and productivity. Mass production, however efficient in economic terms, did not produce conditions in which workers would produce their best. As a result, interest turned away from scientific solutions towards a human relations or behavioural approach.

The attitudes and performance of people at work are influenced by the degree of job satisfaction they enjoy. Alone this will not motivate the employee to peak performance. As Peter Drucker points out, a responsible attitude is needed that replaces the externally imposed spur of fear with an internal self-motivation for performance.

Modern writers recognize the following types of motivation in this context:

(a) *Security of Livelihood* is given the greatest importance. A recent study of attitudes by bank managers towards their jobs carried out by the author revealed that this was more important than levels of income or any other factor in this case. The security-mindedness of the British worker is now notorious.

(b) *Levels of Income* tend to motivate within certain limits. People are in fact less concerned about the actual amount of their wages once they have achieved an acceptable standard of living than with comparisons with those in similar jobs.

(c) *Social Status* and status within an occupation are potent motivators. The status of occupations is closely related to the stratification of social class, and is highly valued. Professional codes of conduct are an important part of this, and people will strive towards positions with greater status even where financial rewards do not increase commensurately.

(d) *Group Affiliation* is a motive that is often independent of economic or status considerations. It may explain the willingness to obey an unofficial strike leader, for example. The power of the influence of the work group on the individual was first identified by Elton Mayo in his series of experiments at General Electric's Hawthorne works in Chicago.

(e) *Management Attitudes* were shown by the same experiments to be a powerful factor. Workers who felt themselves to be valued by management performed significantly better than those who were resentful against the suspicions of management.

(f) *Achievement Orientation* describes employees who tend to attempt good performance in more or less everything they do. Working conditions can do much to inhibit or encourage this attitude.

The list is not comprehensive. Other influential factors influencing job satisfaction include the altruistic motive; the desire for independence; the need for variety; the degree of utilization of personal abilities; the need for a definite aim or purpose, opportunities for responsibility, the ability to control the routine details of a job; and the availability of enough activity to employ the energy that the individual wishes to apply to his work. The more active and energetic employees may also seek the new and unfamiliar in adventure, exploration, research, and creative work.

People differ in their mental abilities, emotional demands, personality characteristics, and physical and sensory capacities. The factors that influence their attitudes to work will differ accordingly and there is no single best answer to the problem of motivation. In recent years however a number of different approaches have been tried with varying degrees of success. There has been an underlying trend away from the structured payment-by-results (PBR) schemes towards attempts to increase the worker's involvement in and commitment to his work by the use of behavioural science techniques. The following illustrate this trend.

11.91 *Profit Sharing*

The trend towards industrial democracy has revived interest in profit sharing as a logical extension of participative management. This topic is dealt with in detail in the next chapter. However the motivational value of profit sharing is not universally accepted, and the trade unions are not generally in favour.

11.92 *Management–Trade Union Relations*

Developments toward participative management have included attempts to increase the involvement of representative bodies in the running of companies. This has sometimes taken the form of tentative moves to open up management–union negotiations by attempts at joint problem solving before the actual bargaining process begins. Early discussions are held at workshop level and a joint discussion of principles takes place with the unions before the presentation of formal proposals. In principle this approach should replace the traditional pattern in which management seeks to obtain agreement to a plan that is worked out in final form before the negotiations begin. This inevitably develops into a confrontation, but the newer approach requires an element of trust and a willingness by both parties to make themselves vulnerable that has usually been lacking.

The failure of the last Labour government's scheme for Planning Agreements illustrates this problem, and the unwillingness of managements to disclose confidential details about their business to trade unions representing their employees is another manifestation of it.

11.93 *Management by Objectives*

MBO in the contexts of Management, Planning, and Control is discussed in Chapter 5. Its role in bringing the aims of the individual closer to the company's goals is however relevant here. Objective setting is a deliberately joint exercise between senior and subordinate in which the latter is encouraged to commit himself to a course of action based on what he feels should be done. MBO requires each manager to set the objectives of his unit himself, and there is a close relationship between this process and his own personal development.

11.94 *Job Enrichment*

Awareness that mass production can produce boredom and alienation on the part of the worker, which in turn reduces his productivity, followed from the work Herzberg in which motivators were shown to be associated with work itself, rather than as extraneous elements to be added independently. Attempts were made to make the work more interesting by varying the tasks of individual workers and increasing the range of functions they fulfilled.

Thus a salesman could be given discretion to negotiate prices, and factory workers could be rotated between different jobs. Clearly these changes had impact on other workers, and the idea of autonomous work groups evolved.

In th Philips works at Eindhoven and the Saab and Volvo plants in Sweden, attempts were made to group assembly-line operations so that the worker could recognize the output of his labour and gain some satisfaction from it.

There have been some difficulties with this approach, partly because it seems to run counter to the trend towards work fragmentation associated with greater specifialization. However surveys indicate that enriched sections tend to be more content; less supervision is needed; better job attitudes are developed, together with more recognition of the importance of good customer relations; and staff tend to have a better sense of participation in worthwhile work.

11.95 *Human Relations Training*

The recognition that managerial work activity is predominantly inter-personal or social in character has led to the growth of human relations training schemes for managers. Grid training is one example. Blake's grid (*see* page 26) is available in the form of a six-phase training package. It aims to develop a greater awareness of roles at the work place and encourages the manager to move towards an acceptable balance between concern for people and concern for production.

Another example is T-group training and the other group methods that have superseded it. They aim to improve the performance of employees by developing a greater awareness of their impact on others and applying this in their work. Groups of trainees are placed in unstructured problem-solving situations, often under some emotional pressure or stress. Through systematic observation, they improve their ability to deal with such situations in real life. It needs to be emphasized that these methods should only be used by properly qualified personnel as psychological damage may result from inexpert use.

11.96 *Organization Development (OD)*

The term 'OD' covers a wider range of behavioural methods than those relating simply to organization considered in Chapter 2. Its chief techniques are those of group skills and interpersonal relations applied to the work team, together with 'action research' which feeds back data to group members who plan their activities in the light of its results. Training tends to be less concerned with theory and specific job knowledge and skills than with participation in real problems, developing creativity in problem-solving and confidence in decision-making. OD programmes are characteristically run by a professionally qualified third party, usually an outside consultant, who acts as arbiter, catalyst, counsellor and facilitator.

Team-building is perhaps the most widely used OD technique. A team can be any permanent or semi-permanent group with a reason for working together. Its members must be interdependent, and the group must be accountable as a functioning unit within a larger organizational context. The functioning of a team is hindered by certain task and interpersonal issues. Team-building aims at improving the problem solving ability among the team by developing a better understanding of each member's role in the work group, increasing communication and mutual support between members, and developing a sense of interdependence in the group. Typically the team is withdrawn from its normal working environment for a couple of days and a series of 'instruments' that include personal interviews, games, and simulations are used to make the team aware of its own 'group process' and how this affects the quality of its work. Conflicts are brought out and used constructively to air hidden or latent issues. Members' communication patterns, decision-making approaches and leadership styles are examined. In the team-building session itself the team criticises its own style of working and works on problem areas in order of priority.

Motivation is of particular interest to the marketing manager because so much of the work of his staff is not controllable by direct supervisory methods, depending largely on the amount of personal effort exerted or the quality of the creative thinking applied. What makes the successful salesman out on his lonely 'patch' make that extra call at the beginning or end of the day; what makes the product manager burn the midnight oil to produce effective campaigns for his product range; and what makes the visualizer or copywriter undertake that extra piece of research that ensures the quality of his advertising? The answer lies in one of the many forms of personal motivation.

11.10 Manpower Planning

This chapter so far has concentrated on the personal aspects of manpower, dealing with their human characteristics and their legal rights as people. Staff also have to be considered as a 'resource' to be allocated and utilized in objective and economic ways. Investment in human resources has to be planned as carefully as investment in any other resource. This has become increasingly true in recent years because:

employees represent a growing cost to most companies;
technological changes mean that the company's needs in terms of knowledge, expertise, and skill are constantly changing;
statutory regulation and the strength of trade unions make it very difficult to dismiss an individual worker despite demonstrable unsuitability for his job.

Management needs a means of ensuring that it has the right mix of people, with the right types of skill, in the right numbers at the right time and place to meet its corporate objectives in a satisfactory way. A major group may well produce a wide range of products sold in many different countries, requiring a complex variety of abilities and skills from widely differing social backgrounds. The size of the task may be very considerable.

Thus GEC's total bill for wages, salaries, national insurance and pensions accounted for 35% of sales revenue and 34% of the total cost of materials, services, and labour in 1981.

Table 11.1 illustrates how important the gross remuneration of its employees was to a sample of companies of different size in 1977–8.

Table 11.1

	Total turnover (£m)	Number employees in UK (000)	Aggregate gross remuneration in UK (£m)
GEC	2343	156.0	655.0
Boots	883	67.0	131.1
Turner and Newall	414	24.6	79.0
Chubb and Son	199	12.1	42.9
Associated Newspapers	157	13.3	58.8
Sidlaw Industries	38	3.4	10.5

Source: Company Reports 1977–78

The Industrial Relations Code of Practice defines the functions of Manpower Planning as:

(a) taking stock of existing manpower resources
(b) working out future manpower needs
(c) identifying what should be done to ensure that future manpower resources match those needs.

This approach compares closely with the planning techniques described in Chapter 5, and indeed Manpower Planning is an integral part of the Corporate Plan since without people of appropriate calibre and number it is significantly less likely to be achieved.

11.101 *The Corporate Plan*

The process starts with a detailed examination of the company's Corporate Plan combined with discussions with the heads of various departments to review the organization of their workforce and to estimate their requirements in meeting the plan. The Manpower Plan should cover the same duration as the Corporate Plan. Usually this is divided in two with an Operating or Short Range Plan covering 1–2 years and a Long Range Plan covering 3–5 years.

The objectives of the Manpower Plan are simply to provide the management and workforce needed to achieve the Corporate Plan, and the task is to derive a manpower demand forecast that meets this purpose. It is first necessary to determine the relationship between the workload implied in the company's corporate objectives and the manpower needed to perform it. There are three common methods for doing this:

11.1011 *Direct analysis:* By study of past performance it is possible to calculate a ratio between a level of manning and the results historically achieved from it. In a simple example it could be established that in the past a salesforce of four salesmen achieved £4 million annually. A plan to sell £6 million of merchandise might be expected to require six men. This of course implies that the ratio is a constant one. In practice this is seldom so. Economies of scale may increase the marginal sales yield; alternatively diminishing returns may come into play. Multiple Regression Analysis is one technique that allows manpower to be estimated from a number of independent variables.

11.1012 *Development of standards:* It is also possible to base forecasts on some form of standard relationship between manpower and productivity. A manning standard can be derived by using Work Study techniques. For example if a factory expects to make 50,000 items per year and work studies have shown that it takes on average ten skilled men to produce 50 items a day, the man days required will be

$$\frac{50,000}{(5 \text{ items per man day})} = 10,000 \text{ man days.}$$

If 250 days are worked per year, an average of 40 skilled men will be required. Again this is an oversimplification because there will be changes in productivity over the period, and values will need to be checked on a regular basis.

11.1013 *Management experience:* A third method is for management from Marketing, Finance, and Production to estimate requirements on the basis of their past experience. This routine provides a valuable part of the normal planning cycle as it involves disciplined procedures for reviewing and updating estimates. It does however tend to be more reliable in the short than in the long run.

11.102 *Internal Manpower Review*

The purpose of manpower forecasting is to estimate the size of future shortages or surpluses in particular groups of employees so that redundancies and early retirements on one hand and panic recruitment on the other can be avoided. The next step is therefore detailed analysis of the company's existing manpower resources.

It is not possible to overstate the importance of adequate personnel records in this respect. In general companies keep data on:

personal details: such as name, sex, marital status, etc.
company history: including date of joining, job, absence record, etc.
qualifications: for example formal education, training record, business and trade qualifications and performance appraisal.

In addition material gathered for the production of the payroll is a useful source of information, as are records required to be maintained by Government legislation.

The first task in producing the forecast is to decide on the basic units for fore-casting. These could be a subsidiary group, a department, or a function such as Production or Marketing. It is then necessary to decide on the most significant manpower groupings, skill categories, or job clusters. The basic occupational groups that most companies recognize are:

Managers
Professionally qualified workers
Supervisors
Technicians and other technical staff
Clerical workers
Skilled manual workers by type
Semi-skilled and unskilled employees.

These are broadly in line with the Department of Employment's categories in its annual occupational survey in the manufacturing sector.

The Review will also include detailed analysis of:

the level of skills and status
qualifications, experience and skills
the age distribution of employees
the likely output of company training schemes.

It is more valuable to express this data in terms of changing ratios or relation-ships over time than simply as raw statistics. The ratios of indirect to direct labour or of professional to technical staff can for example be a positive aid to future planning. This approach can also sometimes identify structural changes in the workforce that would not otherwise be apparent. The most commonly used index is that of labour turnover or wastage, expressed as

$$\frac{\text{Number of leavers during period}}{\text{Average number of employees in the period}} \times 100$$

The index may however be misleading during times of change, and further analysis may be needed to determine which category of staff is being lost, particu-larly if there is evidence that a key group, such as skilled operatives, is involved.

Labour turnover is made up of four elements:

natural wastage, comprising death, illness, disability, or retirement
voluntary wastage, relating to such factors as conditions at work, job satisfac-tion, morale, and opportunities elsewhere
transfers and promotions between departments
involuntary terminations, such as disciplinary dismissals and redundancies.

In most cases the planner can identify from past experience regular losses or patterns of movement that can help him forecast satisfactorily. Effective planning can do much to reduce the impact of wastage. Succession planning for example can help minimize dislocation when a senior employee leaves or is promoted.

11.1021 *Costs of wastage:* When an employee leaves, the company incurs the following costs:

(a)   any termination payment to the leaver
(b)   cost of termination procedures
(c)   lost production caused by the vacancy
(d)   induction and off-the-job training for the replacement
(e)   on-the-job training
(f)   reduced productivity during training.

These can be very substantial. There are wide variations between different industries and between firms within an industry, but control of staff turnover is almost everywhere one of the most important cost containment activities in the company

11.103 *External Sources of Manpower*

If the manpower within a company is insufficient in quantity or inadequate in quality to fulfil the requirements of the Corporate Plan, and the possibilities of transfers, training, and development have been fully explored to fill the gap, it will be necessary to recruit staff from outside.

Often the right type of labour is scarce even in areas of high unemployment. A survey by the Confederation of British Industries in late 1978 revealed that although most companies were working below capacity and some 1.3 million people were unemployed, yet one in five manufacturers complained that his output was limited because of a shortage of skilled workers. This is illustrated by the following chart.

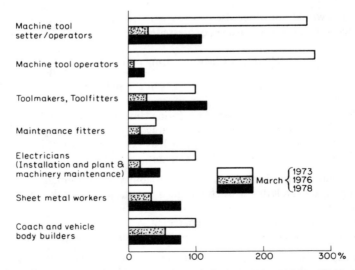

Figure 11.2 Vacancies as a % of registered unemployment for various skilled groups:
Notified vacancies are estimated to be approximately one-third of total vacancies so the propor-
of vacancies to unemployed could be much higher. (Source: Department of Employment)

The reasons are mainly structural, with blame placed on Britain's craft apprenticeship system, lack of skill training, and inadequate differentials between skilled and unskilled men.

Nevertheless the planner needs to be familiar with the conditions in his local labour market and sensitive to the image that his company enjoys as a good or bad employer. Rates of pay must be competitive, conditions at work satisfactory, and the company seen as one that employees would like to work for. Many companies run major public relations campaigns to project their image in the local labour market, and this activity should be included as part of the Manpower Plan.

11.104 *Sources of Manpower*

Depending on the type of staff needed, sources include:

school leavers and university graduates
applicants through advertising
job centres
government training centres and schemes.

In addition it may be necessary to 'head hunt' employees from other firms to fill particular vacancies. The planner should develop his sourcing strategy to co-ordinate his need for people with the availability of particular categories of labour. It may take eighteen months or longer to develop a school leaver or new graduate into a worthwhile contributor. Similarly, apparently unpromising material can sometimes be developed into productive staff by effective training. An important reason for planning is that it provides time to take advantage of these possibilities.

11.105 *Reducing the Level of Manpower*

A manpower plan may well call for a reduction in strength in a particular section, age group, or in the company as a whole. There are four basic strategies to achieve this:

(a) *Stop all recruitment:* This is logical and usually acceptable to trade unions. It is however better to control recruitment selectively if the desired mix and balance of staff is to be obtained.
(b) *Encourage wastage:* This may appear a less painful alternative. It is however open to the objection that the wrong people may leave.
(c) *Encourage early retirement:* This may be applied selectively, but may be expensive in terms of pension rights and other benefits.
(d) *Declare redundancies:* Mention was made earlier of the legal conditions concerning redundancy. This is now a very expensive process, and the costs of redundancy plus those of recruiting new staff when business picks up should be compared with the short-term costs of holding staff in the meanwhile.

11.106 *Construction of the Manpower Plan*

The actual construction of the plan follows the principles outlined in Chapter 5:

overall manpower objectives are defined
forecasts are produced for each significant group or department
additional manpower needed to meet the corporate plan is identified
sources of recruitment are agreed
succession and promotion plans are drawn up
training needs are defined
plans are made to reduce excess manpower.

Table 11.2 demonstrates the basic shape of the plan:

Table 11.2

Manpower Plan for Statistics Clerks

		Year 1	*Year 2*	*Year 3*
S.1	*Plan Summary*			
	(a) Stats Clerks at start of year	30	32	35
	(b) Numbers by year end to meet company growth plan	32	35	40
	(c) Additional clerks needed	2	3	5
S.2	*Projections from Manpower Analysis*			
	(a) Clerks required at start of year (as 1(a) above)	30	32	35
	(b) Projected turnover during year:			
	Retirements	2	—	1
	Normal staff turnover	1	3	3
	Dismissals	1	1	1
	Promotions/Transfers	2	1	2
	Other causes	1	2	1
	(c) Total Labour Loss	7	7	8
S.3	*Recruitment Plan*			
	(a) Clerks needed for growth plan (as 1(c) above)	2	3	5
	(b) Clerks needed to replace turnover losses (as 2(c) above)	7	7	8
	(c) Manpower gap: net gain (loss) in clerks needed each year	9	10	13

With modifications this format can be used for each planning unit up to the whole company itself. The plan's achievement depends on the actions of management and staff, and it must be kept up to date with regular reviews and amendments in line with changes in the company's needs and in the condition of the labour market. As with any other plan, progress must be monitored against target so that corrective action may be taken in good time. Table 11.3 is a simple form of control for this purpose.

Table 11.3

Manpower Report as at 31 May 19........

	Current Strength	Planned Strength	Variance
Accounts Office			
Manager	1	1	Nil
Deputy Managers	2	1	+ 1
Section Heads	8	9	− 1
Senior Clerical Officers	16	14	+ 2
Clerical Officers	89	100	−11
	116	125	− 9

11.11 Conclusion

There are two aspects to the effective management of human resources. Firstly, employees are human beings, that is individuals with emotional and psychological needs. Because of the scale of modern business and industry it is usually necessary to treat them in aggregate on many questions, using an intermediary like a trade union or staff association for the purpose. Nevertheless they perform better if their individuality is recognized and conditions at work are organized so that at least some of these personal needs are met. Secondly however they represent a major category of cost to the company, and many of the techniques of planning, allocation, and control that apply to other resources apply to human resources also.

The difficulty of achieving the right balance is fully recognized at our guinea pig company, Consumer and Electrical. The concept of the Personnel Officer as a sort of 'man in the middle', mainly concerned with being nice to people and dispensing welfare has long been superseded. The MD is quite clear also that the line manager must be responsible for his people as for other aspects of the unit under his control if he is to be held accountable for results in a realistic way. The complex of industrial relations in a multi-operation group like C & E, combined with the fact that so many of the employee privileges of the past have become the legally enforceable rights of today, amply justify the seat of the Personnel Director on the Board.

Following its normal practice, C & E does its best to avoid legal proceedings in staff matters, recognizing that press coverage is seldom favourable to the company, and that a controversial case can embitter staff relations unnecessarily. Theft is one of the few offences that have been prosecuted in recent years by the group. To its surprise however, it finds that a rejected job applicant has recently complained to the Industrial Tribunal that she was discriminated against on the ground of her sex in the recent recruitment of security staff, and may be eligible for compensation.

The Chairman in his heart rather regrets the days when 'people just did as they were told', but he knows the high value of good employee relations and, as an accountant, knows how many extra sales have to be earned to compensate for the slightest disruption of production. He is also aware that good Public Relations can influence the quality of staff applying to the group, whilst bad publicity can deter those scarce skilled grades of worker that C & E so badly needs to attract. In recent years therefore it has become the practice to include an Employment Report after the statutory Directors' Report in the Annual Report and Accounts, outlining the group's staff policies. This year's edition will include the following:

1 *General*
   The employment policy of C & E creates an environment in which individuals are encouraged to develop their full potential, and first class career opportunities are offered. Just over 20% have five years or more service.

2 *Recruitment*
   Recruitment is based entirely on suitability for the job in the interest of seeing staff working productively. C & E have taken part in the Work Experience schemes of the Manpower Services Commission to initiate young people into the working environment and, incidentally to provide the group with a pool of tested potential employees.

3 *Training*
   C & E's training policy is to exceed the standards laid down by the Industry Training Board, and it is a cardinal tenet that all categories of staff should receive systematic training throughout their careers.

4 *Health and Safety at Work*
   All aspects of health, hygiene and safety are included in training courses throughout the company. The Health and Safety Act (1974) is rigorously applied, close contact is maintained with the British Safety Council, and a medical insurance scheme is offered to employees on a shared cost basis.

5 *Communication*
   C & E is constantly seeking to improve the flow of information at all levels. The staff appraisal scheme makes a major contribution, as does consultation with the managers' associations in each division.

6 *Pensions*
   C & E run a pension scheme open to all full-time permanent employees who contribute 5% of pensionable salary whilst the company contributes the balance of the cost of benefits. Members are contracted out of the State Earnings Related Scheme which began on 6 April 1978.

7 *Social*
   The group runs a Country Club near to the Head Office complex where employees may take part in a full range of sports, social and cultural activities for a nominal membership fee.

8 *Industrial Relations*

The group enjoy sound working relations with the trade unions with membership among employees. Recognition and procedural agreements jointly agreed and co-operatively followed are felt to have proved the benefits obtainable from Management and Unions working constructively together.

Many companies have not shared C & E's experience of favourable Industrial Relations. In a period of rapid social and economic change they have often been an area of particular difficulty. The next chapter considers this subject in more detail.

12. *Industrial Relations*

The British labour market has come a long way since labourers attended hiring fairs to obtain their day's employment. The institutions that play a central role today have a history of development that spans almost two hundred years.

By the middle of the eighteenth century industrial change was proceeding apace and journeymen had begun to combine separately from their employers to enforce wage demands and to improve conditions. The modern age did not really begin until 1824 however when the repeal of the Combination Acts, dating from Edward I's reign onwards, removed the main legal restraints to peaceful combinations of masters or workmen for furthering their trade interests. Progress was slow, and the struggle to secure legal status for trade unionism did not take place until the late 1860s and early 1870s. The Trades Union Congress (TUC) was founded in 1868. The period to 1900 was one of growth under the influence of the 'Great Depression'; it saw the birth of the special relationship between the unions and the nascent Labour Party, and the number of trade unionists exceeded two million for the first time in 1900. It was a period of intense struggle with many ups and downs; the Taff Vale decision (1901) which re-emphasized the liability of union funds for damages caused in the course of a dispute, was a potentially crippling blow, reversed by legislation some four years later. The bitterness of industrial relations in the impoverished inter-war years is hard to appreciate in the relative affluence of the Welfare State of the 1980s. It culminated in the General Strike of 1926 and the staggering loss of 162 million working days, a total not remotely approached since. The Second World War improved the public image of the trade unions considerably as they worked closely with the Government to improve industrial relations and to increase output in the interest of the war effort. It was in this period that the basis of the movement's strength and influence was laid. Yet any understanding of Britain's industrial relations problems today depends on an understanding of this turbulent history and the attitudes deriving from it that still bedevil negotiations between labour and management.

12.1 Marketing Implications

Marketing management seldom has a direct involvement in industrial relations. It does however have a direct interest in maintaining the motivation and productivity of the workforce. Interruptions in production can prevent the free flow of products to the market; where supply has been planned to take advantage of seasonal trends or to co-ordinate with increased demand following promotion or advertising, these can result in sales losses that cannot be made up, as well as wastage of scarce marketing budget funds.

200

Where the product affected is a component or essential accessory, industrial action may have a chain effect, damaging the end-product as well as the item directly involved. British Leyland cars have often suffered in this way as their falling share of the home UK market in the last five years bears ample witness. The technique of secondary picketing in which suppliers, customers, and other associates of the company suffering industrial action are put under pressure although not involved in the dispute, may also spread the damage caused by a breakdown in industrial relations.

Stoppages in service industries such as road, rail, or air transport can destroy carefully built up sales and distribution channels in a very short time. The Calcutta bargemens' strike of Spring 1979 decimated India's exports of jute goods at a time when her main competitor, Bangladesh, seemed well placed to snatch a large part of her market share. In the event strikes and power cuts in Bangladesh prevented her doing so. Many would-be users of hessian and sacking found themselves unable to obtain supplies, and had to turn to other materials, synthetics, or mechanical handling methods, causing irreparable harm to the jute industry's future markets.

In recent years the unionization of salesmen has brought marketing closer to mainline industrial relations. Traditionally difficult to organize because they are generally widely dispersed, the salesman has become the target of ASTMS and other white-collar unions. Thus the vast sales forces of the Prudential Assurance Company are organized, and have taken part in industrial action in the past. Shop stewards, consultative councils, grievance procedures, and wage negotiating machinery are foreign to the traditional sales manager, bred on hire-and-fire methods. In Sweden however the union salesman is the rule rather than the exception, and these developments may be expected to herald a revolution in the management and motivation of sales forces.

12.2 Industrial Relations Today

Today the personal element of individual negotiation between employee and employer has virtually disappeared in most trades and occupations. The levels of wages and other conditions of employment are generally negotiated between trade unions on one side and employers' associations on the other with the government often participating as principal, legislator, or arbitrator. The field of industrial relations is regulated by a complex body of legislation, but its scope is in fact wider still, encompassing every aspect of the relationship between an employer and his employees.

12.3 The Current System: Legal Framework

The current system of British industrial relations operates within the framework of two major Acts, the Trade Union and Labour Relations Act of 1974 and the Employment Protection Act of 1975, modified by the Employment Acts of 1980 and 1982.

The former replaced the Industrial Relations Act of 1971, abolished the National Industrial Relations Court, and replaced the Commission on Industrial Relations with the new Advisory Conciliation and Arbitration Service (ACAS). It also abolished the emergency procedures introduced in 1971 for 'cooling off' periods and compulsory ballots whenever proposed industrial action threatened the economy or public health.

The 1974 Act reversed the presumption created by the 1971 Act that collective agreements in writing were legally enforceable. Such agreements are now presumed not to be legally enforceable unless they contain a provision making them so.

A worker's right of appeal to an industrial tribunal against unfair dismissal and the right to take part in strikes and engage in peaceful picketing were retained. But the statutory right under the 1971 Act to belong or not to belong to a trade union was repealed. It became unfair to dismiss an employee for belonging to an independent trade union, but it was also unfair to dismiss an employee for refusing to join a union held to be under the control of the employer.

With the repeal of the 1971 Act, closed shop agreements were once again lawful since the right not to belong to a trade union had gone. Pre-entry closed shop agreements, excluding individuals from a job unless they were already members of a specified union were permissible, as were post-entry union shop agreements by which employees were required to join the union within an agreed period after starting work.

The Employment Protection Act of 1975 encouraged the extension of collective bargaining and established new rights for unions registered as independent.

This Act provided for guaranteed weekly earnings within specified limits for employees who lose their wages because of short time working or lay-off caused by shortage of work. It protected the job of employees absent through pregnancy; established the right to paid leave for trade union activities; and required employers who planned redundancies to notify the Department of Employment and to consult with the appropriate union if ten or more workers are affected. In addition the Act improved the unfair dismissal provisions of the 1974 Act, widened the powers of Wages Councils to regulate wages and other conditions of employment, and established an Employment Appeal Tribunal to hear appeals from decisions of industrial tribunals. A Central Arbitration Committee was set up to deal with rights to trade union recognition, disclosure of information, and the imposition of binding arbitration awards.

The Employment Act 1980 contained provisions for reforming the collective behaviour of trade unions in critical areas like union recognition, coercive recruitment, and secondary action. It also provided for secret ballots and codes of practice on picketing and the closed shop. It was, however, the 1982 Act that made the most fundamental change; it removed the almost complete immunity from actions in tort that trade unions had enjoyed since 1906 and made unions themselves liable for damages for unlawful industrial action if the unlawful acts were done on their behalf. In addition, injunctions could be issued against unions rather than just against individuals.

12.4 The Current System in Practice

In Britain today there are two 'systems' of industrial relations in operation rather than one system. The Donovan Commission found a formal system embodied in the official institutions and an informal system covered by the actual behaviour of trade unions, employers associations, managers, shop stewards, and workers.

The formal system comprises industry wide organizations capable of imposing their decisions on their members.

In this system most matters of collective bargaining are covered by written industry wide agreements, normally restricted to a narrow range of subjects. Pay for example is determined by industry-wide agreements. Industrial relations at factory level are assumed to depend on joint consultation and the interpretation of these agreements.

The informal system on the other hand rests on the wide autonomy of managers in industrial companies and factories and the power of industrial work groups.

In this system bargaining at factory level is as important as that at industry level, and the range of collective bargaining is far wider, including discipline, recruitment, redundancy, and work practices. Important decisions on pay are taken at factory level, and tacit arrangements and custom and practice are as important as formal agreements. There is no clear distinction between collective bargaining and joint consultation or between disputes of right and disputes of interest.

The Commission's emphasis on these conclusions in its report published in June 1968 caused a major stir. In retrospect it is easy to see the relationship between these findings and the emphasis on the importance of informal systems in the earlier chapters of this book. As important was the Commission's finding that the formal and informal systems were in conflict. 'The overriding need is to put an end to the conflict between the pretence of industry-wide agreements and the realities of industrial relations'.

12.5   The Institutions in the System

12.51   *Trade Unions*

There are in all nearly 500 separate trade unions, representing a membership in excess of 12 million workers. In recent years membership has grown rapidly as the traditionally non-unionized professional employees of banks, insurance companies and other white-collar occupations saw the advantage to be gained from industrial organization.

The national centre of the trade union movement is the Trades Union Congress (TUC). It meets for one week each year, but maintains a permanent secretariat. It is recognized as the official channel of consultation between government departments and representatives of organized labour on matters affecting the interests of workers generally. It also nominates members to serve on the National Economic Development Council.

There are however a number of small unions outside the TUC whose existence has been highlighted by the need to obtain formal recognition as bargaining units under the Acts. The Government has tended to discourage them because it regards the proliferation of bargaining units as contrary to better industrial relations. One example, the United Kingdom Association of Professional Engineers (UKAPE), won an important recognition case against ACAS in mid-1978. These unions often represent managerial, technical, or professional staff and have little in common with the broader based unions of the TUC.

Recent years have seen a major increase in the power of the trade unions. The Acts of 1974 and 1975 represented major additions, and it is sometimes maintained that this power has been misused. The case against the unions is that

they have insisted on manning levels that have, as in the car industry, destroyed Britain's chances of competing on world markets;

outdated rivalries between Britain's multiplicity of unions have delayed the introduction of new technologies and processes;

their legal immunities allow them to usurp the role of government and to threaten the freedom of the individual.

However the evidence does not support the view that Britain's strike record is particularly bad, as Table 12.1 shows.

Table 12.1

Working days lost per 1,000 employees

Annual average	1975–9
West Germany	92
Japan	142
France	324
Britain	990
United States	1,042
Canada	1,956
Italy	1,810

Source: *ILO*

It is clear moreover that weak managements have sometimes contributed to the situation. Over-manning and under-use of production capacity must also be blamed on poor managerial skill.

12.511 *Categories of unions:* The organization of individual trade unions derives from the social, economic and political environment in which they were formed. There are four basic patterns:

1 *Craft Unions*
The basis of association here is the possession of certain trade skills and the job in which they are employed. This is a 'horizontal' form of organization since it may cover many industries in which one stratum of workers is employed. They are the descendents of the medieval trade guilds, and today include unions like the National Graphical Association (NGA) and the Amalgamated Union of Engineering Workers (AUEW).
2 *Occupational Unions*
These unions organize workers who belong to a particular classification or related group of occupations (e.g. non-manual unions). Examples are the National Association of Local Government Officers (NALGO), the Unions of Shop Distributive and Allied Workers (USDAW) and the National Union of Public Employees (NUPE).

3 *Industrial Unions*

As the name implies, these unions seek to organize workers of whatever grade in a specific industry. This contrasts with the two types already described as it is a 'vertical' form of organization, with members in successive processes of an industry. Both the National Union of Mineworkers and the National Union of Railwaymen belong to this category, but neither has succeeded in representing all categories of workers in their industries.

4 *General Unions*

These are the largest unions, catering for all workers, regardless of their character of work or industrial qualifications. Both the Transport and General Workers and the General and Municipal Workers are of this type; both have memberships in excess of one million.

12.512 *Internal Union Organization:* Within the administrative system of a trade union, the key local unit is the branch, and the official who directs and organizes the branch is the branch secretary. Typically the union is a national body with branches in many localities. The general secretary assisted by a clerical and specialist staff is in charge of the central office and is responsible to a national executive council whose members are elected by the annual conference of branch delegates. Union policy is generally determined at the conference.

The branch secretary represents his union at the most local level but it is clear from the description of the four types of union organization that he may represent members in different locations and with different skills whose interests may conflict. In most factories in which trade unions are strong therefore, their members in each workplace elect a representative usually called a shop steward. His formal duties include recruiting new members, collecting subscriptions, and communicating between the union and its members. His informal functions may be very much wider however, and he may bargain on behalf of his members, even against the official policy of his union.

The national newspapers provide an example of how powerful this 'informal' element can be. There is some doubt over the extent to which national officials can exert control over the largely autonomous 'chapels' for each newspaper which have some 360 separate bargaining units throughout Fleet Street. Nationally agreed procedures for disputes, for reduction of manning levels, and for the introduction of new computer-based typesetting equipment have proved impossible to implement because of the fierce independence of the chapels from their national union leadership.

The Donovan Commission gave three instances where it felt trade union organization contributed to the unsatisfactory state of British industrial relations.

the existence of two or more unions in most industries and factories contribute to inter-union disputes, cumbersome negotiating machinery and ineffective communications;

many branches consist of a small number of members from a number of different factories or offices. Apathy is therefore widespread; a small clique can exert disproportionate influence; and such branches may be remote from the workplace;

poor communications between the trade union leadership and the rank-and-file may mean that it is out of touch with the real issues that concern them.

12.52   *Employers Organizations*

There are over 1,000 employers associations and over forty national federations
dealing with industrial relations. The British Printing Industries Federation and the
British Iron and Steel Federation are major examples. The tendency has been for
associations to amalgamate, and the Donovan Commission recorded the existence
of some 1,350 employers associations in 1968. Many of these associations are
affiliated to national institutions such as the National Federation of Building Trades
Employers which embraces some 250 local organizations.

12.521   *The Confederation of British Industry:* The main central employers'
organization is the Confederation of British Industry (CBI) with a membership of
over 1,000 individual companies and more than 200 employers associations. Founded in 1965, it combines in a single voluntary association the roles formerly played
by the British Employers Confederation, the Federation of British Industries, and
the National Association of British Manufacturers. It maintains regional offices
throughout Britain and is represented overseas in every country where Britain
trades. The CBI is the national employers' association and its role in industrial
relations is comparable to that of the TUC. It represents the employers' case in
national negotiations with the government, and it sits on many consultative bodies
as the counterpart of the TUC. Thus both bodies have six seats on the National
Economic Development Council, and the same tends to apply wherever the
tripartite principle of consultation is employed.

The CBI provides a means of formulating and influencing general policy in
economic, social and industrial matters and it acts as a spokesman for industry as a
whole. As legislation has strengthened trade unions, so the CBI has become more
active in industrial relations, and held its first national conference on the TUC's
model in 1978.

Nevertheless it is misleading to regard employers' associations simply as the
'bosses unions'. It implies that employers have been forced to combine together
to protect their interests in the same way as employees. Although this has sometimes been the case, employers such as ICI, Royal Dutch Shell, and Unilever have
often been able to protect their interests better without combination. Moreover
employers' associations deal with a much broader range of issues than trade unions.
All are concerned directly or indirectly with the negotiation of wages and working
conditions; many are also involved in such questions as the standardization of
products and trading contracts and the provision of a range of commercial services
to their members. The extent that employers' associations are active in industrial
relations will depend on how closely their organization matches the prevalent
bargaining structure. Where bargaining is concentrated at the local level, local
associations or national associations with local affiliates will tend to play a greater
role than purely national organizations.

The Donovan Commission concluded that whilst industry-wide collective
bargaining inevitably involves associations of employers, they often represent
a mere formal facade with other influential negotiations taking place within an
informal structure.

Employers and managers sometimes act informally and unofficially in much
the same way as the shop stewards, valuing their membership of employers

associations for the trade and commercial services that they provide rather than as a part of their mainline industrial relations activity. Sometimes this informal activity can inhibit the operation of orderly pay structures; the following are some examples:

concessions of claims in excess of national agreements
payment by results schemes
merit pay, grade rates, and extra payments for special conditions
excessive overtime payments.

At the same time management may well consult with workers on other conditions like manning levels, pace of work, new jobs and machinery, and discipline, thus developing a network of agreements which are informal, tacit and outside the scope of co-ordinated personnel policies. A similar result occurs if the manager uses his prerogative to make changes on his own initiative without consultation.

12.53 *The Government*

Successive governments have in general followed two policies since the end of the Second World War:

the state has stood aloof from collective bargaining in the private sector, only imposing a few restrictions on strikes and lock-outs, and accepting that the parties to collective agreements should be bound by honour rather than law; Parliament has traditionally held that free collective bargaining is the best system to settle industrial relations affairs and has acted accordingly.

As the size of the public sector grew however, and the Government's role as employer and paymaster became progressively more important, its impact on the nation's industrial relations also grew. Since many nationalized industries are critical to the country's economy, they became natural targets for strikes and other industrial action. A Department of Employment study of the period 1966—76 showed that five industries predominantly nationalized, coal mining, docks, motor transport, ship-building, and iron and steel, accounted for a quarter of strikes and a third of days lost. The National Health Service, the biggest employer in the country with a total workforce of one million, has some of the most intractable industrial relations problems, centering on the question of ancillary workers pay. ACAS has reported the fundamental failure of the present joint procedures and the lack of properly organized industrial relations machinery. The twelve TUC-affiliated unions are in conflict with the professional bodies over the right to strike, whilst the latter maintain that the trade union strategy as operated in the industrial sector is inappropriate in the health service.

Governments have departed from these previously established policies in two important ways during the 1970s.

12.531 *Legal Regulation:* The Industrial Relations Act of 1971 established the National Industrial Relations Court with the same powers and privileges as the High Court and Court of Session to enforce its orders, and to require the attendance and examination of witnesses. The Act met with great opposition from the trade unions, and was repealed after a change of government, but not before a number of trade unionists had been imprisoned for contempt.

12.532 *Pay Policy:* Attempts by successive governments to regulate the size of potentially inflationary wage settlements with a series of semi-voluntary controls, ranging from total 'freeze' to 'Social Contract' have met with only limited success. The contradiction between conceptual support for collective bargaining and the actual imposition of pay guidelines of varying rigidity has been a continuing bone of contention between trade unions and successive governments. Thus the Ford strike in late 1978 followed rejection of the company's offer based on the Government's 5% pay guidelines and demands for a settlement based 'on the company's ability to pay'.

12.54 *Statutory Wage Regulation*

From 1909 to 1959 a series of Trade Boards and Wages Councils Acts empowered the Government to establish machinery for wage regulation in industries where adequate arrangements between employers' associations and trade unions did not exist and which were usually characterized by low pay. The Catering Wages Act (1943) and the Agricultural Wages (Regulation) Act of 1947 are examples. It was understood that such regulation would continue only until it was possible for normal collective bargaining to operate and a Joint Industrial Council could be set up. Commonly known as Whitley Councils, these bodies were set up with works committees at individual establishment level. However national and local government are now practically the only fields in which they have survived.

The Terms and Conditions of Employment Act (1959) provided other powers for wage regulation. An employer under certain circumstances may be required to observe terms and conditions not less favourable than those established in his industry by collective bargaining, and nationalized industries are obliged to seek agreement with trade unions to establish negotiating machinery for setting the terms and conditions for their employees.

12.55 *Conciliation Mediation and Arbitration*

The Government has an important role to play as arbiter of last resort between employers and trade unions. Because of its direct involvement in many disputes, an independent organization, the Advisory Conciliation and Arbitration Service (ACAS) was established under the Employment Protection Act (1975) to carry out these functions. The Service is run by a Council consisting of a chairman, three members nominated by the CBI and TUC respectively, and three independent members.

The Law gave ACAS 'the general duty of promoting the improvement of industrial relations and, in particular, of encouraging the extension of collective bargaining'. Its main functions are to provide:

advice on industrial relations and the development of modern personnel practices;
conciliation in trade disputes;
conciliation in certain disputes between individual employees and their

employers;
arbitration and mediation services;
help in improving collective bargaining;
advice on trade union recognition problems.

Conciliation is voluntary. When parties are involved in a trade dispute they can ask for an independent conciliator to help them reach agreement. The eventual level of settlement will be the joint decision of both parties. The conciliator does not impose or even recommend what that level should be.

Arbitration is also voluntary. Parties may wish to ask ACAS to appoint an arbitrator or board of arbitration to examine the case for each side and make an award. Arbitration awards are not legally binding but since arbitration is chosen by both parties as a means of settlement such awards are normally accepted. Before seeking arbitration, the parties should try to settle a dispute by conciliation.

Mediation is also voluntary. Sometimes the parties to a pay dispute may ask for the help of an independent third party to mediate and make recommendations for a settlement or to suggest a basis for further discussion. If so ACAS may appoint a mediator from outside the Service.

Any independent trade union may refer a recognition issue to ACAS. When ACAS receives such an application it will examine the issue and try to settle it by conciliation if appropriate. If a settlement cannot be reached by agreement ACAS makes further inquiries. ACAS has to find out the views of the workers concerned and consult all parties who it considers might be affected by the outcome. Unless the reference is withdrawn, ACAS is required to prepare a written report setting out its findings and any recommendations for recognition, with reasons. The reasons must also be given if ACAS does not recommend recognition. Copies of the report are sent to every trade union and employer concerned.

If an employer does not comply with a recommendation, the trade union may complain to ACAS, who will try to conciliate. If this is unsuccessful the trade union may complain to the Central Arbitration Committee about the employer's failure to comply and at the same time enter a claim that the contracts of the employees should include specified terms and conditions. Any award that the Committee makes as to terms and conditions is legally enforceable as part of the contracts of employment.

ACAS involvement in recognition disputes has been surrounded by controversy. In the cases of Grunwick, the North London photographic processing firm and UKAPE (quoted earlier) it sustained damaging judgements in the Courts. The Law on recognition is ambiguous and the TUC has proposed that ACAS should be withdrawn from this area.

12.6 Industrial Relations in Practice

It is important to appreciate that the national strikes featured in the press represent only a very small proportion of all disputes. A Department of Employment study shows that between 1971–3, a period of comparatively high strike activity, 95% of manufacturing plants were strike-free, whilst in an average year 98% of plants do not experience strikes. The following process is intended to illustrate how the system works, and is not intended as a typical example therefore.

In the first instance a worker normally raises an issue with his superior on the shop floor. Thereafter a shop steward can take it further, and it may come before a joint committee in the factory. If it is not settled, the full-time trade union officer and the employers' association are involved.

In many factories there are arrangements for Joint Consultation between management and employees about matters of concern that are outside the scope of official negotiating machinery. These often take the form of joint committees, although less formal methods may be used. It would be unusual for an issue raised by an individual worker to pass this stage in normal circumstances.

Industry-wide negotiations may be involved, either by bringing the question before a national joint body or by sending a joint investigation sub-committee to the factory. If agreement is not forthcoming either side may call on the services of ACAS for mediation or arbitration.

At some stage either side may undertake industrial action to force a desired advantage. This may take the form of an official strike by the union or a lock-out by the employer. More often action is likely to be 'unofficial', that is it lacks the approval of the appropriate trade union authority, or 'unconstitutional', meaning that action is taken before the appropriate disputes procedure is completed. Industrial action may stop short of complete withdrawal of labour however, particularly where only a limited section of the company is concerned. It may include such practices as:

working to rule, i.e. delaying work by meticulous attention to every regulation;
refusing to work overtime;
'blacking' suppliers or other departments;
extending breaks for lunch, tea, and union business;
withdrawal of labour for limited periods;
refusing to co-operate with first-line management;
'go-slows'.

In a final trial of strength the striker has many advantages. *The Economist* stated baldly in early 1979 that 'Britain is engulfed in strikes because strikers think they will gain'. An official striker often receives strike pay from his union, unemployment benefit from the state, and social security payments for his family. The Employment Acts of 1980 and 1982 began the process of restoring a rational balance, undoubtedly aided by depressed business conditions. The withdrawal of the immunity of trade unions to civil action in tort and other measures for union reform made a radical change in the climate of industrial relations and 1983–4 was characterized by a considerable move of litigation across the whole range of industrial relations and employment protection questions.

12.7 Maintaining Good Industrial Relations

A strike is final evidence of the breakdown of relations between employer and employees. In the short run either side may register gains; in the longer term all parties concerned, including the country as a whole, usually lose. Good industrial relations are therefore a major objective for most responsible managements. But what does this mean in practice?

12.8 Industrial Relations Code of Practice

The 1974 Act makes provision for a code of practice containing practical guidance on the promotion of good industrial relations. Nothing in the Code is enforceable by law, but it will be admissible in evidence in proceedings that go before industrial tribunals. It is supplemented by a new code on the closed shop, effective from May 1983.

The Code covers much wider ground than that covered by the Act, which is a reminder that constructive management–union relations must be considered in the context of all that goes on at the place of work. The Code is divided into seven sections, and the following summary is taken from the Industrial Society's guide to the Trade Union and Labour Relations Act.

12.81 *Responsibilities*

'Primary responsibility' for good industrial relations is placed upon management and this is seen as covering the development of fair and effective industrial relations policies, effective organization of work and the provision of training in industrial relations for all members of management, including the supervisor who is identified as a key member of management. Union organization and internal communication are examined as well as union aims, and the obligations of the individual employee are described.

12.82 *Employment Policies*

There are individual sections on: planning and use of manpower, recruitment and selection, training, payment systems, status and security of employees, and working conditions.

The Code lays stress on the need for soundly based pay policies, and payment systems which employees can understand. Differences between employees that are not related to the responsibilities of the job should, the Code says, be progressively removed.

12.83 *Communication and Consultation*

The need for systematic communication down the line to employees is emphasized and the essential information that each employee needs is listed. Face-to-face communication is identified as the most important method of communication. There are guidelines on the establishment and operation of consultative committees and the Code stresses the need to link negotiation with consultation.

12.84 *Collective Bargaining*

The Code recognizes that bargaining may take place at various levels, but stresses the need for an agreement to be capable of application at the place of work. It lays down guidelines on the nature, composition and establishment of 'bargaining units'. It lists the factors affecting recognition of trade unions and indicates what management's and unions' responsibilities are after recognition. It distinguishes between procedure agreements and substantive agreements and indicates what each type of agreement should contain. Facilities for trade union activities and the status and function of shop stewards are among those matters which the Code says should be included in a procedure agreement. It lists those matters which are appropriate to an industry level agreement, and asks that the relationships between industry and plant agreements be clearly defined.

On disclosure of information, the Code states that management should try to meet all reasonable requests from trade unions for information relevant to a negotiation.

12.85 *Employee Representation*

The Code states that there are advantages to employees and to management in having properly accredited employee representatives. It concentrates on shop stewards and includes sections on appointment and qualification, status, functions, facilities, senior shop stewards and convenors, and training. The issue of joint credentials, the shop steward's responsibility for observing agreements, the minimum facilities to enable him to do his job as a representative are some of the matters covered. Both management and the trade unions are identified as having responsibilities for the training of stewards and guidelines are given on what these responsibilities are.

12.86 *Grievance and Disputes Procedures*

Individual grievances and collective disputes are often dealt with through the same procedure. The Code states that, where the procedures are separate, they should be linked so that an issue can pass from one to the other if necessary. It lists the characteristics of a grievance procedure, and the stages that might be included in a procedure for settling disputes through to conciliation and arbitration.

12.87 *Disciplinary Procedures*

'Management should ensure that fair and effective arrangements exist for dealing with disciplinary matters.' The rules of work should be made known as well as the procedure and the type of circumstances which can lead to suspension or dismissal. The Code lists the characteristics of a disciplinary procedure, e.g. the steps involved, the right to union representation, the need for written records, and the right of appeal.

12.9 Industrial Democracy

Although legislation now exists to protect people from unfair dismissal, bad conditions, and exploitation, British industrial relations are still tainted by conflict. There remains a major gap in the development of the employee role.

It is sometimes maintained that further progress will depend on employees in companies and nationalized concerns alike being given the opportunity to take part in the development of corporate strategy, to contribute to decisions before they are taken, and equally important, to share in the responsibility for their implementation.

The White Paper, 'Industrial Democracy' published in May 1978 explained the concept in the following terms:

'In a democratic society, democracy does not stop at the factory gate or the office door. We spend a large part of our lives at work and invest our skills and energies in industry. There is growing recognition that those of us who do so should be able to participate in decisions which can vitally affect our working lives and our jobs. This development is no longer a question of 'if' but 'when and how'. Industrial democracy stands for the means by which employees at every level may have a real share in the decisions within their company or firm, and therefore a share in the responsibility for making it a success. The objective is positive partnership between management and workers, rather than defensive co-existence.'

12.10 The Bullock Report

The Bullock Report, published in January 1977, suggested a framework for implementing these proposals. The majority report recommended:

equal numbers of union and shareholder representatives ('2 x') on existing boards, together co-opting a third group ('y');
participation through union channels only;
legislation to impose the new structure on companies employing more than 2,000 workers (including subsidiaries of foreign-based multinationals);
union directors to be chosen for three years, to be paid no fee, and to be removable if all unions agreed;
establishment of an industrial democracy commission (IDC) to encourage participation generally.

The Bullock Report caused a major storm. The three main points of the CBI's objection to the proposals were summed up by Alex Jarratt, chairman of Reed International, as follows:

1 'We reject completely the imposition of so-called worker directors over the heads of our shareholders;
2 'We reject completely the single channel of representation; all employees must have equal rights under the law;
3 'We reject completely any legislation that would force a rigid formula on companies when the real hope for participation lies in flexibility of application.'

The principle of participation itself was not at issue and it is the CBI's policy to develop and promote a voluntary code of practice to encourage high standards of participation within companies.

The Government's White Paper adopted a more conciliatory note than the original Bullock proposals, both on the question of legislation and the representation of non-union employees. It was proposed that a two-tier system of company boards should be introduced into company law, consisting of a Policy Board and a Management Board.

The functions of the policy board included appointment of the management board; determining company policy over the full range of its operations, setting objectives and approving strategic plans, monitoring the performance of the management board, and supervising its conduct of the company's financial affairs in particular through the approval of programmes for capital investment. It would also convene general meetings of shareholders, making recommendations to the shareholders as appropriate.

The management board, appointed by the policy board, would normally consist of the executives of the company at the most senior level, sitting under the chairmanship of the chief executive. It would be assigned the responsibility for the day-to-day management of the company.

It was envisaged that in general the existing duties of directors under the Companies Acts would apply to the management board except where they are specifically assigned to the policy board to enable it to perform its statutory functions.

The new boards were expected to help create a framework in which those among the workforce and in management who are most closely concerned with achieving real co-operation in industry could come together to share responsibility for the future prosperity of the companies in which they worked.

The political and economic climate in the United Kingdom during 1983–7 is unlikely to favour a major extension of industrial democracy in the sense of the Bullock Report, although both major political parties are committed to improving the working relations between management and labour. However both the EEC and the Labour Party place major emphasis on this topic and further developments may be expected in future.

12.11 Employee Participation in Practice

In the meantime gradual but significant progress is being made towards participation. Some nationalized industries have statutory obligations to promote industrial democracy. Management and the unions in these industries are already developing new arrangements for participation. The Post Office has begun an experiment, lasting for two years, based on agreed proposals put forward by the management and the unions for a new board with, in addition to the chairman, seven management and seven union members, and five independent members including two with experience in consumer affairs.

In some nationalized industries the management and the unions have put the emphasis on the development of their existing procedures. For example in the energy sector the recently established national Joint Co-ordinating Council in the electricity industry and the Planning Liaison Committee of the British Gas Corporation discuss policies over a wide range of the industries' activities. Tripartite discussions of coal industry strategy involving unions, management and Government began in 1974.

Elsewhere progress has been slower. The appointment of a new 15-man supervisory board at Harland and Wolff, the Belfast shipyard, comprising one-third trade union representatives, one-third management, and one-third Government appointees has proved the exception rather than the rule. The system of planning agreements and worker participation at Talbot has proceeded very slowly.

Most large companies in the private sector have some arrangements to enable staff to participate in the running of the business. GEC and Boots are examples:

(a)   *The Boots Company*

The participation of staff in the business of the Boots Company is through the linked channels of the Staff Council structure and trades unions. Direct representation of Industrial Staff is arranged through seventeen staff councils, while in its shops, committees have been established in the two hundred larger branches, which together employ half its retail staff. This structure will be extended to cover two-thirds of the total staff. At the apex of the council structure are the Wholesale and Retail Central Staff Councils. These, meeting in Nottingham four times a year under the chairmanship of the Staff Director, are valuable as a further means of consulting staff and involving them in the decisions of the business.

(b)   *GEC*

GEC regards consultation with the unions and participation by employees as very important. Managers are required to encourage employees to participate as much as possible in the conduct of the business, and discussions take place on a wide range of topics covering market trends, production plans, investment, new methods, training, health and safety, and employment. These topics and others are discussed from the overall standpoint by management and national trade union officials within the formal framework of GEC's National Joint Consultative Council.

Figure 12.1   From GEC's 1979 Annual Report

It should however be noted that participation by employees is significantly further advanced in most Western European and Scandinavian countries than it is in the UK, and that this establishes what is thought most likely to be the trend there also.

Two other aspects of the growth of industrial democracy merit mention at this stage:

12.111 *Profit Sharing*

Shared profit is a logical corollary of shared responsibility for management decision-making, and the Government issued a consultative document in early 1978, proposing tax concessions to encourage the development of schemes increasing employees' share ownership.

The distribution may be in shares or cash, or a combination of the two. Until the 1950s, profit sharing in Britain was limited mainly to a few closed co-partnerships. Trustees rather than individual workers owned the shares, and the employees built up no stake to take away when they left or retired. The best known today is the John Lewis Partnership, whose profit-sharing scheme began in 1929. Until 1970 the firm paid an annual 'benefit' in non-voting fixed-interest shares, tradeable on the stock exchange. Now it pays cash: employees preferred it, and share performance was disappointing. All the employees (more than 25,000) are partners; they earn benefit (15% of pay) from the day of joining.

In the 1950s, partly under the threat of nationalization of chemicals, cement and sugar, ICI, Rugby Portland Cement and Tate and Lyle began profit sharing. ICI's scheme, the best known, began in 1954. Immediately marketable shares in the company are distributed as an annual bonus at the middle market price. They are taxed as income, and most employees sell them at once.

1977 saw a great increase in interest in profit-sharing schemes, and British Home Stores, H.P. Bulmer, House of Fraser, ICL, Lloyds Bank, and Marks and Spencer were among the companies putting forward schemes. In January 1978 there were only about 100 schemes open to all employees (as distinct from directors only) covering some 2% of the total. In spite of the tax concessions in the 1978 Finance Act, the number of schemes has remained low compared with other countries. USA has nearly 200,000 schemes, often however designed in the absence of other forms of company pension.

In principle it is a good thing that employees should get a fair share of the wealth they create, that the ownership of capital should be widely spread, and that they should feel a commitment to the enterprise for which they work. In practice the link between a share-handout and output may be tenuous; immediately marketable shares on the other hand may not be retained. Deferred shares that are not vested in the employee until a number of years after allotment can leave him with 'too many of his eggs in one basket', penalize him severely if he leaves and may inhibit mobility of labour when needed. Questions of fairness to other shareholders also arise. It is clear that there is a significant degree of apathy among unions to profit sharing, and this could well reduce the desired results. Collective ownership of shares under union control is unlikely to find favour with many employers. American evidence suggests that well-designed schemes may give employees a greater feeling of commitment, but shareholding is only one small part of the process. Companies like IBM and Texas Instruments have many other systems for ensuring that its employees feel involved. Profit sharing is no substitute for good employee relations and effective personnel management.

12.112 *Worker Co-operatives*

The co-operative principle has been influential since the earliest attempts at industrial democracy and employee participation. The effects of the Department of Industry in 1974 to save the co-operatives at the Meriden motorcycle factory, the Scottish Daily News, and Kirkby Manufacturing and Engineering provided a stimulus for development in the 1970s.

British Co-operatives have fallen into three main groupings. Firstly there are those born out of industrial failures — Meriden and Kirkby, springing from the sit in form of defensive worker reaction to imminent redundancy. Secondly there are 33 co-operatives, mainly in woodworking, plastics, and similar trades that have been funded under the Manpower Services Commission's (MSC) job creation schemes. The third group is centred on the Industrial Common Ownership Movement and enhances 15 collectively owned enterprises.

12.113 *Management Buy-outs*

Management buy-outs are another way in which employees have become more involved in the management of their organizations in recent years. Management and staff buy the assets of the company and manage them through a new commercially run company, owned by the employees, but with conventional management and shareholders.

The National Freight Company and Ansafone are two major examples, but the average deal is much smaller. ICFC, the leader in this field of finance, has arranged over 200 buy-outs over the last eight years, averaging in the £250,000 — £300,000 range.

12.12 Industrial Relations in Other Countries

As an industrial nation, Britain's performance is most often compared with that of the USA and the Federal Republic of Germany. There are a number of important differences in the field of industrial relations.

Britain's Industrial Revolution pre-dated those in the other countries; as with many aspects of industrialization, the legacy of an early start is often a handicap. The struggle to establish effective trade unionism demanded an involvement in politics that has continued. Today trade unions provide the Labour Party with the bulk of its adherents and its finance, and the block votes of the five biggest unions dominate both the Annual Conference and the elections to the NEC. This political orientation does not exist in USA or Germany, and it is alleged that worker—management relations have benefitted from non-involvement in such highly charged issues as nationalization, social justice, and redistribution of wealth. German unions have come to terms with the mixed economy and are anxious to see it work efficiently and profitably. In Germany it is sometimes claimed that worker participation within a mixed economy has made public ownership redundant. US unions are also pro-private enterprise.

The German system of supervisory boards, another major difference, is illustrated in Figure 12.2.

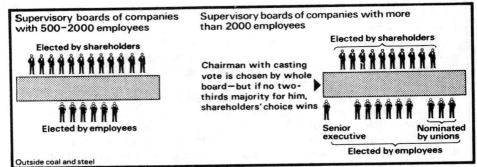

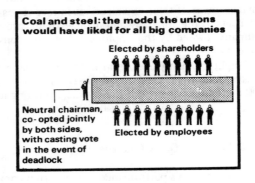

Figure 12.2
(Source: *The Economist*)

But German worker-participation begins on the shop floor. Every concern with more than five employees elects a works council by secret ballot. Hiring, firing, allocation of work and transfers all need the advance consent of the works councils, and they have an equal say with management in manpower problems ranging from job evaluation and wage structures to training, discipline, promotion and holidays. Conflicts go to the labour courts for compulsory arbitration, and it is illegal for a council to call a strike. Although they have little say in wage determination, a topic covered by regional agreements, they provide a means of bargaining at plant level without industrial unrest.

The position of the unions in the USA is much weaker. Since 1955 union membership has fallen from 34% of the workforce to 20% in 1979. In the anti-union South only 15% of workers are union members. The National Right to Work Committee is only one indication of the hostile climate unions face. Twenty states have adopted right-to-work laws banning compulsory union membership, and the closed shop is illegal under federal law.

American unionism also has its violent past, and the AFL–CIO has not developed the respectability or the closeness to government that European unions have. Violence is seldom far below the surface of labour organizing drives, particularly in the South. Names like the corrupt Jimmy Hoffa of the Teamsters and the murderous Tony Boyle of the mineworkers, still give the movement a bad name.

Many American firms, particularly in the new technologies and service industries follow the example of the giants like IBM, Eastman Kodak, and Texas Instruments in developing the sort of positive personnel policies that make it hard for unions to exploit grievances. This type of 'paternalism' has fended off demands for worker participation and industrial democracy; the unions still have to justify their existence to the American worker.

12.13 Conclusion

In spite of the impression sometimes given by the Press, most industrial relations is not about strikes, lock-outs, and unremitting power struggle; it is rather a routine, painstaking process of day-by-day detailed negotiations within a structure of procedures that are often tedious and time-consuming. It is the effort to find a *modus vivendi* between the aspirations of labour in a time of intense change, and the desire of management to get on with the job and make profits.

Our guinea-pig company, Consumer and Electrical, has not had a strike since its re-organization. It inherited from its constituent companies a mixed bag of unions and agreements, but took advantage of the provisions of the Trade Union and Labour Relations Acts of 1974 and 1976 to conclude a series of union membership agreements that have restored a degree of perspective. Most production workers are unionized, but very few of the white-collar workers in C & E (Distribution) and C & E (International) belong to unions. Drivers are an exception, and the Chairman suspects that both TGWU and ASTMS are stronger in the group than anyone thinks.

The group's policy is to co-operate closely with its unions. There are national agreements between the unions and the whole of the UK engineering industry, but most matters are discussed and settled locally. Negotiations between unions and management at the factory follow simple procedures in which subjects like pay increases or matters affecting individuals can be talked over in an orderly way. Discussions between factory shop stewards and management are sometimes reinforced by local trade union officials and, exceptionally, by national trade union leaders. There are seven unions at C & E, and although the Personnel Director is responsible for industrial relations negotiations and procedures, the Chairman, through his contacts with senior union officers, is able to play an effective 'elder statesman' role. Line management is also closely involved with the process.

Most C & E employees are not members of unions, but the Board has encouraged participation and consultation through the Staff Association which has staff consulting committees in all operating units. All employees are informed about the group's activities through a well-established house magazine and an annual staff report, covering trading performance, finance and personnel matters.

C & E is in no sense anti-union, but, in line with most British management, it would not welcome worker directors on the board; in fact its unions are also showing less enthusiasm for this development at the moment. Wages are a topic of continuing negotiation but have not led to actual disputes. A difficult time was experienced when Phase 2 of the late Labour government's pay policy was followed by Phase 3 instead of by free collective bargaining as expected; C & E's policy has been to maintain its wages and other employment conditions marginally above those of other local employers, and this, combined with the skill of C & E's industrial relations staff, has paid dividends in a virtual absence of official disputes and a containable number of unofficial ones. The C & E Employees Share Participation Scheme was launched successfully early in 1979. The Board believes strongly in the concept of a property owning democracy, but remains to be convinced that this type of scheme is effective as a staff motivator.

13. *The Role of Marketing*

Today there is widespread acceptance of the 'marketing concept' in most of the world's developed countries. The degree of application however differs widely. In some companies marketing is no more than a smart name for sales management whilst in others marketing is the lead function that determines not only the scale of the company's operation but also the activities of other major departments.

The tasks of the marketing department in a business usually include some or all the following:

(a) identifying opportunities in the market and producing sales forecasts
(b) initiating and co-ordinating new product innovation and development
(c) planning and developing a profitable product range
(d) maintaining the personal selling effort at a high level of performance and cost efficiency
(e) ensuring that the physical distribution of goods meets the needs of company strategy
(f) developing and implementing advertising and sales promotion plans
(g) providing the planned level of customer and technical service
(h) monitoring product pricing and initiating desirable changes.

This list of activities, broad though it is, does not explain why so much attention has been given to the marketing concept in recent years, and why its role in the business organization should be regarded as central and unique.

The Institute of Marketing's definition explains in a nutshell why the importance of marketing to a business is infinitely greater than the functional expertise of its managers in advertising, promotion, selling, and the traditional marketing tasks, critical though these often are.

13.1 The Institute's Definition of Marketing

'Marketing is the management process responsible for identifying, anticipating and satisfying customer requirements profitably.'

Marketing should not be regarded as a specialized activity, but should be basic to everything the company does. It may be said to encompass the entire business because it provides the interface with the customer who determines in the final event the scope, scale and success of the company. Peter Drucker would say that since it is the purpose of any business enterprise to create and satisfy the customer, it has two — and only these two — basic functions: marketing and innovation. Similarly, Theodore Levitt in his famous article 'Marketing Myopia' wrote:

'the entire corporation must be viewed as a customer-creating, and customer satisfying organism. Management must think of itself not as producing products but as providing customer-creating value satisfactions. It must push this idea (and everything it means and requires) into every nook and cranny of the organization'.

Thus in a market-orientated business, that is one that gears its efforts consciously to the demands of the market place, the needs of customers are constantly considered and taken into account:

1   They will be consulted regularly through market research
2   The product will be designed according to their preferences
3   It will be manufactured in the quantities they want to buy
4   Distribution will meet their buying habits and delivery requirements
5   Pricing will take account of what they are prepared to pay
6   Post-sale service will be geared to their operating needs.

The potency of this concept cannot be denied. The problem is to integrate it in a corporate organization structure that will effectively produce what customers want in a given product, in the required quantities, at a price they will pay, where and when they want it, and yet avoid the frustration and expense of trying to follow every vicissitude of short-run demand.

13.2   Application of the Marketing Concept

The implication so far has been that the marketing concept is of universal application to all businesses and organizations. Its area of influence is already very wide, covering not only consumer goods companies, but also companies manufacturing consumer durables, repeat and capital industrial goods, retailers and wholesalers, and the big financial institutions. Public sector bodies, such as the Manpower Services Commission and the Department of the Environment are adopting marketing techniques to develop and promote the social services they provide. Professional firms, like architects, solicitors, and accountants are one exception, but even here progress is being made. There are however a number of situations in which the marketing approach is sometimes maintained to be inappropriate. The following are some examples:

(a)   *A Sellers Market*
      In a sellers' market, i.e. in conditions where the seller not the buyer is the key influence, for example when goods are in short supply this situation may arise.

(b)   *High Technology*
      Where the company's future is believed to depend on its technical research ability to keep ahead of competition above all else. This attitude has been common in the electronics industry for example.

(c)   *Other Bottlenecks*
      Where other influences than the market provide the critical factor that

determines the company's profitability and its ability to grow. These might include:

management limitations
contractual or legal restrictions on the company's operation
shortage of skilled labour
inability to expand production capacity
availability of finance.

In each example a case may be made that certain conditions are more important than the market and require special treatment. Yet such orientation towards technology, procurement, or production, can prove dangerous in the longer term. The company that loses sight of the proposition that it produces customer satisfactions rather than merchandise takes an unnecessary risk. Shortages have a way of turning into gluts; technical research out of a market context becomes a mere theoretical exercise; and other bottlenecks tend to disappear in the medium term. None of these approaches can provide a corporate sense of direction that is valid in the longer term in the way that the disciplines of the market do.

Nevertheless the marketing concept is not a substitute for management experience and discretion. The manager who slavishly follows consumers' tastes to the extent that his efficient mass production process degenerates into a series of small-run job shops is serving nobody. The second principle of the concept therefore is that the customer's wants should be satisfied at an acceptable profit to the company. Some writers have also added a third, that account should be taken of the longer term interests of society in the process, involving the marketeer in the social and ecological consequences of his actions.

13.3 Marketing and the Corporate Plan

In Chapter 4 Planning and Control were discussed in detail. Emphasis was placed on the need to give a company a sense of direction and to provide a monitoring system to ensure that it did not stray too far from the chosen route. The whole process was summarized into four simple questions:

Where are we now?
Where do we want to go?
What do we have to do?
How are we getting on?

Thus the corporate plan is a collection of strategies, tactics, and intentions designed to achieve its goals and objectives. Marketing's role will appear wherever any of these aspects is influenced by developments in the market place.

The first step is to take stock of where the company and its products are. Current performance is analysed and strengths and weaknesses are identified. Some of the factors concerned are internal to the company and relatively easy to control. Others are external and may be outside the company's power to influence at all except in a marginal way. A large proportion usually relate to the markets in which the company is active or potentially active. A detailed market review is an essential part of any corporate plan because it will not only indicate

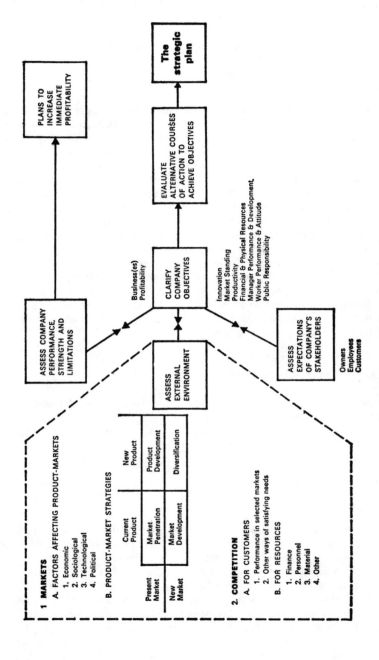

Figure 13.1 Developing the Strategic Plan

From Humble: *Improving Business Results*. Reproduced by permission of the author and publisher, McGraw-Hill Book Co. (UK) Ltd.

(Copyright ©1968 John Humble.

where current performance can be improved but should also provide the factual basis for identifying and appraising the threats and opportunities that face the company. This is one of marketing's most creative tasks, and the quality of this input will determine the scale and momentum of the corporate plan.

Marketing is not the only discipline involved at this stage, but Figure 13.1 illustrates its special position in the early, critical phases of the planning cycle.

The clarification of company objectives is the start of a chain that penetrates through the whole of the business. Company objectives must be broken down into unit, divisional, and departmental objectives so that every manager is clear about the part he is expected to play in the plan. Similarly the strategic plan is exploded into a series of tactical plans designed to meet these objectives. Figure 13.2, which can best be read as a continuation of Figure 13.1, illustrates this process.

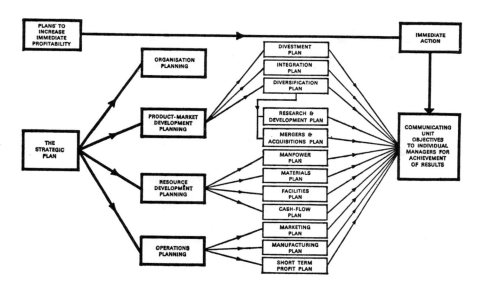

Figure 13.2   A Typical Range of Tactical Plans
(Source: Ibid)

It will be seen that the functional Marketing Plan covering the eight activities listed at the beginning of this chapter is included among the other tactical plans.

Thus the whole of a company's planning, down to the role of the individual manager, should be based on its analysis and interpretation of its position in its markets, and its success will rely heavily on the skill and flair of its marketing department in fulfilling this role.

13.4   Marketing's Day-to-Day Involvement

As the interface with its customers, the Marketing Department has a vested interest in anything that influences the degree of satisfaction that customers obtain from its range of products or services in the day-to-day running of the business. Questions of product quality and availability will involve it with Production; delivery performance and stock levels, with Distribution; cost control, credit policies and pricing with Finance; bought out products with Purchasing; and staff policies and manning levels with Personnel. Then it will have a special relationship with Research and Development because of its responsibility for developing the existing range to exploit market trends and for the introduction of new products.

The mechanics of marketing's working relationship with the other major functions in the company are examined in the following paragraphs.

13.5 Production

The critical input by marketing into the production or manufacturing process is the demand forecast. Whether a company is marketing- or production-oriented, any decision made about the future implies some forecast about demand. A factory manager who drafted his manufacturing schedule without taking into account what he believes he can distribute will clearly run into trouble soon. The actual basis for his planning may be no more than a crude adaptation of the volume he produced last year or simply be based on hunch. In times of stable demand conditions this may serve well enough. Few markets enjoy these conditions today however, and the development of the best possible sales forecast should be a high priority, because a company's scale of activity, growth prospects, range of products or services, and operating efficiency, are among the critical factors that are radically influenced by the view of sales opportunities that it takes now.

The demand forecast provided by Marketing Department to Production Department is specifically designed to be the basis for Production Planning and Control. It is Marketing's statement of the volume of goods it can distribute with an indication of when they will be needed. It therefore needs to be as realistic as possible:

> it should not include an incentive or 'stretch' element that is often included in the Sales Department's own forecast;
> it should allow for the likely effect of any planned activity in the market, either by the company or competitors;
> it should take an objective balanced view of growth opportunities.

The sales forecast in most companies is expressed in value and volume terms, and is then broken down into individual sales regions and territories by product group, covering periods that relate to the company's financial reporting periods. Most commonly this period is one month.

The demand forecast for Production may differ in a number of ways:

13.51 *Detail of Forecast*

In the final event somebody has to decide how many of the smallest component are going to be manufactured or purchased. In practice this type of 'forecasting' is termed 'scheduling', and is carried out within the Production Department. Product grouping is carried out at this stage and an important change of emphasis between the two departments takes place.

The marketing manager forecasts sales for product groups that are faced by a common demand; the production manager requires a forecast for product groups that utilize the same production process.

In some cases the two may coincide. In the case of domestic refrigerators both parties will think in terms of cabinets of a particular capacity, since variations in colour, handle position, and interior furniture are relatively superficial. The end uses of other products however may associate products in the market that are totally diverse as far as production planning is concerned. Jute hessian, sacking, and carpet-backing are examples.

13.52 *Period Covered by the Forecast*

The period of time covered by the forecast depends on the demand pattern facing the product and the time constraints involved in producing it.

Where demand varies only insignificantly from period to period, the time span of the forecast can be quite short.

If the product experiences seasonal variations or fluctuations relating to the business cycle, the forecast must cover at least one demand cycle from one peak to the next, to guide production and inventory planning. Ice-cream and oil tankers would represent extreme examples of this type.

Lead time plus at least one manufacturing cycle will represent an absolute minimum span.

There are three major purposes for which demand forecasts are used. They are:

(a) *Capacity and Equipment*
To determine the optimum scale of production capacity required and to decide when expansion or contraction of facilities is needed.

(b) *Production Planning*
To plan ongoing production for existing and new products to be manufactured with the existing equipment and facilities. ·

(c) *Production Scheduling*
To schedule short-term manufacture of existing products with existing equipment and facilities.

Table 13.1 describes the degree of detail and time span applicable to each.

Manufacturing cycles for a wide range of consumer and semi-durable items are measured in hours rather than days. A typical schedule of demand forecasts might be as follows:

1 A long range forecast covering three to five years in broad outline
2 An annual forecast specifying volume in broad product groups
3 A monthly or quarterly forecast in sufficient detail to aid scheduling.

Regular updating and review are of critical importance, and it is common practice to review all forecasts monthly or quarterly so that the full span of the forecast is maintained on a rolling basis with new estimates being added as time elapses.

Table 13.1

Type of Forecast	Degree of Detail	Time Span
Capacity and Equipment	Demand pattern with expected maxima for broad product groups	Pay back period
Production Planning Forecast	Volumes of product by groups related to categories of production process/facility	Several manufacturing cycles or at least one demand cycle
Product Sales Forecast	Individual product types based on orders expected or sold forward	Lead Time plus at least one manufacturing cycle

The demand forecast is the main mechanism by which marketing injects customer orientation into the factory, but there are many other aspects where production performance has a direct impact on the final satisfaction obtained by the customer. Adequate stocks of finished goods, product quality, cost control, spares availability, and new product development are major examples where the interests of the two departments may be at odds. Table 13.2 characterizes some typical attitudes.

Organization of the interface between the two departments has to be handled with care if friction and conflict are not to result. The following are some of the means used by management to foster interdepartmental co-operation:

the appointment of brand, product, or business managers with broad responsibility for their product or service that includes co-ordination of production aspects;

job rotation of managers to include both marketing and production responsibilities early in their career;

informal interfunctional task forces and committees including people at all levels in the organization, both to tackle specific problem areas and to provide ongoing co-ordination and liaison;

training courses designed to promote knowledge and understanding in managers from both functions;

regular formal liaison committees of senior managers meeting as part of routine performance monitoring procedures.

13.6 Distribution

Marketing planning starts with the identification of a target market, and the selection of channels to reach it must come very soon afterwards. A distribution system outside the context of the company's marketing objectives makes little sense, but it often happens that the Distribution Department is not under the direct control of the Marketing Director. Very often it forms part of the Production Department because it fits functionally on the end of the factory line and because the control of

Table 13.2

*Marketing/manufacturing areas of necessary
co-operation but potential conflict*

Problem area	Typical marketing comment	Typical manufacturing comment
1 Capacity planning and long-range sales forecasting	'Why don't we have enough capacity?'	'Why didn't we have accurate sales forecasts?'
2 Production scheduling and short-range sales forecasting	'We need faster response. Our lead times are ridiculous.'	'We need realistic customer commitments and sales forecasts that don't change like wind direction.'
3 Quality assurance	'Why can't we have reasonable quality at reasonable cost?'	'Why must we always offer options that are too hard to manufacture and that offer little customer utility?'
4 Breadth of product line	'Our customers demand variety.'	'The product line is too broad — all we get are short, uneconomical runs.'
5 Cost control	'Our costs are so high that we are not competitive in the marketplace.'	'We can't provide fast delivery, broad variety, rapid response to change, and high quality at low cost.'
6 New product introduction	'New products are our life blood.'	'Unnecessary design changes are prohibitively expensive.'
7 Adjunct services such as spare parts inventory support, installation, and repair.	'Field service costs are too high.'	'Products are being used in ways for which they weren't designed.'

Source: Benson P. Shapiro, *Harvard Business Review*, September–October 1977

many aspects of distribution as a physical operation has more in common with factory than marketing management. It is not critical that marketing controls the day-to-day details of the transport system; it is however vital that the distribution mix is the best possible available for achieving marketing objectives, and Marketing Department has a very real interest in this function.

The distribution mix is essentially composed of two mixes:

1 *Distribution Channels*
   Selection of channel and the determination of channel strategy has always been an integral part of marketing planning. To obtain a cost or tactical advantage over competition by an adroit choice of channels can be very valuable indeed. The 'Avon lady', the Tupperware Party, or the industrial manufacturer who decides to 'go direct' after traditionally using a chain of middlemen, are examples.

2 *Physical Distribution*
   Physical distribution concerns the delivery of goods from supplier A to customer B, and involves the technical skills of managing company transport, selecting outside means of delivery, scheduling, routing, and stock control. Often it also encompasses documentation, particularly where exporting is concerned. Traditionally the distribution manager has not been a marketing man in the accepted sense.

Marketing is nonetheless deeply concerned with what he is doing. Its interest in the satisfaction of its customer should not stop at the factory gate. Physical distribution includes a broad range of activities concerned with the efficient movement of goods from the end of the production line to the customer. In addition to freight transportation, it encompasses warehousing, materials handling, protective packaging, order processing, stock control, plant and warehouse site selection, and after-sale customer service. Moreover the delivery man may be the only member of the company outside Marketing Department who has direct personal contact with the customer, and each item in the list may provide either a competitive advantage or prejudice the customer against the company. Alert marketeers can use physical distribution as a powerful tool in providing on improved customer service but in most cases there is a trade-off between cost and benefit. Thus:

   air freight will be faster but rates are higher than by land or sea;
   higher stock levels will reduce out-of-stock situations but increase working capital;
   better packaging may reduce breakages but will increase cost;
   faster order processing may require new equipment or additional clerks;
   improved materials handling may demand a fresh investment in machinery.

Today physical distribution management is claimed to represent one of the few areas where there are major opportunities for potentially large cost reductions, combined with possibly lower prices to the customer, and improvements in internal efficiency.

A creative approach to distribution facilities can often add a fresh dimension to the product itself. Packaging is a prime example. Its basic function is to protect the product, but it can contribute to the convenience of usage, as does the Flymo oil pack; it can provide an after-use item like the decorative honey pot;

and also reinforce the brand personality and support the product's advertising though effective graphic surface design. Similarly the introduction of refrigerated rail wagons opened up the world's market for cheap meat, and the use of air freight has produced a lucrative market in early season fruit and vegetables. The list is far from comprehensive, but illustrates the depth of marketing's interest in physical distribution.

The relationship between Marketing and Distribution Departments sometimes suffers from the sort of friction encountered with Production. The distribution manager's priorities tend to be minimum transport costs, low stock levels, and the most efficient scheduling and routing. These may conflict with the marketing manager's attempts to minimize stock-outs and to provide the delivery service that the customer wants. Often the interface with Distribution is neglected as simply one more aspect of Production and it is seldom that separate co-ordinating machinery exists, except when specific questions arise. An alert marketing manager should however maintain ongoing contact and keep changing rates and practices in this area under review.

13.7   Finance and Accounts

Sales forecasting for the company brings marketing into direct contact with the finance and accounting functions. For most companies in manufacturing or trading sales represent the largest form of revenue. In the financial year ending in 1978 the giant GEC earned less than 10% of its profit before tax from net investment income whilst for Tesco the figure was about 5%. This perspective underlines the importance of reliable sales forecasting in financial planning.

There are five main activities in which marketing shares a role with accounting. They are:

Budgeting
Cost Control
Pricing
Profit Planning
Credit Policy and Control

13.71   *Budgeting*

The company's overall budgeting procedure begins with the master budget in which the total sales forecast in value terms is compared with the total costs likely to be incurred in achieving it, and the planned profit for the year is extracted. The cost side of the equation is then exploded into the individual expense budgets of each department. Because the company must cut its coat according to its cloth, the scale of each part of the operation should be planned in proportion to the sales income likely to be earned. The sales forecast in this way determines the level of expense of each part of the company.

'Sales budget' may have two meanings therefore. It is both:

the amount of revenue that is expected from sales by the company as a whole;
the expense budget for the sales department, covering the cost of salesmen,

sales administration, and other sales activities.

13.72 *Cost Control*

Marketing is involved in two distinct exercises in cost control. The first is the relatively routine tasks of ensuring that departmental expense does not exceed the levels budgeted. Sometimes flexible budgets will be designed to vary with sales revenue, but often the budget set at the beginning of the year remains as the standard of performance. Marketing will be monitored by the budget controller's department in the same way as any other cost centre.

Marketing is however concerned with what are sometimes termed 'managed costs'. Items like advertising and sales promotion, often extending into many hundreds of thousands of pounds, are regarded as tactical weapons in the market place and may be varied widely to meet changing conditions. They tend to be treated separately by top management, both because of their size, and because flexibility needs to be retained to manoeuvre at short notice.

A dichotomy of interest appears between the departments. It is extremely difficult to establish the exact effect of advertising, and the budget is particularly vulnerable to reduction in hard times when there may well be a strong case for extending or at least maintaining effort. In the period 1972—5 television time costs rose over 50% whilst the average expenditure by advertisers rose only 2%. Thus either a major re-assessment of the value of the medium took place, or the advertising budget once again proved vulnerable to accountants in search of cost reductions. It is a clear responsibility of marketing to see that the optimum course of action is taken in these cases.

13.73 *Pricing*

Price planning and policy is usually the province of marketing. In setting prices the seller attempts to optimize his return. He has to juggle three balls in the air at the same time — volume, cost and price. They are however interdependent and an increase in price will usually, other things being equal, depress the volume sold to a degree dependent on the price elasticity of demand in the market segment concerned. The marketing man will attempt to evaluate this relationship with a number of techniques at his disposal. The accountant with an eye on cost and the margin of profit may take a different view of the best pricing strategy. It is therefore important that both departments work toward agreed objectives in pricing. Maximization of profit is only one goal; others may include maintaining a high level of employment, increasing or maintaining market share, or extending the life of the product range.

13.74 *Profit Planning*

The marketing concept not only implies the philosophy of customer-orientation, but also emphasizes the need to implement it with optimization of profit rather than maximization of sales volume. Marketeers need to be aware of the financial implications of their plans and understand how their decisions and strategies will enable them to realize their planned profit objectives. This responsibility involves the use of professional and financial techniques that require close co-operation with accounting staff to be used effectively. The calculation of discounted cash flows and return on capital employed are best carried out by specialists.

13.75 *Credit Policy and Control*

Credit control is one of the most sensitive areas in a company's relationship with its customer. Nevertheless prompt payment may be essential to a company's cash flow and resources may not be available to finance a customer's operation with trade credit to a major degree. Again the controller and the marketing man are on opposite sides of the fence. It is however seldom that a credit-worthy customer resents a fair and consistent credit policy. Both managers have a creative role to play. In some companies debt collection is a sales responsibility, and the marketing manager can sometimes make good promotional use of extended credit. The controller's function is to realize outstanding revenue as quickly as he can and maintain bad debts at an acceptable minimum. Both areas are important, and a high degree of mutual understanding and co-operation is desirable.

13.8 Inter-departmental Attitudes

There is a cultural gap between the marketing man and the accountant that needs to be recognized before really effective co-operation can take place between them.

A recent attitude study by the author suggests that the marketeer is often seen by the accountant as a bit of a rogue, lower on integrity than most other professionals, with suspect accuracy and an intellect towards the bottom of the range. On the other hand the marketing man tends to see the accountant as being rather formal and difficult to approach, whose professionalism sometimes seems designed to stifle rather than encourage enterprise and whose commercial practices are no better than they ought to be.

There would seem to be a clear cut need for closer liaison between the two functions. One approach that has received increasing acceptance in recent years has been the appointment of a 'marketing controller' or 'marketing cost accountant'. He should be qualified in financial accounting and control, but should ideally have practical sales and marketing experience. He should report to the Controller, but his role is to help marketing men take full advantage of the best and newest financial and accounting techniques in the interest of improved decisions and planning to insure maximum return on investment for the company as a whole. (See R.H.S. Wilson's book on *Management Controls and Marketing Planning* in this series.)

13.9 Research and Development

Sooner or later every product becomes obsolete, or becomes uneconomic for one reason or another, and is replaced. Competition, technological advance, changing life styles, and changing business needs contribute towards the process of secular decay.

Most products have a market life not unlike that of a living organism; they are born, they mature, and they decline. The emphasis on new products must not be allowed to distract attention from the current earners. The real skill in product management is to exploit them to the full, knowing when to extend their life with a judicious face-lift and when to withdraw, leaving production and marketing resources free to concentrate on range members with better prospects. This knowledge comes from regular monitoring of performance in the market place against pre-determined standards for such factors as sales volume, margins, distribution, and of course, competition. Sales revenue increases rapidly in the introduction, growth and maturity phases, slackens as the market becomes saturated, and declines as competitive new products are introduced, so that the product becomes obsolescent. Margins however develop out of phase with sales revenue, and may begin to decline before maturity is reached because more promotion is needed to maintain sales growth and price competition begins to erode them. It is obvious that if total profits are to continue to grow, a new product will be required to take over the running even before its predecessor is in decline. The life-cycle process is illustrated by Figure 13.3.

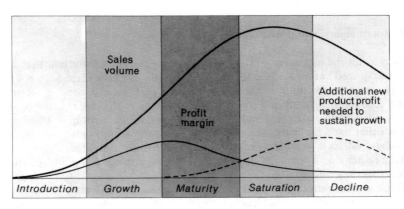

Figure 13.3   Product life-cycle
(Source: R.J. Williamson, *Marketing for Accountants and Managers*,
Heinemann, 1979)

Marketing's role in identifying the needs of the market is central to the corporate task of managing change and innovation, covering not only the development of new products but also the threat of obsolescence to the existing range and the opportunities for extending its life-cycle. Thus Drucker defines five innovation goals for a typical business:

1 New products and services to attain marketing objectives.
2 New products or services to meet technological changes that may make existing products obsolete.
3 Improvements to existing products for reasons covered in 1 and 2.
4 New processes and improvements to all processes either to meet marketing objectives or to offset obsolescence.

5 Innovations and improvements in all areas of activity to keep up with advances in knowledge and skill.

Although other disciplines are involved, marketing is basic to all. Even where the emphasis is on innovation in areas of knowledge, skill and technology, the identification of the need and the justification of the allocation of resources required should be related to market considerations.

Relationships between Marketing and Research & Development may often be sensitive. The scientist engaged on original research may resent the application of business disciplines to his area. It is certainly true that the company inherits the fruit of yesterday's research, and tomorrow's prosperity will depend on the work of R & D today, yet the company that gets its research effort out of proportion to its total business runs a major risk either because it is under-investing when change is inevitable or because it is spending large sums without prospect of ultimate profit.

It may also be that there is lack of balance between development on the company's range of products and application development carried out for customers. Careful cost control is needed to ensure that the company is not giving away expensive services unnecessarily. Marketing men often have difficulty in placing this possibility in its true perspective, particularly if a new sale is involved. Budgeting each activity separately however provides a good guide.

An R & D strategy is not confined to in-house activity:

original research can often be delegated to an industry body;
consultancies like PA Management Consultants PATSCENTRE in
Cambridge can develop a component or assembly from market brief
to manufacturing specification;
companies with complementary products can be acquired;
joint ventures may be organized with sympathetic partners.

The chosen method will depend on the company's overall research objectives. A desire to be the first in the field implies a relatively intensive R & D effort; the company that wants to be best rather than first will need a more modest budget with different priorities, whilst the company satisfied with 'me too' products may need very little R & D at all.

13.10 The Interface between Marketing and R & D

In most companies the R & D department is part of Production, although in rare cases it may be part of Marketing, or, as in some high technology companies, a division reporting in its own right to the Managing Director. Its form of organization will depend on the nature of the product and its markets.

Its work differs from that of regular production because it is project-based rather than ongoing, although some projects may enjoy very extended lives. A marketing executive should be a member of the project team and is likely to be product or brand manager for the product where that system of management applies. Where marketing aspects influence the projects' day-to-day progress, he may well be chairman of the team's regular work sessions.

It is impossible to overstate the potential value of active cross-fertilization between the two disciplines. The scientists of the Corning company had developed a new material to withstand high temperatures for use in the nose cones of missiles. By chance a marketing executive visiting the laboratory where development was under way pointed out that the glass would be a great new material for cooking ware. Corning still makes a few missile cones, but the market winner was the cooking ware.

13.11 New Product Development Committee

Many companies appoint a permanent New Product Development Committee whose functions are to review progress, make recommendations on development priorities and new projects, and to ensure that all departments of the organization who are likely to be involved are kept informed, and their efforts co-ordinated. Again there is a case for the chairman of the committee coming from marketing because he has a continuing interest in the project from the initial pilot market research through to the final launch and market promotion. It is indeed a characteristic of his function that he can bridge this range of activities. The Committee should represent all departments with a direct part to play, and will usually include Production, Cost Accounts, and Purchasing, as well as Design and R & D of course. Others, like Distribution or Legal may well maintain a watching brief.

13.12 R & D Strategy

Research is a creative activity that does not always yield its benefits according to plan. It is nevertheless amenable to management planning, financial control, and measurement of results within the structure of the corporate plan. Thus an old family company had a major share of the world's market for fine artists oil colours. No stone was left unturned in developing the range and pigments were developed from an extremely wide selection of esoteric materials. Yet market studies showed that the artists' sector represented a small and declining part of the market, and that major growth lay in oil colours for students and amateurs at a lower price level. The company's research effort was directed almost exclusively towards original research into pigments, and it took a major effort to turn it towards products that had hitherto been regarded as cheap and nasty.

The balance between pure research and the development of commercial applications is a prime consideration in every R & D strategy. Imbalance can again be costly, both in cash cost and market opportunity cost. Thus when Sir Arnold Weinstock took over GEC's famous Hirst Lighting Laboratories he found it necessary to cut back original research in favour of commercial and applications development.

A research centre should be a highly flexible industrial resource, but it is often a problem to keep a unit that is tuned to medium and long-term objectives responsive to the demands and pressures of the industry in which the company is operating. It is a question of effective management control without stifling innovation.

At ICI's Corporate Laboratory near Runcorn strenuous efforts are made to prevent R & D becoming isolated from real business problems. One way is through 'relevance groups' — small groups of divisional directors set up as avuncular critics of some portion of the research programme. Their function is to dissuade the unit from chasing lines of research felt to be more suitable for one of the other divisions, or perhaps projects where only a non-viable share of the market would be available. Another means is to encourage top management to visit regularly. The main board directors for research and engineering are frequent visitors, and divisional deputy chairmen and engineering directors make a point of keeping in touch.

13.13 New Product Development

In spite of the mystique and excitement that surrounds this topic in marketing circles, it is now accepted that the inevitable risk associated with new products can be minimized by a systematic planning process based on an established set of proven principles. Many of the dangers and pitfalls are self-inflicted and can be avoided by a rational, step-by-step approach.

Nevertheless entrepreneurial risk cannot be eliminated, and competitors will go to great lengths to prevent the preemption of their markets. There are probably more uncontrollable elements in new-product introductions than in any other aspect of marketing, and the ability to change direction quickly is of the essence.

James Neill, the Sheffield-based hand-tool group, had developed a world-first electronic digital micrometer, planned to revolutionize the traditional manual micrometer market. Development and worldwide market testing had proceeded in 1975 and 1976, and a roll-out launch was envisaged in the UK in mid-1977. Then in early 1977 technical intelligence spotted a similar programme being carried out in the US, patently to the same time scale. James Neill girded up its loins, and both products, the British Micro 2000 and the American Q Mike were launched together at Inspex 77 in March.

The following six-stage pattern represents the basic management process of new product development, providing manageable stages for planning and control.

Stage 1 Exploration

The search for product ideas to meet company objectives starts with a broad-based exercise in which virtually anybody can participate. Salesmen, customers, production staff and senior management should be regular contributors. The first task, however, is to determine the product fields that are of primary interest, taking into account the company's principal resources and external opportunities, such as expanding markets or technological breakthroughs. An original idea is a delicate plant that needs to be nurtured with care, and there is no standard procedure for producing it; but systematic efforts can be made to collect ideas, and comprehensive idea-collection procedures can be valuable. Planned idea generation is less widely accepted, but excellent results have been achieved with techniques like 'brainstorming', which minimize distractions from current problems and expose creative personnel to idea-generating facts. 'Gap analysis' is a technique that identifies gaps in the market where customer demand is not satisfied by existing products and where opportunities for a new entrant may exist.

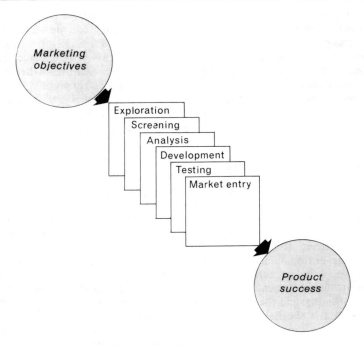

Figure 13.4   Stages of new-product development
(Source: R.J. Williamson, *Marketing for Accountants and Managers*,
Heinemann, 1979)

Stage 2 Screening

Since a productive brainstorming session can produce over 100 ideas, the purpose
of screening is to reduce them to manageable numbers and expand each into a full
product concept. An objective method of comparison and evaluation is needed,
because managers tend to have the same feelings towards their idea that a mother
hen has towards day-old chicks. All ideas must, however, be treated seriously and
be seen to have been fairly considered. One effective approach is to design a
checklist of important features which can easily be converted into a system of
evaluation ratings. The example in Table 13.3 is used by a large manufacturing
company with general engineering capacity. The idea is awarded marks out of
ten for each feature, and it soon becomes apparent whether it should be progressed
or not although a marginal idea should always be given the benefit of the doubt at
this stage. In the case of this company a potential revenue of £1 million plus within
3 years merits 10 marks, and there are marking guide scales for each feature. The
list itself is not statistically significant, and no detailed costing has been done at this
stage, but a general picture of the idea's potential value to the company has been
provided.

Table 13.3

Feature	Rating
Sales volume potential	6
Element of risk	3
Competition	4
Scale of promotion	7
Technical opportunity	3
Use of existing capacity	10
Size of investment	4
Relation to current range	7
Effect on present products	6
Compatibility with objectives	8
General rating	6

Stage 3 Business Analysis

Very little cost has been incurred so far, but perhaps three quarters of the ideas originally submitted have been eliminated or amalgamated into other projects. The aim now is to reduce the proposed idea to a specific business proposition in terms of time, costs, manpower, profits, and benefits.

It is necessary to determine the characteristics of the market and the detailed specification of product features and performance. It will not be possible to be specific in every respect, and it is good practice to develop a number of planning cases, representing perhaps the favoured plan, with best and worst alternatives showing 10–20% variances on either side of it. At this stage experimental market and technical research should be carried out, and a timetable should be drafted, with cost estimates for each successive stage. A formal product proposal is also common at this point.

Stage 4 Development

During this stage the concept becomes an actual product, which will be producable, demonstrable, and saleable. A product team representing all aspects of the business concerned should be nominated, and responsibilities defined and allocated. The product proposal needs to be exploded into as many sub-projects as are necessary, and progress procedures established varying from full networks in complicated cases to simple bar charts in less intricate ones. The first models are built to the specifiations developed in laymen's terms by the marketing manager from his field research. Market studies will continue as a basis for improving the product's saleability, and, after appropriate laboratory evaluation, it will be released for testing.

Stage 5 Testing and Decision-making

The commercial experiments necessary to confirm the earlier business judgements can now be carried out. Enthusiasm and optimism verging on euphoria are not uncommon at this stage and the need for careful and objective market testing cannot be overstated, bearing in mind any security precautions. Above all it is essential to establish before the tests begin what results will justify further investment and what will not. A simple algorithm can demonstrate this process. Failure against one test criterion does not justify terminating an otherwise successful programme, but the reasons need to be understood before progressing to the next step. Figure 13.5 assesses the test results achieved by a new male hairdressing. The procedure ensures that significant aspects are not overlooked.

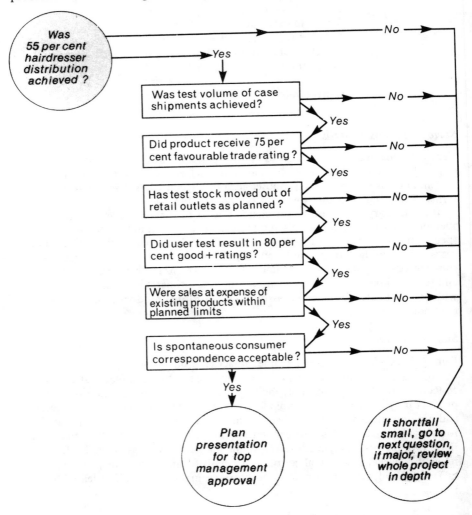

Figure 13.5 Procedure for assessing test results
(Source: R.J. Williamson, *Marketing for Accountants and Managers*,
Heinemann, 1979)

Market-testing includes usage tests by potential customers in real-life conditions as well as market place assessments. The following programme carried out by an international food group illustrates the length and complexity of this process:

March Year 1	Concept-testing with a series of group discussions throughout the country.
March Year 1	Small-scale product tests, using imported product presented 'blind', i.e. in unidentified packs.
June Year 1	An attitude survey among purchasers, following a demonstration in a small number of outlets.
March Year 2	Test marketing in a regional marketing area with local press and TV advertising.
March–October Year 2	Retail audits in the test-marketing area.
May/June/October Year 2	Product-awareness studies in retail stores and consumers' homes.
June Year 2	Special audits to identify impact on manufacturer's other products.
January/September Year 3	Regional rollout, with studies of the pattern of the introduction in each new area.
September Year 3	Pack-size survey to assess prospects of two new smaller packs.

The best conceived and run test programme in the world still leaves management with one of its most important functions, the making of the decision on whether to go to market or not. In recent years a great deal of work has been applied to the development of decision theory, mainly as an adjunct to operational research. These systems can become very complex if used to trace and evaluate the impact of the possible decisions in any given situation: a relatively simple case, with two levels of production capacity, three price policies, three sales forecasts, two alternative promotion policies, and three product variations has already generated 108 different possible developments. Usually a computer is needed to trace through all the possible options.

Statistical decision theory (sometimes referred to as Bayesian decision theory) may also require a computer to reach the ultimate decision, but may offer the manager confined to manual techniques some guidance on the way. He needs to identify the decision alternatives that face him, and distinguish the key uncertainties associated with each, before estimating the probability of each outcome, by calculating the expected value of each decision. His final step is to choose the decision with the highest expected value.

The estimates of probability are based on the judgements of the manager and his colleagues. For each decision alternative they assign the probability of a fair, poor, or good outcome by allocating a total of 10 points between them. The profit from each alternative is then calculated with the use of conventional costing and sales forecasting techniques, and the expected value is this profit figure factored by the allocated probability rating.

A company considering the launch of a new product is faced by a market situation that may develop in a number of ways. It regards the probability of a poor outcome in which its best choice of action would be not to proceed as 0.4. On the other hand a fair outcome producing a profit of £1.0 million is seen as a 0.5

probability and would justify the launch. A very good outcome yielding a profit of £4.0 million is only given a probability of 0.1, however. The expected value of profits is calculated in Table 13.4.

Table 13.4

Outcome	Probability of outcome	Best choice given outcome	Profit (£m)	Expected Value (£m)
Poor	0.4	No-go	0.0	0.0
Fair	0.5	Go	1.0	0.5
Good	0.1	Go	4.0	0.4
	1.0			0.9

The manager still has to decide whether the expected value of £0.9 million does justify the launch, but he now has a numerical criterion to aid him.

Stage 6 Market Entry

The successful product is now ready for launching into full-scale production and sale. Co-ordinated production and selling programmes come into effect, and results are carefully monitored with an eye to removing 'bugs' and introducing improvements. There is no definitive pattern for a successful new product. A Nielsen study has however, identified some of the critical factors for a new grocery product, and has analysed eight successful 'million pound' new products in the light of them:

1 All enjoyed a constant basic demand; sold regardless of general economic conditions; reinforced the present product line.
2 Seven were a definite improvement over existing products; enjoyed a wide range of customers; had access to prime markets via their existing channels.
3 Six expected at least a moderate increase in customers; had promotable features that compared favourably with competition.

13.14 Conclusion

This chapter has emphasized Marketing's central and co-ordinating role in an integrated organization. This is not to belittle its functional tasks and activities. Our guinea-pig company, Consumer and Electrical, recognize this distinction and provide for it in their formal organization. The Marketing Director sits on the main Board with group-wide responsibilities. This position is necessary if he is to play his full part at corporate level; a non-Board Marketing Manager would be unable to obtain agreement to group-wide policies that affected other departments, and might find himself restricted to the provision of marketing services.

At group level, C & E's Marketing Director is supported by a small group of specialists consisting of Marketing Information, Advertising, and Sales Promotion managers, each with a threefold role. They contribute to corporate planning; they offer advice to the divisions as required; and they provide a specialist service. In this way the group can employ a better calibre of management than any of the divisions could alone afford, but care is taken not to dilute the responsibility of the Divisional General Managers who, at least in theory, have a free hand in using or not using the services available.

Each division has a marketing organization appropriate to its needs. C & E (Distribution) has its own industrial and retail sales forces with a sales manager in charge of each. It also has a Marketing Manager, with three Brand Managers, each responsible for one range of products. They report on a line basis to the General Manager, but have functional responsibility to the Marketing Director. C & E (Production) sell most of their volume to Distribution, but about 30% goes outside for incorporation in other equipment. They therefore employ a single Sales Executive for these sales, otherwise depending on Group for marketing services. C & E (International) have three Marketing Managers with responsibility for groups of overseas countries. They undertake selling trips themselves, and make extensive use of group services when producing their plans.

Two other aspects of C & E's marketing organization are worthy of note. A Marketing Accountant is attached to the Marketing Director with the tasks of keeping an eye on the financial implications of marketing proposals and giving assistance to marketing management in constructing its plans. A permanent New Product Committee sits at monthly intervals for each group of products, under the chairmanship of a brand or marketing manager, to review progress and to recommend future action.

14. *Managing Change*

The common element running through the work of all managers is that they are responsible for 'getting things done through other people', and the function of the business organization is to provide an environment in which they can do this effectively in the pursuit of its corporate objectives.

A manager running a business works on at least two timescales; he is vitally concerned with the pressures of day-to-day operations, but he must also plan for the medium- and long-term future if his organization is to survive and prosper. Most managers find difficulty in providing time for the vital business of looking ahead. They tend to fail 'to see the wood for the trees' because they are unable to step back from the immediate present to take a broader view. This can be very dangerous because it is a characteristic of business that nothing stops still; a company is either growing or contracting and there is no equilibrium point at which it can rest on its laurels. New threats and opportunities are constantly emerging.

The manager cannot avoid change, but he is far from being a passive bystander, although the extent to which he can influence conditions in the market-place will depend on his size and general market strength. Monitoring change and planning to exploit developments as they occur is probably his most important single function. Changing conditions mean revised objectives, new methods and possibly modifications to the organization. Unfortunately change is seldom a smooth-flowing process. A new technology may render a whole industry obsolescent at a stroke.

Most people will say that they are in favour of 'Progress' in principle, but in practice many are fearful of changes they do not really understand and would truthfully prefer a quiet life. Change is uncomfortable and the threats always appear greater than the opportunities to the majority. At the beginning of the eighties, technological advance has outstripped the ability of management to harness it for the good of mankind. The main problems are human and organizational. At a pinch the manager can always buy the latest technology, but he cannot buy a contented workforce and a productive organization. These problems are often very complex and may appear intractable. We still know relatively little about the behaviour of a human being at his place of work. It is over a decade since the perfection of electronic typesetting for newspapers. The technology is available for a journalist to telephone in his story and for it to be set electronically in one process. Fleet Street however is still edging painfully towards the systems and procedures that will make this method acceptable to its staff.

This is not the blind destructiveness of the English Luddites or the French 'saboteurs'. It is not pre-evident that every new technology should be implemented to its final degree. Technology has to advance in line with human society's ability to digest and live with it. The manager only benefits from a

244

technological cost saving if other elements do not frustrate him. The original introduction of the computer brought neither the savings nor the unemployment widely
forecast, often involving a net increase in staff. The need for a comprehensive
feasibility study before implementation began was seldom realized.

The keynote should therefore be 'appropriate' rather than 'maximum' technology, whatever may be available and affordable. The capital-intensive technologies
of the West are not necessarily sensible for countries where capital is scarce, labour
cheap, but technical management at a premium, for example. Again there are
human and political difficulties in this approach; a third world country might well
see it as a device for the rich countries to dispose of outdated technologies to the
poor at a profit. Even in a major company management may have difficulty in
accepting that the latest and most sophisticated equipment is not necessarily the
best for them.

But what are the changes that are likely to take place in the next ten years, and
what will their impact be on business? They fall into three broad categories:
technological, socio-economic, and international.

14.1 Technology

14.11 *In Production*

The micro-chip revolution has been described as doing for the twenty-first century
what James Watt did for the nineteenth. These silicon micro-circuits are often
capable of processing millions of pieces of information per second, and have an
extremely wide range of potential applications, as is shown in Figure 14.1.

Automation of production processes will be an important application for
micro-chips. The following are examples of what can be done:

numerically controlled machine tools guarantee the planned degree of accuracy;
computerized scheduling of changes in the raw materials needed reduces the
possibility of stock-outs;
computer-aided design (CAD) ensures *inter alia* that a new design is compatible
with existing tools.

Microprocessors have also enabled robots (i.e. programmable automatoms) to
be developed. These can now help to make goods more cheaply than can conventional machines operated by human workers. The vast majority of today's robots,
numbering 6,000–7,000 worldwide are used for simple 'pick and place' tasks like
feeding pieces to a lathe for machining. But others do slightly more complex jobs
such as cutting metal, spraying paint or welding. The next step will be to use
robots for assembling complicated products like car gearboxes or washing machines.

Production management is notoriously slow to recognize the benefits of new
techniques and the acceptance of numerically controlled machine tools has been
very slow. There has been a traditional resistance to all forms of automation from
organized labour. Pioneering users of robots like Volvo in Sweden however have
found that it has not had to make workers redundant because of automation. The
real threat of unemployment may not come from replacing workers doing boring
repetitive jobs with robots but from failure to compete at home and abroad in

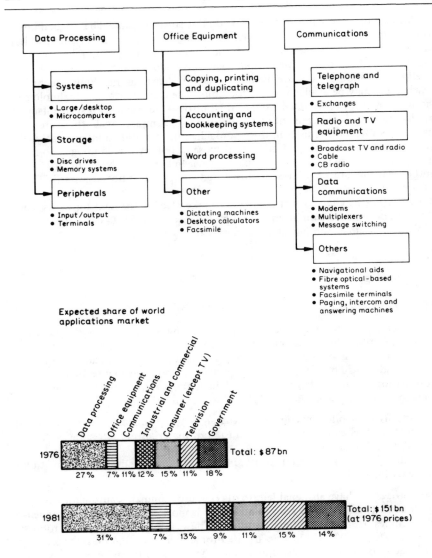

Figure 14.1　Applications for Microprocessors
(based on Booz, Allen & Hamilton, extraction from public data)

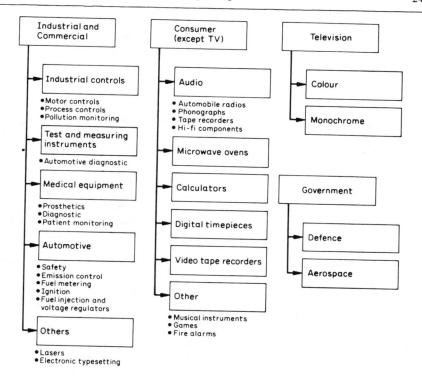

Figure 14.1 (continued)

terms of price and quality. This however implies that in addition to harnessing microprocessors in production, new ranges of products that employ microprocessors will be required, representing another challenge to management.

14.12 *The Office of the Future*

New electronic technology is also giving rapid growth and diversity to the range of office equipment available. The boundaries between the old familiar products are breaking down as mechanical parts begin to be replaced by electronic circuits. *The Financial Times* put it like this:

'Thus computers are starting to control telecommunications networks at the same time as telecommunications become an integral part of computing. Electrostatic copiers, which a few years ago appeared to be straightforward rivals to stencil duplicators, are now being linked to them. Copying machines are being plugged into telephone lines. Typewriters, television displays, computers and tape recorders are forming a somewhat mysterious alliance under the term "word processor". Then it turns out that word processors may not after all be machines to make typing more efficient, but the start of a communications revolution which will challenge the familiar Telex and surface mail at the same time.'

Word processors are one of the most important but least understood of the new office machines. Initially they have been presented as an advance on the electric typewriter, plugged in to a magnetic memory. The memory records what has been typed and can be played back to produce an additional copy or extra draft. There is also a correcting or editing facility that employs a video screen to enable the typist to see what she is doing. The next generation of word processor is likely to be very like a computer terminal or perhaps a computer on its own. In addition to typing documents and letters, they may well be able to extract information from the company's main computer and use it to compose letters and perform calculations. Above all they could be able to communicate with similar machines across telephone lines.

Perhaps the central part of the office of the future will be the private branch telephone exchange (PABX) that may be computer controlled and will convert all speech signals into computer-like pulses or data streams. The exchange will not only be a communications centre, but may also have extra computing power located within it. Word processors may be linked together through the exchange into a single communicating network.

These developments face management with a host of problems, not least the selection of which systems to employ. The plethora of data available will also place new strains on the manager. With instant data from his desk terminal, there will be added emphasis on imaginative planning and closer co-operation with production and other departments. The virtue of a computer is that it can do in seconds or minutes what man takes weeks or months to accomplish, and managers are gradually learning to use computers to help them manage more effectively rather than as simple processors of data. Yet it is clear that the new systems will call for new forms of business organization and new attitudes from employees. A video desk terminal combined with a telephone suggests the opportunity for some staff to work from their homes rather than in centralized offices.

A step in this direction is the market trial that GUS, one of the largest mail order companies, is carrying out on the Post Office's Prestel system. Prestel sets, accommodating the company's catalogue reference code, have been installed in the homes of a panel of selected agents, putting them in effect on line to the computer. Confirmation orders or notification that a requested item is out of stock will be instantaneous.

14.2 Socio-Economic

Social and economic factors will continue to make a deep impression on business. The speed of change will be influenced particularly by the interventionalist or non-interventionalist posture of the government in power and its success in controlling the combination of low investment, high inflation and pay rises in excess of productivity increases that has become known as the 'British disease' but is now endemic in many other countries as well.

Changes in fiscal policies and in provisions for social security can radically affect the business climate. Rewards for risk-taking and the need to ensure that work is more attractive than idleness are at the root of business motivation. Thus Volvo's famous experiment in 'group production' made production line assembly work more interesting, but did not succeed in reducing absenteeism. High Swedish pay and social security still kept workers in bed on Mondays.

The strength of trade unions in relation to management, their political orientation, and willingness to accept change are other critical factors. The length of the working week, the place of women in commerce and industry, and the organization of work are likely to change. The threat of long-term unemployment at unacceptably high levels will also generate organizational changes, although recent efforts at job creation and work sharing have been only partially successful. The changing age composition of society will also make an impact on employment as well as consumption.

New techniques, new machines, and new styles of management require new skills and sometimes new categories of staff that may not be easy to recruit. They also generate demand for different facilities and accommodation. The development of office design illustrates thus. The open plan office with rows of desks arranged in strict rectangular order was developed under the influence of work study techniques in the early years of the century to accommodate an army of desks carrying out innumerable small transactions manually. Its objective was the efficient use of masses of low level clerical skills, and banking and insurance contained many examples. By the 1960s a new kind of office worker had emerged. The computer programmer for example was below management status but needed privacy as well as contact and required access to manuals and references. To meet his needs, screen based furniture was developed with separation between work places achieved by linked screens, perhaps attached to the desks themselves, which also served to hang reference material.

During the 1980s employees may be expected to take a progressively greater share in the running of their organizations. The German model of two-tiers boards, each including worker representatives, is the most widely accepted pattern. A series of papers published by the Institute of Chartered Secretaries and

Administrators in 1979 considered other areas of corporate governance and accountability where change may be expected. These included:

the aims and objectives of corporate bodies;
the function of ownership and the role of institutional shareholders;
the relationship between public companies and their shareholders;
the structure of corporate boards;
the nature of board accountability.

It is clear that business organization will look very different at the end of the next decade. In Britain a major new Companies Act is overdue and in many countries impending product liability legislation will alter the relationship of companies with their customers.

The major economic issue is of course energy. The pricing policies of the Opec nations since 1974—5 and the failure to re-cycle the resulting funds in fruitful ways have dampened the economic climate of the rest of the world. Energy management has emerged as a discipline in its own right, and may well become more important, particularly in the USA where the high price of imported fuel has contributed to the continuing weakness of the dollar.

14.3 International

Two trends should be recognized in the international sphere:

(a) *The European Economic Community*
The influence and power of the EEC is likely to grow, and Britain is unlikely to withdraw. British business will come to regard Europe as increasingly its major area of operation. The reduction of trade barriers and restrictions could well provide a real common market by the mid-1980s, and companies that do not adjust will find the strength of foreign competition increased without the counter-benefit of access to major new markets. The transition period will be a painful one, but may provide the stimulus that the country needs to strengthen its ability to compete. Membership of one of the world's most powerful trading blocs will also enhance national influence in dealings with the rest of the world.

(b) *China*
The emergence of China as an international trading nation may be expected in the 1980s. Its sheer size will present both threats and opportunities, and could well change the balance of expert effort in many cases, with the need for changes in attitudes and organizations.

14.4 Conclusion

This book has examined and discussed current principles and methods relating to the major aspects of business organization today. These however are not stable and immutable; rather they are dynamic and are constantly changing. The marketing manager knows that if he does not keep his product up-to-date it will soon decline;

a recent survey of the post-war performance of thirty-four brand leaders in consumer goods markets shows that the two-thirds that retained their leadership all made major product and packaging improvements not once but many times over the fifteen-year period monitored. The same is true of business organizations, methods, systems, and procedures. A problem is answered not once but many times as internal and external conditions change.

Perhaps the last word should go to our imaginary guinea-pig company, Consumer and Electrical, who have adopted a sensibly practical approach throughout.

Although not a high technology group C & E have some manufacturing interests and are also deeply involved with the general public. The Chairman says that he does not like surprises and that his job is to minimize risk. Some of his younger executives feel that this sounds unenterprising but do not question the common-sense of the approach.

The process of reacting to change is continuous, and is an integral part of each manager's day-to-day thinking. The annual corporate planning process starts with a formal audit of the group's current situation and those of its constituent divisions, with appraisal of their strengths and weaknesses and the threats and opportunities facing them. C & E also carry out monthly retail audits for their main consumer products and quarterly surveys to identify changes in usage patterns, whilst the sales force is trained to report other market developments promptly.

On the production side, the Engineering Manager has the responsibility defined in his Job Specification of keeping in touch with machinery developments and reporting any that are significant. This aspect is less important however than on the materials and methods side. A Value Analysis section meets regularly and there is a small but permanent Work Study Unit. Machinery purchases are infrequent, but the Investment Appraisal procedure requires an analysis of other options available and a technological forecast of expected industry development in the next five years.

Consumer and Electrical do not own their own computer, having postponed the purchase until their needs after the re-organization were clear. Instead they use a bureau and are currently well satisfied. The payrolls and customer invoicing of all three divisions are computerized; C & E (Distribution) have their finished goods stocks on the computer; and C & E (Manufacturing) have a fully integrated Management Information System covering costs and productivity ratios as well. It has taken longer than expected to get the bugs out of this system but it seems certain the group will buy its own mainframe in due course. A word processor is not expected to be justified in the near future. The Board is conscious that a high proportion of its operating costs lie in clerical and administrative systems and procedures and is experimenting with a micro-fiche filing system and dictating machines for directors and outside managers. Management makes a positive effort to keep abreast of developments in the office by keeping in touch with computer manufacturers and office product suppliers, by subscribing to the trade and professional press, and by membership of appropriate professional societies.

Finally, C & E watch for changes within the ranks of their own staff. Communication should be a two-way process, and through its formal channels of industrial relations and its less formal Staff Association, it tries to keep in touch with changes in the attitudes of its employees. As the Chairman says, 'a loyal, contented, and motivated staff is at least two-thirds of the battle nowadays'.

Revision Exercises

Chapter 1 Principles of Organizations

1 Give a brief definition of the following organizational terms:

 (a) Patterns of Leadership
 (b) Functional Authority
 (c) Decentralization

2 The term Unity of Command means that each subordinate should be accountable to only one superior. Describe *two* situations where this principle might reasonably be violated by a company.
3 Describe the contribution made to Management Theory by F.W. Taylor.
4 Explain the purpose of an Organization Chart, using as an example that of a company with which you are familiar. What are the advantages and disadvantages of Organization Charts?
5 What is meant by the expression 'Informal Organization'? Indicate in what ways its existence may contribute towards, or inhibit, the achievement of organizational objectives.
6 The concept of line and staff organization is in common use, especially in large organizations. Explain the meaning of the term, using a typical line and staff example. What potential difficulties could such a system produce?
7 Explain the meaning of the term 'Organization Development'. What factors have led to the increasing importance of this technique?
8 Explain the meaning of the term, 'Functional Organization'. What are its main advantages and disadvantages as an organizational system?
9 What are the symptoms of a malfunctioning organization?
10 What is the technique of Organization Development (OD) and what are its commonest uses?

Chapter 2 Functions of Management

1 What are the advantages of the Committee, as a form of Management? Illustrate your answer by reference to the work of a typical committee to be found in an industrial organization.
2 What are the functions of a manager, and do you agree with Henri Fayol's list?
3 Distinguish between a 'professional man' and a manager.
4 What are the three forms of authority that a manager may employ in his work?

5   How far is it true to say that a manager is born, not made?
6   What is delegation, and what conditions are necessary for delegation to be successful?
7   'MBO is a results-oriented approach to management'. What part does the average middle manager play in this technique?
8   How important is leadership to the manager?
9   Is it possible to improve a manager's performance? Outline some of the methods in current use.
10 'The ability to make decisions is one test of a good manager.' Discuss with reference to three different sorts of decision that the manager may have to make.

Chapter 3   Structure of Business

1   How far do you consider the operations of Multinational corporations are dangerous to the countries in which they operate? In what respects do you think their activities should be subject to control?
2   What differences in structure would you expect to find between:

   (a)   a company manufacturing and selling chemical plant world-wide
   (b)   a company manufacturing and distributing fast-moving domestic appliances in its home market
   (c)   a company operating a chain of retail supermarkets?

3   Explain the meaning of the term 'vertical integration' and indicate the advantages to a company of such a policy.
4   What motives lead some companies to merge with, or take over, others and what kind of problems may be the result of such combinations?
5   The activities of Multinational Companies are being regarded with increasing concern by the governments of many countries. What aspects of multinational business concern the government of your country? (State country to which you refer.)
6   Your company is considering moving part of its production into a new factory in a Government Development Area. State the arguments in favour of such a move and indicate some of the difficulties which might arise.
7   What are the main advantages and disadvantages in the use of Committees in the management of a business organization? Indicate briefly the function of any one committee commonly found in such an organization.
8   Outline the problems a small firm might have in competing with a very large company. What particular advantages might the small firm have in such a situation?
9   Compare and contrast *any two* of the following types of business structure, under major headings of (a) Formation, (b) Ownership and Control, (c) Membership, and (d) Advantages and Disadvantages:

   1 Sole Trader   2 Partnership
   3 Public Limited Company   4 Co-operative

10 Many companies achieve growth as a result of a deliberate policy of acquisition and merger. What are the advantages and disadvantages of such a policy?

Chapter 4   Channels of Communication

1   Communication is regarded as an essential ingredient of successful management. Describe the main areas of internal communication to which management should devote their attention.

2   Why are good communications crucial to organization structure design?

3   What channels or flows of communications are available to the manager?

4   Give some examples of non-verbal communication, and explain why a manager will ignore them at his peril.

5   Outline the major obstacles to effective communication, and suggest how the manager may counteract them.

6   What are the symptoms of inadequate communications in a company?

7   Committees are frequently used in organizations to serve particular purposes. What are the main advantages and disadvantages of committees?

8   Good internal communications are essential if a business is to function effectively. Describe the main methods and media which a company might use in order to achieve this.

9   How can the production of Employee Financial Reports effect the working environment in a company?

10   What is a Communications Audit? Why might a company decide to commission such an audit?

Chapter 5   Planning and Control

1   The basic elements of a Manager's job have been described as Planning, Organizing, Controlling, Co-ordinating and Commanding. Explain the role of a Marketing Manager in relation to these elements.

2   Many companies have adopted the system of Management by Objectives; what does this mean and how is it applied in a Marketing Department?

3   Planning is an important management function. Explain the main steps in the planning process.

4   What is the Situation Audit, and what is its role in the planning process?

5   Which areas should be the subject of corporate objectives, and what distinguishes a good objective from a bad one?

6   What information should be included in the Master Plan?

7   What is Budgetary Control, and how does its control element work?

8   Why is it necessary for companies to establish and periodically review their objectives? What objectives should a business aim to achieve?

9   In defining the basic principles of Management, text books often list Planning and Control as two separate and distinct functions. How far can they be regarded as independent of one another?

10   Many companies attempt to forecast sales many years into the future. Why do they do this, and what possible dangers may result?

Chapter 6 Business and the Law

1 'The policy of the Board of Directors of a Limited Company should be concerned primarily with earning the maximum profit for the shareholders.' How far do you think this advice is true in the present day?

2 What is a Public Limited Liability Company? What are the advantages and disadvantages of this form of business organization?

3 Contrast the outlook of the EEC, as laid down by the Treaty of Rome, on Monopoly and Fair Competition, with that revealed by the comparative legislation of the USA.

4 Describe the typical areas of business activity which would be the subject for decision by the Board of Directors.

5 In what ways has the advertising industry been affected by State intervention in the last five years?

6 How is a Limited Company 'wound up'?

7 Give a brief summary of Agency Law in the UK or any other country with which you are familiar.

8 What are the legal remedies available when one party breaks a contract?

9 Describe the main ways in which the Law protects consumers from unfair business practices.

10 Outline the essential differences between the attitude of the EEC towards Monopoly and Restrictive Trade Practices, and that of the USA or any other named country outside the EEC, with which you are familiar.

Chapter 7 Financial Management

1 What is meant in a company balance sheet by:

(a) the firm's equity;
(b) an issue of preference shares;
(c) debenture stock?

2 What is meant by the term 'Liquidity' in connection with a business? What steps can Management take to reduce the likelihood of problems arising in this connection?

3 Explain briefly the meaning of any three of the following terms:

(a) Working capital
(b) Discounted Cash Flow
(c) Break-even Point
(d) Semi-variable cost
(e) Prime Cost

4 What is meant by Marginal Costing? What advantages does it have over the conventional methods of arriving at product costs?

5 A number of Accounting Ratios are commonly used in measuring the efficiency with which a company's resources are managed. Describe any five of these ratios, indicating how they are applied.

6 The continuing increases in the costs of labour, materials and services make

cost reduction an important objective for management. Suggest the important areas, in a retailing or manufacturing business, where cost reduction measures could usefully be applied, indicating briefly, in each area, the ways in which cost reductions might be achieved.

7   Explain briefly what is meant by the following terms:

Marginal Costing   Flexible Budget
Standard Costs   Variance Analysis
Fixed Costs   Break-even Chart

8   Explain the purpose and application of any *six* of the commonly used financial ratios relating to the operation of a business.

9   Many companies use a system of Standard Costing to eliminate the need for frequent cost revisions. Explain briefly how the system works and indicate in what ways the marketing department of a manufacturing company might benefit from its adoption.

10 Write a brief explanatory note in relation to any *three* of the following financial terms:

Absorption costing   Contribution
Marginal costing   Break-even analysis

Chapter 8   Sources of Funds

1   Explain what is meant by Long-term, Medium-term and Short-term Capital and outline the normal means by which a business would raise these categories of finance.

2   'A market for second-hand securities'. Is this an adequate description of the functions of the Stock Exchange?

3   Outline the main responsibilities that are usually allocated to the Finance Director.

4   What are 'internally generated funds', and why are they the prime sources of finance for investment in the UK?

5   What are the main categories of external funds available to companies? Write short notes on the advantages and disadvantages of any three.

6   Outline the main ways of issuing equity capital.

7   What part do the 'institutions' play in financing companies and to what extent do they take a direct part in the management of companies in which they invest?

8   What is 'venture capital', and why is it normally provided by specialist institutions?

9   What steps have successive UK governments taken to release funds for investment?

10 What services do London merchant banks normally provide?

Chapter 9 Sourcing and Materials Management

1 Nowadays many companies consolidate Purchasing, Stores, and Inventory Control under the functional authority of a Materials Controller. What are the advantages of such an organizational change, and what problem areas might be encountered?

2 Stock Control is becoming increasingly important as an area for management's attention. How can it increase the efficiency of:

(a) The Production Department
(b) The Purchasing Department, and
(c) The Finance Department?

3 The scope of the activities of the Purchasing Department may vary from company to company, but there are a number of common activities which are essential. Describe these vital activities.

4 Explain the meaning of the term Value Analysis. What is the importance of this technique to the Marketing Department of a company?

5 Outline the essential elements of an Inventory Control system.

6 What are the main objectives of efficient purchasing? To what extent is it desirable or necessary that the purchasing activity should be carried out by a separate department?

7 Why is it necessary for companies to hold stocks of finished goods or materials? What are the principal factors which determine the cost to a company of holding stock?

8 Describe a typical paperwork system, covering the purchase of required material, from the request from the originating department to the payment of the supplier's invoice.

9 Give a brief account of the part that computers can play in Materials Management.

10 What opportunities may there be for the marketing manager in the area of Materials Managenent?

Chapter 10 Production Management

1 Standardization and Simplification are terms frequently encountered in Manufacturing. What do you understand by them and what is their importance in securing greater industrial efficiency?

2 Contrast the tasks involved in Production Planning prior to the first operation in:

(a) a jobbing shop manufacturing to order its own specially designed products;
(b) a batch production shop manufacturing a range of standard products for stock and sale;
(c) a flow production shop manufacturing a few varieties of a standard product for stock and sale.

3 There are many ways by which productivity or industrial efficiency may be

increased. Review briefly the main methods.

4   In relation to manufacturing activities, write a brief explanatory note on any *three* of the following:

> Batch Production;
> Automation;
> Method Study and Work Measurement;
> Standardization.

5   Deviations from the Sales Forecast in terms of either the total quantity or the mix of products sold, can have a significant effect on the efficiency of the Production Department. Explain why this is so.

6   Describe the technique of Value Analysis. Explain how it is applied and its objectives.

7   What is the significance of the adoption by a manufacturing company of standardization to:

(a)   the Marketing Department, and
(b)   the customer?

8   Describe the essential features of a system of Production Planning and Control.

9   Quality Control is an activity which has been described as 'adding additional cost to a product without adding value or benefit to the purchaser'. How far do you think this statement is true?

10   Work Study can be divided into two distinct functions, Method Study and Work Measurement. Describe what is involved in each of these functions.

Chapter 11   Management of Human Resources

1   A number of companies make use of the services of consultants in selecting candidates for senior posts. Discuss the merits and demerits of this practice,

(a)   for the company concerned, and
(b)   for those seeking employment.

2   Describe the main areas that you think are embraced by a company's Personnel Policy.

3   What is meant by the term Job Enrichment (sometimes also called Job Enlargement) and why are many companies now concerned with its practice? Give a brief example of Job Enrichment to illustrate your answer.

4   In what ways can the Personnel Department be particularly useful to the Marketing Department?

5   Many companies provide an induction training course for their new employees. What subjects do you consider should be covered in such a course?

6   Discuss the reasons which induce a company to undertake programmes of staff training and development and show how job evaluation and staff appraisal techniques can contribute to these programmes.

7   It has been said that a worker's performance will tend to lie somewhere between the minimum necessary to ensure that he holds his job, and the

maximum effort of which he is capable. What methods might a company adopt to induce the worker to select a position towards the upper limit of his discretionary performance?

8 What are the main features of a Job Grading system? Indicate the factors that you would consider essential in any system for appraising the performance of salesmen.

9 What are the key factors which determine the success of a Personnel Department in an organization?

10 In the selection of new personnel, what deficiencies can you see in the interview method of selection? By what means might its efficiency be improved?

Chapter 12 Industrial Relations

1 In what ways did the conditions in the inter-war years influence the climate of industrial relations in Britain in the early 1980s?

2 Why is a Marketing Manager concerned with the quality of industrial relations in his company?

3 The current system of British industrial relations operates within the framework of two major Acts. What are they? Outline their main provisions.

4 Name the four categories of Trade Unions and give examples of each.

5 Describe and comment on the functions of the TUC and CBI.

6 What is ACAS, and what is its role in industrial disputes?

7 Describe how a dispute arising on the shop floor might develop in a typical manufacturing company.

8 What are 'good industrial relations'? Outline the main contents of the Industrial Relations Code of Practice.

9 What is meant by 'Industrial Democracy'? Write brief explanatory notes on *two* of the following:

The Bullock Report	Profit Sharing
Employee Participation	Workers' Co-operatives

10 Britain's industrial relations have been described as 'notorious' and are the cause of some unfavourable comment abroad. Yet the country's strike record is significantly better than that of the United States and notably less violent. What factors account for this situation?

Chapter 13 The Role of Marketing

1 In the present-day marketing operation, tomorrow's products are very important. But existing products and product lines are closer to the cash register and are the basis of the company's survival. On what criteria do you consider existing products should be evaluated, in order to ensure the continued contribution to the company's marketing performance?

2 The failure of a new product to achieve market acceptance can be costly and serious. In what ways can management organize their New Product Development, in order to minimize the risk of such failure?

3   In what ways would the Marketing Manager of a large company be able to a more effective job if he were appointed to the Board as Marketing Director? How would his responsibilities change?

4   Consider the means by which research and development may be successfully co-ordinated with marketing investigations.

5   In what ways can the Personnel Department be of particular service to the Marketing Department?

6   Explain the main factors which affect the design of a new product.

7   Consumerism is a phenomenon of the post-war years, and is a fact of life for many companies. How is it likely to affect the work of:

(a)   the Marketing Department, and
(b)   the Production Department

of a company marketing consumer durables?

8   Standardization and simplification are goals which are important to a Production Manager, because they lead to savings in production costs. What is the significance of the adoption by a manufacturing company of standardization, to:

(a)   the Marketing Department,
(b)   the customer?

9   The Board of a company manufacturing a range of consumer durables has decided to set up a New Product Committee, under the chairmanship of a director, to consider every aspect of all proposals for new products and to make appropriate recommendations to the Board. What sections of the business do you think should be represented on that Committee and why?

10   Discuss the role of the Research, Development and Design functions in relation to the Marketing activities of a firm.

Further Reading

The following reading list has been designed to supplement the coverage of the text. It has been drawn up with the help and advice of the Librarians of the Institute of Marketing and British Institute of Management, which is gratefully acknowledged.

A high proportion of the books listed are available from one of these libraries, and both are prepared to supply reading lists to meet specific needs on request.

1 Principles of Organization

Brech, E.F.L., *Organisation: the framework of management* (Longmans, 1965).
Brown, W., *Organisation* (Heinemann Educational Books, 1971).
Clark, P.A., *Organisational Design: theory and practice* (Tavistock, 1972).
Child, J., *Organisation: a guide to problems and practice* (Harper and Row, 1977).
Newman, D., *Organisational Design: an analytical approach to the structuring of organisations* (Edward Arnold, 1973).
British Institute of Management, *Company Organisation Structure*, ed. by H. Johannes.
Pugh, Hickson and Hinings, *Writers on Organizations* (Penguin, 1978).

Periodical Articles

'How should you organize manufacturing?', *Harvard Business Review*, January—February 1978.
'A structure to ensure every job gets done but only once', *Rydges*, February 1977.
'Where the companies place the administrative function', *Administrative Management*, March 1977.
'Personnel and organisation structures factors in planning', *Managerial Planning*, May/June 1977.
'The managed metamorphosis of ICI's cure', *Management Today*, December 1976.
'The business unit — all things to all men?', *Management Accounting* (UK), December 1976.

2 Functions of Management

Argenti, J., *Management Techniques: a practical guide* (Allen & Unwin, 1969).
Dale, E. and Michelon, L.C., *Modern management methods* (Penguin Books, 1969).
Dale, E., *Management: theory and practice* (McGraw-Hill, 1973).
Drucker, P., *Effective Management Performance* (BIM, 1974).

Falk, R., *The Business of Management, Art or Craft?* (Penguin, 1969).
Hall, L., *Business Administration* (Macdonald & Evans, 1969).
Hiner, O.S., *Business Administration: an introductory study* (Longmans, 1969).
Liston, D.J., *The Purpose and Practice of Management* (Hutchinson, 1972).
McAlpine, T.S., *The Process of Management: major features of management per-
    formance* (Business Books, 1973).
Stewart, R., *The reality of Management* (Pan Books, 1967).
Wild, R. and Lowes, B., *The Principles of Modern Management* (Holt, Rinehart &
    Winston, 1972).

3 The Structure of Business

Allen, G.C., *The Structure of Industry in Britain* (Longmans, 1972).
Boswell, J.S., *Small Firms Survey* (ICFC, 1967).
Branton, N., *Economic Organization of Modern Britain* (Hodder and Stoughton,
    1975).
Cook, P.L., *Effects of Mergers* (Allen and Unwin, 1958).
Turner, G., *Business in Britain* (Eyre and Spottiswoode, 1969).

Government Publications

Monopolies and Restrictive Practices Commission; Reports on a number of industries,
including *Electric Lamps, Insulin, Rubber, Footwear, Pneumatic Tyres, Chemical
Fertilisers, Man-made Fibres, etc., etc.* (from 1951 on, HMSO).
Annual Report of the Director of Fair Trading, HMSO, 1978/9
A Review of Restrictive Trade Practices Policy, CMND 7512 (HMSO, 1977).
Trade and Industry (weekly, HMSO).
Report on the Census of Production (quinquennial, HMSO).
Acquisitions and Mergers of Companies (Business Monitor M7; quarterly, HMSO).

4 Channels of Communication

American Management Association, *Leadership on the Job* (AMACOM, 1970).
Chilver, J.W., *The Human Aspects of Management* (Pergamon, 1976).
Drake, J.D., *Interviewing for Managers* (AMACOM, 1972).
Davies, A., *A First Course in Business Administration* (George Allen and Unwin,
    1971).
Gowers, Sir E., *The Complete Plain Words* (Pelican, 1962).
Kegel and Stevens, *Communication: Principles and Practice* (Wadsworth, 1961).
Lillico, M., *Managerial Communications* (Pergamon, 1972).
Radford, K.J., *Managerial Decision Making* (Reston Publishing Co., 1975).
Little, P., *Communications in Business* (Longmans, 1977).
Harvard Business Review Library, Ref 2.141, *Effective Communication.*

5 Planning and Control

Ansoff, H.I., *Corporate Strategy* (Pelican, 1973).
Harvard Business Review Library, *Marketing Planning and Strategy* (Pt IV 1978).
Kotler, P., *Marketing Management: Analysis, Planning and Control* (Prentice Hall, 1978).
Lewis, R.F., *Planning for Control and Profit* (Heinemann, 1975).
Perrin, H.F., *Focus the Future* (Management Publications Ltd., 1975).
Taylor, B., *Business Strategies for Survival* (Heinemann, 1976).
Rawnsley, A., *Manual of Industrial Marketing Research* (Marketing Research Association, 1978).
Taylor, B., and Sparkes, J.R., *Corporate Strategy and Planning* (Heinemann, 1977).
Welsch, *Cases in Profit Planning and Control* (Prentice Hall, 1970).
Wilson, R.M.S., *Management Controls and Marketing Planning* (Heinemann, 1979).

6 Business and the Law

Dewis, M., Hutchins, D.C., and Madge, P., *Product Liability* (Heinemann, 1980).
Gower, L.C.B., *The Principles of Modern Company Law* (Stevens, 1979).
Hamies, J., *Your Business and the Law* (Oyez Publishing, 1975).
Livermore, J., *Legal Aspects of Marketing* (Heinemann, 1981).
Marsh, S.B., and J.Soulsby, *Business Law* (McGraw-Hill Book Company UK, Ltd., 1978).
Schmitthoff and Godwin Sarre, *Charlesworth's Mercantile Law* (Stevens, 1977).
White and Jacob, *Patents, Trade Marks, Copyright, and Industrial Design* (Sweet and Maxwell, 1978).
Woolley, D., *Advertising Law Handbook* (Business Books for IPA).

Government Publications

Annual Report of Director of Fair Trading (HMSO).
Review of Restrictive Trade Practices Policy, Cmnd 7512 (HMSO).
Changes in Company Law, Cmnd 7291 (HMSO).
Restrictive Trade Practices Act 1976, White Paper (HMSO).
Fair Trading Act 1973, White Paper (HMSO).

7/8 Financial Management and Sources of Funds

Allen, D., *Funds Flow Management* (Heinemann, 1980).
Boland, R.G.A. and Oxtoby, R.M., *DCF for Capital Investment Analysis* (Hodder & Stoughton, 1975).
Cohan, A.B. and Wyman, H.E., *Cases in Financial Management* (Prentice-Hall, 1972).
Coleman, A.R., *Financial Accounting* (N.Y., Wiley, 1970).
Gilbert and Forman, *Factoring and Finance* (Heinemann, 1977).
Halsall, J.H., *How to Prepare an Operating Budget. A programmed book* (London, Longmans in association with the International Centre for Advanced

Technical and Vocational Training, Turin, 1974).

International Labour Office, *How to read a balance sheet* (Geneva, 1972).

Midgley, K. and Burns, R.G., *Case Studies in Business Finance and Financial Analysis* (Macmillan, 1971).

Rogers, L.A., *Business Analysis for Marketing Managers* (Heinemann, 1978).

Shaw, E.R., *The London Money Market* (Heinemann, 1978).

Thornton, N., *Management Accounting* (Heinemann, 1978).

Welsch, G.A., *Budgeting* (Englewood Cliffs, N.J., Prentice-Hall, 1976).

Wilson Committee, *Reports and Working Papers* (HMSO, 1976/7).

Wood, F. and Townsley, J., *Accounting* (Stockport, Polytech. Publishers Ltd., 1970).

Wright, M.G., *Case Studies in Financial Management* (McGraw-Hill, 1971).

Sourcing and Materials Management

(a) *Purchasing*

Aljian, G.W., *Purchasing Handbook* (McGraw-Hill, 1975).

Anderson, R.G., *Business Systems* (ch. iv) (M & E Handbooks, 1977).

Baily, P.J.H., *Purchasing and Supply Management* (Chapman and Hall, 1969).

Lee and Dobler, *Purchasing and Materials Management* (Tata McGraw-Hill, 1977).

Pitfield, R.R., *Business Organisation* (ch. xi) (M & E Handbooks, 1978).

(b) *Inventory Control*

Battersby, A., *A Guide to Stock Control* (BIM, 1962).

Greene, J.H., *Production and Inventory Control Handbook* (McGraw-Hill, 1970).

Hobbs, J.A., *Control over Inventory and Production* (McGraw-Hill, 1973).

Van Hees and Monhemius, *An Introduction to Production and Inventory Control* (Macmillan, 1972).

'Planning the Material and Production Control System', *BPICS News*, September–October 1977.

(c) *Materials Handling*

Baily, P. and Farmer, D., *Managing materials in industry* (Gower Press, 1972).

British Institute of Management, *Materials handling* (1972).

Hemphill, C.F., *Preventing loss in handling merchandise* (AMACOM, 1974).

Hulett, M., *Unit load handling* (Gower Press, 1970).

Peckham, H.H., *Effective materials management* (Prentice-Hall, 1972).

(d) *Physical Distribution*

Aylott, D.J. and Brindle-Wood-Williams, D., *Physical distribution in industrial and consumer marketing* (Hutchinson, 1970).

Benson, D. and Whitehead, G., *Transport and distribution made simple* (W. H. Allen and Co., 1975).

Hussey, D.E., *Corporate Planning for Physical Distribution* (Bradford, MCB Physical distribution management Ltd., 1973).

Murphy, G.J., *Transport and distribution* (Business Books, 1972).

Wentworth, F., *Handbook of Physical Distribution Management* (Gower Press, 1976).

10 Production Management

British Institute of Management, Managing manufacturing operations (1976).

Buffa, E.S., *Modern Production Management* (Wiley, N.Y., 1973).

Burbridge, J.L., *Production Planning* (Heinemann, 1971).

Burbidge, J.L., *The principles of production control* (Macdonald & Evans, 1971).

Greene, J.H., *Production and inventory control handbook* (McGraw-Hill, 1970).

Harvard Business Review Library, *Production Management* (Heinemann, 1978).

Hoggett, R.H., *The supervision of production* (Gee & Co., 1970).

Hull, J.F., *The control of manufacturing* (Gower Press, 1973).

King, J.R., *Production planning and control* (Pergamon Press, Oxford, 1975).

Lines, A.H. and Beart, J., *Production control techniques* (Industrial and Commercial Techniques Ltd., 1972).

Lowe, P.H., *The essence of production* (Pan, 1970).

Lockyer, K.G., *Production control in practice* (Pitman, 1975).

National Computer Centre, *Computerguide 9*, production control report to DTI on the use of computers for production control in UK manufacturing industries by P.E. Hall, G.K. Holden and A.H. Green (Manchester, 1973).

Radford, J.D. and Richardson, D.B., *The management of production* (Macmillan, 1972).

Riggs, J.L., *Production systems: planning, analysis, and control* (John Wiley and Sons, 1976).

Starr, M.K., *The management of production* (Penguin, 1970).

Van Hees, R.N. and Monhemtus, W., *An introduction to production and inventory control* (Macmillan, 1972).

Weld, R., *Management and production* (Penguin, 1972).

Whitmore, D., *Work measurement* (Heinemann, 1977).

Periodical Articles

'Production Control Systems', *Computer Management*, July/August 1976.

Wild, R., 'The Management of Capacity', *Management Services*, October 1978.

Fadel, H., 'Measuring the Performance of Production Systems using Management Ratios', *Managerial Finance*, 1976.

Harrison, F.C., 'Production Planning in Practice', *Omega*, 1976.

Kennedy, R.L., 'How to Audit Production Control', *Internal Auditor*, January/February 1976.

Collins, J., 'Modern Small Batch Production', *Production Engineer*, December 1978.

Martin, M.D., 'Production Control', *Work Study*, September 1975.

Rowan, T., 'Computers as Manufacturing Control System', *Rydge's*, September 1978.

Rowan, T. and Chatterton, A.N., 'Production Systems Audit', *Production Engineer*, February 1974.

Voss, C., 'Delivery Times., *Chief Executive*, June 1978.

11 Management of Human Resources

Towrington, D., *Encyclopedia of personnel management* (Gower Press, 1974).
Barber, D., *The practice of personnel management* (Institute of Personnel Management, 1970).
Beach, D.S., *Personnel: the management of people at work* (Macmillan, N.Y., 1970).
Brandis, J., *Manpower: personnel management* (Educational Explorers, 1972).
Collingridge, J. and Pitchie, M., *Personnel management: problems of the smaller firm* (Institute of Personnel Management, 1970).
Cuming, M.W., *Theory and practice of personnel management* (Heinemann, 1972).
Department of Employment, *Training for the management of human resources* (HMSO, 1972).
Dickinson, A.W., *The industrial manager's guide to personnel practice* (Gower Press, 1974).
Drucker, P.E., *People and Performance* (Heinemann, 1977).
Dunn, J.D. and Stephens, E.C., *Management of personnel: manpower management and organisational behavior* (McGraw-Hill, 1972).
Finnigan, J., *The right people in the right jobs* (Business Books, 1973).
Graham, H.T., *Human resources management* (McDonald and Evans, 1974).
Harvard Business Review, *Personnel management series*, Reprints from Harvard Business Review (Boston, Mass., Graduate School of Business Administration, Harvard University, 1968).
McFarland, D.E., *Personnel Management* (Penguin, 1971).
Matteson, M.T., Blakeney, R.N. and Domm, D.R., *Contemporary Personnel Management* (Canfield Press, San Francisco, 1972).
Pocock, P., *Personnel management handbook* (Business Books, 1971).
Singer, E.J. and Ramsden, J., *Human Resources* (McGraw-Hill, 1971).
Thomason, G.A., *A Textbook of Personnel Management* (IPM, 1978).

12 Industrial Relations

British Institute of Management, *Conflict or consent in industrial relations* (BIM, 1973).
Clegg, H.A., *The system of industrial relations in Great Britain* (Oxford, 1972).
Flanders, A., *Management and unions:the theory and reform of industrial relations* (Faber, 1970).
'Working Together Campaign', *Readings in Industrial Relations* (London, 1975), BIM M.37
Marsh, G.B., *Employer and employee* (Shaw and Sons Ltd., 1977).
O'Higgins, P., *Workers rights* (Society of Industrial Tutors, 1976).
Payne, D., *Employment law manual* (Gower Press, 1978).
Slade, E., *Tolley's employment handbook* (Tolley Publishing Co., 1977).
Belling, H., *A history of British trade unionism* (Pelican, 1965).
HMSO, *The industrial relations handbook.*
HMSO, *Industrial democracy*, Cmnd 7231.
HMSO, *Report of the Royal Commission on trade unions and employers' associations*, Cmnd 7231 (1968).
Lowndes, R., *Industrial relations* (Holt Rinehart and Winston, 1972).

13 Role of Marketing

Baker, M., *Marketing, theory and practice* (Macmillan Press, Ltd., 1976).
Kotler, P., *Marketing Management: analysis, planning and control* (Prentice-Hall, International, 1978).
Krier, B., *Your Marketing Department: its organisation and structure with job descriptions of the principal functions* (Business Books, 1975).
Levitt, T., *Marketing for Business Growth* (McGraw-Hill, 1974).
Rodger, L.W., *Marketing in a Competitive Economy* (Associated Business Programmes, 1974).
Rowe, K.L., *Communications in Marketing* (McGraw-Hill,Book Co., Ltd., 1978).
Stanton, W.J., *Fundamentals of Marketing* (McGraw-Hill, 1978).
Willsmer, R., *Directing the marketing effort* (Pan, 1975).
Wilmshurst, J., *The Fundamentals and Practice of Marketing* (Heinemann for the Institute of Marketing and CAM Foundation, 1978).
Williamson, R.J., *Marketing for Accountants and Managers* (Heinemann, 1979).
Fundamentals of Marketing Series (Pergamon Press, 1976–8:
  Johnson, A.S., *Marketing and Financial Control*
  Hugo, I. St. J., *Marketing and the Computer*
  Dow, R., *Marketing and Work Study*
  Keay and Wensley, *Marketing through Measurement.*

Periodical Articles

Baligh, H.H. and Burton, R.M., 'Marketing in Moderation — the Marketing Concept and the Organization's Structure', *Long Range Planning*, April 1979.
Hibbert, E.P., 'The Cultural Dimensions of Marketing and the Impact of Industrialisation', *Management Research*, January 1979.
Ardnt, J., 'The Proper Scope and Content of Marketing', *Management Decision*. 1978, Vol. 6.
'Sales to Marketing, the Crucial Transition', *Management Review*, July 1978.
'How to Work Out the Right Price for the Product', *Company Directors Letter*, 1975.
Kehos, P.T. and Dole, P.D., 'The Marketing Audit Way to Higher Profits', *Rydges*, November 1977).
Michell, P.C.N., 'Financial Analysis and Marketing Strategy', *Management Accounting* (UK), February 1979.

Index

Abbey Life Assurance Co. Ltd., 65
Accountants, categories of, 105
Acquisitions, 44
Advisory Conciliation and Arbitration
    Service (ACAS), 202, 207–9
Advertising Standards Authority, 100
AEU, 204
AFL–CIO, 219
Agricultural Mortgage Corp, 131
Allied Breweries, 45
Anglia Building Society, 45
Ansoff, H. Igor, 263
Argyris, Chris, 9
Ashridge, 28
Associated Newspapers Ltd., 107, 110, 191
ASTMS, 201, 219
Avis Car Rental Ltd., 65
Avon Lady, 230

Bader, Ernest, 217
Balance sheet, 105
Balance sheet analysis
    Authorized and issued capital, 110
    creditors, 111
    debtors, 111
    fixed assets, 110
    loan capital, 110
    ratios 111–12
    stock, 111
Barclays Bank Ltd., 28, 117, 138
Blake, Robert, 9, 26
Blake's Grid, 189
Block discounting, 127
Board of Trade, 86
Body Language, 55
Bolton Committee, 36, 124
Boots Company Ltd., 191, 215
Booz, Allen & Hamilton, 246
Boyle, Tony, 219
Brech, E.F.L., 3, 7
Breakeven charts, 120
British Code of Advertising Practice, 100
British Direct Mail Association, 100
British Gas Corp., 214

British Home Stores, 216
British Leyland, 35, 72–3, 141, 201
British Poster Advertising Association, 100
British Printing Industries Federation, 206
British Safety Council, 198
Brown, Wilfred, 4
Budgetary Control, 75, 114, 231
Bullock Report, 213
Bulmer H.P. Ltd., 216

Capitalism, 31
Case Law, 80
Cash flow budget, 115
Chartered Association of Certified
    Accountants, 83
Census of Production, 140
Centralization, 8
Centrally planned economies, 31
Charles, Prince, 50
Charterhouse Development, 130, 135
China, 250
Chubb and Sons Ltd., 139, 191
Citicorp International Capital, 130
Clayton Act, 90
Classes of share, 104
Combination Acts (1824), 200
Commercial Union Assurance Co. Ltd., 28,
    181
Committees, 23, 53
Communications, 19
    audit, 62
    channels, 52
    committees, 23, 53
    in practice, 60
    interviews, 54, 179
    manager, and the, 50
    mass media, 60
    meetings, 53
    non-verbal, 55
    obstacles, 56–9
    organization, and the, 50
    symptoms of inadequate, 59
Company Law
    company formation, 83

Company Law (continued)
  duties of directors, 85
  European Company Law, 84, 86–7
  exercise of powers, 84
  memorandum, 83
  protection of investors, 85
  public and private companies, 83
Company resolutions, 84
Companies Acts
  1948, 39, 83
  1967, 39, 83
  1980, 39, 83
Competition Law
  abroad, 90–91
  mergers, 89
  monopolies, 88
  resale prices, 88
  restrictive trade practices, 87
Computers
  computer aided design, 245
  materials management, 152
  models, 115
  office of the future, 248
  operational research, 22
  telecommunications, 248
Conciliation and arbitration, 208
Confederation of British Industries (CBI), 100, 194, 206, 213
Consumer Credit Act (1974), 98–9
Consumer Law, 80
Consumer Protection
  advertising, 100
  caveat emptor, 97
  main legislation, 98–100
  product liability, 100
Consumer Protection Act (1961), 98
Contract Hire, 127
Contract Law
  discharge, 93
  legal remedies, 94
  types of contract, 92
Contracts of Employment Act (1972), 184
Convergent thinking, 72
Co-operatives, 217
Corning Company, 236
Corporate Plan, 66, 225
Cost reduction, 154
Credit Control, 124, 231
Cybernetics, 11

Dawson International, 44
Debtor control, 116–17
Decision making, 14, 21
Delegation, 14, 23
Demand forecast, 220
Department of Employment, 194, 202, 207
Department of Environment, 227
Design department, 176
Director General of Fair Trading, 88
Discounted cash flow, 123
Division of Labour, 7
Donovan Commission, 202, 205, 206
Dreamland Group, 108

Drucker, Peter F., ix, 2, 22, 27, 70, 187, 222, 234

Eastwood, J.B. Ltd., 90
Economic development councils, 34
Employee financial reports, 62
Employment Act (1980), 202
Employment Legislation
  contract of employment, 184
  prior to commencement, 84
  rights of employees, 185
  statutes, 184
Employment Protection Act (1975), 184, 201–2
Equity Capital for Industry (ECI), 41, 131
Environmental audit, 69
Estate Duties Investment Trust (EDITH), 130
Euromarkets, 127
European Business Development, 130
European Community
  Convention on Human Rights, 81
  European Court of Justice, 81
  European Investment Bank (EIB), 131
  finance from, 134
  future trends, 250
  policies, 82
  Treaties of Rome, 81, 91
European Community Law
  company law directives, 87
  competition policies, 91
  directive on product liability, 100
European Investment Bank (EIB), 131
Exchange control, 126
Export Credit Guarantee Department (ECGD), 137

Factors' Act (1889), 96
Fair Trading Act (1973), 86, 98, 99
Fairey Aviation, 30
Fayol, Henri, 7, 18
Federal Trade Commission Act (1914), 90
Ferodo, 149
Ferranti Ltd., 46
Finance Corporation for Industry (FCI), 130
Finance for Industry, 130
Financial health and strength, 109
Financial management
  budgeting, 75, 114, 231
  cost control, 124, 232
  credit control, 233
  liquidity, 103
  nature of, 102
  performance, 104
  pricing, 232
  profit planning, 70, 115, 232
Financial Structure
  assets and liabilities, 107
  capital and reserves, 107
  classes of share, 104
  loan capital, 104
Fixed and variable costs, 119
Frequensor, 19
Follett, Mary Parker, 7

Food and Drugs Act (1955), 98
Fordyce and Weil, 10
Funds, sources of
  bank finance, 126
  deferred taxation, 131
  external sources, 125
  institutions, 129–31
  internally generated, 124
  market finance, 127
  trade credit, 124

Gearing, 104, 110
Geneen, Harold, 17
General Electric Company (GEC),
  44, 51, 104, 106, 125, 139, 191, 215,
  236
General Strike (1926), 200
Glacier Metal Company, 9
Goldsborough, Arnold, 46
Gledhow Autoparts v *Delaney*, 93
GMWU, 205
Government
  deferred taxation, 131
  industrial relations, 207
  public sector, 32
  regional policy, 32
  research, 176
Growth, 14
Grunnick, 209
Grunwick, 237
GUS, 249

Haggas, John, 44
Hambros Bank, 130
Harland Wolff, 215
Hawthorne studies, 9
Health and Safety Act (1974), 198
Henley Staff College, 28
Herbert, Alfred, 35
Hill, Samuel, 130
Hire Purchase, 99, 127
Hirst Lighting Laboratories, 236
Hoffa, Jimmy, 219
Hoffman-La-Roche, 91
House of Fraser, 216
Human Resources
  induction training, 180
  interviewing, 179
  job evaluation, 180
  management of, 178
  management consultants, role of, 183
  personnel department, 178
  recruitment, 179
  staff appraisal, 182
  staff policies, 198
Humble, John, 24, 223
Hyde v *Wrench*, 92

IBM, 216, 219
ICI, 28, 175, 206, 216, 237
ICL, 216
ITT Corporation, 17, 48, 65

Imperial Group, 90
Industrial and Commercial Finance
  Corp. (ICFC), 35, 130
Industrial Democracy
  Bullock report, 213
  employee participation, 214
  profit sharing, 216
  White Paper, 41–2, 213–4
  worker co-operatives, 217
Industrial relations
  code of practice, 211
  collective bargaining, 211
  conciliation, mediation, arbitration, 205
  current systems, formal and informal,
    202–3
  employees' organizations, 206–7
  Government policies, 207–9
  industrial action, 210
  industrial democracy, 212–17
  in other countries, 217–19
  in practice, 209–12
  joint consultation, 210
  legal framework, 201
  trade unions, 203–5, 217
Industrial Relations Act (1971), 185, 201,
  207
Industrial Relations Code of Practice, 185,
  191, 211
Industry Act (1973), 34
Inmos, 35
Institute of Chartered Secretaries and
  Administrators, 249
Interviewing, 54, 179
Investment appraisal, 115

Jarratt, Alex, 213
Job enrichment, 189
Job evaluation, 172, 180–82
Joint Stock Companies Act (1844), 38

Kirkby Manufacturing & Engineering Ltd.,
  217
Kredietbank SA Luxembourgeoise, 127

Law
  Agency, 94–7
  Civil and Criminal, 82
  Company, 83–7
  Competition, 87–91
  Consumer, 97–100
  Contract, 91–4
  Employment, 184–6
  International, 80–2
  National, 80
Law of Agency
  agent's authority, 94
  agent's liability, 95
  categories of agent, 95
  definition of agent, 94
  duties between agents and principals, 96
  termination of authority, 97
  unauthorized agent's liability, 95

Leadership in management
  communications, importance of, 51
  decisions, 22
  delegation, 23
  leadership, 20
  on the job, 29
  training and development, 27—30
Leasing, 127
Legal entity, 39
Lewis, John, Partnership, 216
Levitt, Theodore, 222
Likert, Rensis, 9
Linear responsibility chart, 6
Lindsey Oil Refinery, 127
Lloyds Bank Ltd., 216
Lonrho Ltd., 65
Lucas Ltd., 149
Lyons, J. Company, 45

McGregor, Douglas, 9, 26
Management
  by objectives, 24, 188
  buy-outs, 217
  common element, 17
  decision-making, 21
  formal authority, 20
  in practice, 18
  leadership, 20
  liaison, 21
  style, 20–1, 26
Management by objectives (MBO), 24–6,
  188
Management consultants, 183
Managers
  functions of, 18
  ten roles of job, 19
Manbre and Garton Ltd., 90
Manpower Planning
  construction of plan, 196
  external sources, 194
  in corporate plan, 191, 194
  internal manpower review, 192–4
  manpower as resource, 190
  manpower report, 197
  reducing level, 195
Manpower Services Commission, 27, 198,
  217, 222
Marketing
  application, 222
  concept, 222
  customer needs, 222
  definition, 222
  motivation, 190
  new product development, 236–42
  relationships with other departments,
    226–35
  strategic planning, 223
  tactical plans, 225
  tasks, 222
Marketing, interfaces with
  distribution, 227
  finance and accounts, 231
  industrial relations, 200
  materials management, 153
  planning, 225

  production, 228
Marketing, interfaces with (continued)
  R & D, 233
Market review, 69
Marks and Spencer, 216
Mayo, Elton, 9
Meeks, Geoffrey, 44
Meetings, 53
Merchandise Mark Act (1862), 97
Mergers, 44
Method study, 170–1
Micro 2000, 237
Microprocessors, 245, 246
Midland Engineering Ltd., 46
Ministry of Technology, 176
Mirror Newspaper Group, 45
Misrepresentation Act (1967), 98
Motivation
  human relations training, 189
  job enrichment, 189
  management by objectives, 188
  organization development (OD), 189
  participative management, 188
  profit sharing, 188
  types, 187
Morgan Grenfell, 127, 137
Models, computer, 118
Molony Committee, 97
Monopolies and Mergers Commission, 89
Mooney, J.D., 7
Morecrest, 135
Multi-national companies, 37
Muskham Finance Ltd. v *Howard*, 92
MWP Incentives,Ltd., 138

National Association of Local Government
  Officers (NALGO), 204
National and Commercial Development
  Capital, 130
National Economic Development Council,
  34
National Enterprise Board (NEB), 35, 72,
  131
National Film Finance Corporation, 131
National Graphical Association (NGA), 204
National Physical Laboratory, 176
National Research Development Corpora-
  tion (NRDC), 35, 131, 135, 176
National Union of Mineworkers (NUM),
  205
National Union of Public Employees
  (NUPE), 204
National Union of Railwaymen (NUR), 205
Neill, James Co. Ltd., 237
New product development, 140, 154
NFBTE, 206
Nielsen, A.C., Company, 68

Objectives
  corporate, 13, 113
  divisional and departmental, 225
  innovation goals, 234
  management by (MBO), 24, 188
  research, 235

setting, 70
Office of Fair Trading, 100
Office of the future, 248
Offshore Supplies Office, 91
Operational research, 22
Organization development (OD), 10, 26, 28, 190
Organization, approaches to
  applying theories, 12
  classical school, 7
  development of effective organization, 13
  human relations school, 9
  systems approach, 11
Organization, principles of
  charts, 4
  criteria, 1
  development of structures, 42—4
  establishing the structure, 2
  formal relationships, 3
  theory, 7
  types, 3
Ownership, company, 40—1

PA Management Consultants, 176, 235
Parker, Sir Peter, 26
Partnership, 37
Partnership Acts (1890) (1907), 38
PATS Centre, 176, 235
Pay Policy, 208
Pearson Commission, 100
Performance analysis, 68
Personnel department, 179
Personnel development, 178
Philips (Eindhoven), 189
Planning Agreements, 188
Planning
  concept, 66—7
  evaluation, 74
  implementing, 75
  multi-tier aspect, 71
  new product development, 237
  profit, 232
  strategic, 71
  structure of, 73
  tactics, 72
Poisson distributions, 144
Polycell Holdings Ltd., 45
Post Office Telecommunications, 25
Powers of Criminal Courts Act (1973), 98
Powers of companies, 84
Prestel, 249
Prices Act (1974), 98
Pricing, 232
Private sector, 35
Probability theory, 144
Procurement/purchasing
  function, 149
  market intelligence, 149
  organization, 147—8
  process, 150
  receipt of goods, 151
  value for money, 151
  vendor selection, 149

Product development
  new product development, 237
  new product development committee, 236
  planning process, 237—42
  product innovation goals, 234
  R & D, 233
Product life cycle, 234
Production
  concept, 159
  dialogue with marketing, 165
  factory layout, 161—4
  methods, 159
Production Management and Marketing Strategy, 159
Production Planning and Control
  content, 165
  dispatching, 167
  follow-up, 168
  planning, 165
  production programme, 165
  routing, 166
  scheduling, 166
Profit improvement, 70
Profit planning, 118
Profit sharing, 188
Profit and Loss Account, 105, 108—9
Profit and loss forecasting, 121
Proprietory Association of Great Britain, 100
Protection of investors, 85
Prudential Assurance Co., 201
Public and private companies, 83
Purchasing, *see* Procurement

Quality Control, 155, 173

Race Relations Act (1976), 184
Rank Xerox Ltd., 89
Ratios, 74, 111, 112
Recruitment of staff, 179
Redundancy Payments Act (1965), 184
Reed International, 45
Regional policy, 32
Registered Companies
  joint stock, 38
  legal entity, 39
  ownership, direction, and control, 40—1
  private companies, 39
  public companies, 39
  registered company, 38
  ultra vires, 39
  winding up, 40
Registrar of Companies, 83
Resale Prices Act (1976), 88, 98
Resolutions, company, 84
R & D
  design department, 176
  marketing, 235
  materials management, 140
  outside methods, 235
  production department, 175
  research and development, 140, 175, 233, 235

R & D (continued)
    R & D strategy, 236
Restrictive Practices Court, 88
Restrictive Trade Practices Acts (1976 &
    1977), 87–88, 98
Return on capital employed, 70, 104
Revie, Don, 24
Risk, 123–4
Robens, Lord, 26
Robots, 245
Rolls Royce, 35
Rowland 'Tiny', 26
Royal Dutch Shell, 206
Rugby Portland Cement, 216

Saab, 189
Scalar chain, 8
Sale of Goods Act (1893), 97
Scottish Daily News, 217
Sector Working Parties, 34
Sex Discrimination Act (1975), 184
Sheraton Hotel Group, 65
Sherman Act (1890), 90
Sidlaw Industries Ltd., 139, 191
Situation audit, 67–8
Small Business Capital Fund, 130
Small firms employment subsidy, 34
Sole trader, 37
Sources and applications of funds, 112–13,
    136
Span of control, 8
Staff
    appraisal, 182
    management, 8
    policies, 198
Statute Law, 80
Stock control
    analysis, 145
    economic ordering quantities, 142
    interface with purchasing, 146
    methods, 145
    re-order levels, 143
    stock forecasting, 143
    stock holding, 156
    stock investment, 140
    stock-taking, 146
Stock Exchange, 128–9, 137
Stone Platt Company Ltd., 62
Strategic planning, 71, 223
Sundridge Park Management Centre, 28, 57
Supply of Goods (Implied Terms) Act
    (1973), 98
Swiss Bank Corporation, 127
Synergy, 2

Tactical plans, 72, 225
Taff Vale decision (1901), 200
Tate and Lyle Ltd., 90, 216
Tavistock Institute of Human Relations, 12
Taylor, F.W., 187
Teamsters Union, 219
Tesco Stores Holdings Ltd., 109, 179
Texas Instruments, 216, 219

Theft Act (1968), 98
Threats and opportunities, 69
Tootal Group, 118
Trade credit, 124
Trade Descriptions Acts (1968), (1972),
    82
Trade unions, 203–5, 217
Trade Union and Labour Relations Act
    (1974), 184, 201
Trade Union Congress, 200, 203
Training
    appraisal, staff, 182
    induction, 180
    internal manpower review, 192
    management development, 28, 57
    staff development, 27–30
Transport and General Workers Union
    (TGWU), 205, 219
Trist, Eric, 12
Turner and Newall Ltd., 139, 191
Tupperware, 230

UKAPE, 203, 209
Ultra vires, 39
Unfair Contract Terms Bill, 98
Unigate Ltd., 139
Unilever Ltd., 45, 206
United Bank, 91
Unity of command, 8
Unity of direction, 8
Unsolicited Goods and Services Act (1975),
    98
Urwick, L.F., 7
USDAW, 204

Value analysis, 140, 151
Variance analysis, 76, 115
Vertical thinking, 72
Volvo, 8, 189, 245

Wall Paper Manufacturers Ltd., 45
Weights and Measures Act (1963), 98
Weinstock, Arnold, 26, 47
'Which' Magazine, 98
Wilson Committee, 135, 233
Winding up, 40
Work measurement, 172
Work study
    job evaluation, 172
    method study, 170
    simplification, 169
    standardization, 169
    work measurement, 172
Worker co-operatives
    Industrial Common Ownership
        Movement, 217
    Kirkby Manufacturing and Engineering,
        217
    Meriden, 217
    Scottish Daily News, 217
Woodward, T. Joan, 9, 42

OTHER TITLES IN THE SERIES

Marketing Communications
Colin J. Coulson-Thomas

Marketing Research for Managers
Sunny Crouch

Case Studies in International Marketing
Peter Doyle and Norman Hart

The Principles and Practice of Selling
Alan Gillam

Essentials of Statistics in Marketing
C. S. Greensted, A. K. S. Jardine and J. D. Macfarlane

A Career in Marketing, Advertising and Public Relations
N. A. Hart and G. W. Lamb

The Practice of Advertising
N. A. Hart and J. O'Connor

Glossary of Marketing Terms
N. A. Hart and J. Stapleton

The Practice of Public Relations
Wilfred Howard

Legal Aspects of Marketing
J. L. Livermore

A Modern Approach to Economics
F. Livesey

Marketing Plans: How to prepare them; how to use them
Malcolm H. B. McDonald

Case Studies in Marketing, Advertising and Public Relations
Colin McIver

Business Analysis for Marketing Managers
L. A. Rogers

Profitable Product Management
John Ward

Behavioural Aspects of Marketing
K. Williams

The Fundamentals and Practice of Marketing
J. Wilmshurst

Management Controls and Marketing Planning
R. M. S. Wilson

Bargaining for Results
John Winkler

Pricing for Results
John Winkler

Business Organization